WYCLIFFE CONTROVERSIES

What 'Original' Texts Did Dr. John de Wycliffe Use For Translating? Who Were His Associates? Where and When Was He Born? Who Translated and Edited the EV and LV Wycliffe Bibles? And More...

H. D. Williams, M.D., Ph.D.

The Old Paths Publications
142 Gold Flume Way
Cleveland, Georgia 30528

Bible For Today #3363

Disclaimer

The author of this work has quoted the writers of many articles and books. This does not mean that the author endorses or recommends the works of others. If the author quotes someone, it does not mean that he agrees with all of the author's tenets, statements, concepts, or words, whether in the work quoted or any other work of the author. There has been no attempt to alter the meaning of the quotes; and therefore, some of the quotes are long in order to give the entire sense of the passage.

Printed in the United States of America

Library of Congress Control Number: 2008934749

REL015000: Religion: Christianity – History General.

ISBN 978-0-9817339-8-2

All Scripture quotes are from the King James Bible except those verses compared and then the source is identified.

Address All Inquiries To:
THE OLD PATHS PUBLICATIONS, Inc.
142 Gold Flume Way
Cleveland, Georgia, U.S.A. 30528

Web: www.theoldpathspublications.com
E-mail: TOP@theoldpathspublications.com

BIBLE FOR TODAY #3363
Web: www.biblefortoday.org
E-mail: bft@biblefortoday.org

1.0

John de Wycliffe: Man of the Age

"Then arose **the Man of the Age**. Among the brilliant and imposing forms that crowd the arena of that stirring time—the magnificent Edward III, and his chivalrous son, the martial barons, the gorgeous array of ecclesiastical dignitaries—stands alone and preeminent the apostolic form of John Wyckliffe, Rector of Lutterworth.

"We call him **the man of the age**, who into a dead Past drops the seed of a living Future; who infuses into the social mass leavening ideas, which, sooner or later, by their inherent quickening energy, work essential changes in the inner and outer life of society. This John Wickliffe did. The supreme and binding authority of the Holy Scriptures as the guide of Christian faith and life; the right of all men, without distinction, to the possession of the Scriptures; these are the living thoughts which Wickliffe cast into the soil of the fourteenth century. They inspired the labors of his active years; they culminated in that great gift to the Anglo-Saxon race, the Holy Bible in the common tongue."[1]

---

[1] Mrs. Conant, *The English Bible* (Sheldon, Blakeman & Co., J. J. Reed printers, New York, 1856) p. 17.

Wycliffe Said:

"If God's Word is the life of the world, and every word of God is the life of the human soul, how may any Antichrist, for dread of God, take it away from us that be Christian men, and thus to suffer the people to die for hunger in heresy and blasphemy of men's laws, that corrupteth and slayeth the soul." "The sacred Scriptures be the property of the people, and one which no party should be allowed to wrest from them."

DEDICATION

This work is dedicated to my grandsons Brad, Scott, Dean, Jedd, and Luke, and to my great-grandsons Owen and Matthew.

> *"The fear of the LORD is the beginning of knowledge: but fools despise wisdom and instruction. My son, hear the instruction of thy father, and forsake not the law of thy mother: For they shall be an ornament of grace unto thy head, and chains about thy neck." (Proverbs 1:7-9)*

This author is deeply appreciative of those who have helped make this work possible and have helped improve it. All of them cannot be mentioned. Among those who have helped are our neighbors and friends, Pete and Brenda Taylor, who love the Lord and study the Bible with us every week; Tom Eller, my friend in the Lord for many years who has remained steadfast in the Lord's will; and my wife, Patricia, whose unfailing love, patience, and gentleness have sustained me through the years. Also, this work would not have been possible without Pastor D. A. Waite, Th.D., Ph.D. who is Director of Bible For Today and President of the Dean Burgon Society. He is a "watchman" in this age for the Lord. He heard the Lord's command, *"Stand ye in the ways, and see, and ask for the old paths, where is the good way..."* (Jeremiah 6:16).

Throughout this study, God's Right Hand has allowed this author to observe Him at work in history as He guided men to grow in Wisdom and Understanding of His ways and to develop reverence for His Words. I am grateful for this. Many men full of faith in the middle ages in England were determined to guard, protect, watch over, and obey the Words of God and fought to make them available to the common man, even unto death. May they not be forgotten; may they be honored; may we be thankful to them for helping light the way for us.

In Christ,

H. D. Williams, M.D., Ph.D.

Chaucer's Description of Wycliffe

"A good man was there of religioun
That was a pore Persone of a town;
But rich he was of holy thought and werk;
He was also a lerned man, a clerk,
That Christes gospel trewly wolde preche.
* * * * * * *
This noble ensample to his shepe he gaf,
That first he wrought and after that he taught.
* * * * * * *
A better priest I trow that nowhere non is,
He waited after no pompe ne reverence;
Ne maked him no spiced conscience,
But Christes lore and his apostles twelve
He taught, but first he folwed it himselve."
CHAUCER.

CONTENTS AT A GLANCE

TABLE OF CONTENTS

THE LATIN VULGATE

Any Bible translated from the Latin MSS, whether the Latin Vulgate or the Old Latin versions, the Itala and the North African Latin MSS, is summarized by this statement:

> "There can be no doubt nor denying of the massive influence of the Latin Scriptures in the Western World, where for over a thousand years it was 'The Bible'. But it was only ever a version; the Latin language has no standing over against the Hebrew and Greek, so that all translations made from it are doubly at fault. It is true that all Bible texts before the general use of the printing presses are subject to the problems of hand-copying, but the Latin texts more so by their very popularity. Textbooks talk of the Old Latin, the Itala, the Hieronymian (Jerome's 405) and the Vulgate as if there were only a single text of each, but none of these were in any way stable, always begging the question, 'Which particular one?'"[2]

[2] C.P. Hallihan, "The Latin Vulgate" (*Quarterly Journal*, Trinitarian Bible Society, issue 579, April-June, 2007) p. 14.

ABBREVIATIONS & DEFINITIONS

Alexandrian: refers to the city of Alexandria in Egypt where many cults existed in the late B.C. and early A.D. An Alexandrian MS is one whose origin is in Alexandria and is considered a corrupted MS by many excellent scholars. An Alexandrian may refer to one born in Alexandria or a scholar who favors Alexandrian MSS above the Received Text.

Anglo-Saxon: "a member of a West Germanic people who settled in Britain from the 5th century A. D. and were dominant until 1066. They included the Angles, Saxons, and Jutes." The language is the "same as old English" (Encarta)

Archbishop: "a bishop of the highest rank, who heads an archdiocese or an ecclesiastical province" (Encarta)

Bible: may be defined by some as a portion of the Scripture such as the Psalter or the Gospels **or** as a book **containing** the Words of God. One must exercise caution when reading various author's works. Some people consider the sixty-six books of the Canon of Scripture or the sixty-six books plus the deuterocanonical[3] books as the "Bible." Bible is derived from the Greek word biblos (βιβλος). A "Bible" is defined in this work as an accurate and faithful translation by word-for-word translating[4] of the preserved Hebrew, Aramaic, and Greek Words **received** by local sanctified churches with baptized immersed members. Many present and past authors consider a 'book' **containing** the Words of God translated from corrupted manuscripts by dynamic equivalent translating (interpretive translating or paraphrasing) as a Bible. It is not. It is a commentary or something worse. The original preserved Hebrew, Aramaic, and Greek Words found in the Hebrew Masoretic Text edited by Jacob ben Chayyim and printed by Daniel Bomberg, 2nd edition, and the Greek Received Text published by Frederick H. A. Scrivener and printed by the Dean Burgon Society or the Trinitarian Bible Society are the **foundational** texts of any translated Bible.

---

[3] Deuterocanonical is "relating or belonging to a secondary, less well-regarded, or disputed collection of religious scripture, especially the Apocrypha." (Encarta)

[4] H. D. Williams, M.D., Ph.D., *Word-For-Word Translating of the Received Texts, Verbal Plenary Translating* (The Old Paths Publications, Cleveland, GA, 2007).

Bull: in this work “a written statement formally issued by the pope and bearing an official seal” (Encarta).

Canon: is the rule or measurement from the Greek canon (κανον). The canon of Scripture in this work is defined as the sixty-six books of the Scripture; it does not include the apocryphal books included in the Roman Catholic ‘bible’.

C: Circa = approximately; sometimes abbreviated ca.

COS: Canon of Scripture

Curate: a secretary of a priest or a priest’s assistant.

Dark Ages: the period of European history between the fall of the Roman Empire in A.D. 476 and about A.D. 1000, for which there are few historical records and during which life was comparatively uncivilized.

Doctrine: a teaching that may or may not be based upon Scripture.

DR: Douay Rheims Catholic Bible.

i.e.: “that is”

e.g: an example

Eucharist: “the symbolic or consecrated bread and wine eaten and drunk during the ceremony of Communion.” (Encarta).

EV: Early Version of the Wycliffe Bible. Most scholars believe that the earlier versions of the Wycliffe Bible were one stage in the translation process. See LV.

Exegesis: interpretation of a (biblical) text.

Friar(s): “a man belonging to a Roman Catholic religious order, especially a mendicant one. The four main orders of friar are the Augustinians, Carmelites, Dominicans, and Franciscans.) (Encarta).

Gloss: is word-for-word translating between a text without regard to syntax.

Goths: "members of an ancient Germanic people who settled south of the Baltic and founded kingdoms in many parts of the Roman Empire between the 3rd and the 5th centuries." (Encarta).

Herefordshire: a 'county' in western Britain.

Hexapla: a six column parallel work.

KJB: King James Bible.

Lateran: "the site of the cathedral church of Rome and of a palace that was the former home of the popes;" "Christianity held at or originating in the Lateran Palace in Rome." (Encarta) Decrees were often issued from the Lateran Palace where Roman Catholic councils were held.

Latin Vulgate: A Latin version of the 'bible' containing the Words of God translated and edited by Jerome c. 400 A.D., allegedly from the "original" Hebrew and Greek manuscripts. Pope Damasus I commissioned Jerome to make a new translation of the Bible into Latin about 400 A.D., but he used corrupted Alexandrian-type Greek manuscripts. "Most widely used Bible in the West. It was mainly the work of St Jerome , and its original purpose was to end the differences of text in the Old Latin MSS (HDW, but it did not, it only made things worse). In 1546 the Council of Trent pronounced it the only authentic Latin text of the Scriptures (HDW, only after many many revisions and the text was still not settled, q.v.). (*The Concise Oxford Dictionary of the Christian Church*).

Lingua Franca: common language of a people used for trading and communication.

Lollard Tower: The term 'Lollards Tower' refers a tower where under its roof was a small prison where Lollards or followers of John Wycliffe were imprisoned in the 16th century.

Lollard: a Waldensian named after Walter Lollard (Raynard or Reynard); Lollard was a name of derision. They gathered about Dr. John de Wycliffe as a leader during his age. (see Waldensian).

Lollardy: follow the principles or doctrines taught from the Bible by the Lollards and included the rejection of many false doctrines of the Roman Catholic Church.

LV: Late Version of the Wycliffe Bible. Most scholars continue to believe that the LV was edited by John Purvey whereas several recent researchers believe that John Trevisa was the major contributor.

LV: Latin Vulgate.

LXX: see the Septuagint.

ME: Middle English.

Medieval: many meanings, but generally the middle ages; specifically the age of middle English, but often from the fifth to the fifteenth century.

Mendicant: "a member of a religious order such as the Franciscans, Dominicans, Carmelites, or Augustinians that forbids the ownership of property and encourages working or begging for a living." (Encarta)

Middle Ages: "the period in European history between antiquity and the Italian Renaissance, often considered to be between the end of the Roman Empire in the 5th century and the early 15th century," (Encarta), which corresponds to the Dark Ages up to the beginning of the Renaissance. (see Dark Ages and Renaissance).

Middle English: the English language between approximately 1100 to 1500. "The leading dialects of this period were Kentish, West Saxon, West Midland, East Midland, and Northern." (Encarta).

Monk: "a man who withdraws entirely or in part from society and goes to live in a religious community to devote himself to prayer, solitude, and contemplation" (Encarta).

MS: manuscript (handwritten).

MSS: manuscripts (handwritten).

Nominalism: see footnote 64.

OL: Old Latin.

Old English: The Anglo-Saxon language affected by the local dialects in Britain prior to the 12th century.

Old Latin Manuscripts: are the translations into Latin from original language biblical manuscripts that may or may not be corrupted. They are usually parts of the sixty-six and/or apocryphal books; that is, they are not complete. Most emanate from North Africa or Northern Italy. Those from Northern Italy are closer to the "Received Text" than others and were frequently used by the Waldensians.

Pandects: a comprehensive exposition on a subject or topic; "a set of documents containing all the laws of a country or society" (Encarta). Used as an alternate name for the *whole* Bible because the term, 'bible' was used for portions of the Scripture such as the Psalter or Gospels.

Penance: in this work it is a duty or religious devotion imposed by a priest during the sacrament of confession in the Roman Catholic Church. To impose penance is to make someone do something for absolution from some sin.

Popery: "the masterpiece of Satan" (q.v.).

Postmodern(ism): The modern age has given way to a new philosophy that focuses solely on the experiences and knowledge of the individual. The postmodernist assert that environment and experiences lead a person to the only correct interpretation of "truth." The 'belief' of the individual about his interaction with 'reality' becomes "truth" to the exclusion of all external reality. Every written work, including the Bible, can be deconstructed by examination of every word based upon the writer's view and culture. The postmodern age began after the troubling atomic bomb and World War II experiences by the world in the 1950's and accelerated in the 1980-1990's. Doubt concerning the goodness of man emerged. The purpose of the postmodern generation is to "tolerate" all opinions, to accept any belief as possibly true, and to avoid confrontation. The hope of humanistic philosophers is to bring about peace in the world. The religious postmodernists hope to lead individuals to a (false) postmodern construction of Jesus Christ and the Bible based upon an individual's concept of God, cultures, and people. A postmodern "emerging" or "emergent" church incorporates elements from many different religions such as sacramentalism, centering meditation, chanting prayers, relics, and decentralized worship services.

Prelate: "a high-ranking member of the Christian clergy, e.g. an abbot, bishop, or cardinal" (Encarta).

Psalter: a book of the Psalms.

q.v.: which see, used to indicate a cross reference to something within the same book or article (Encarta).

Renaissance: "the period in European history from about the 14th through 16th centuries regarded as marking the end of the Middle Ages and featuring major cultural and artistic change" (Encarta).

Scholasticism: "a medieval theological and philosophical system of learning based on the authority of St. Augustine and other leaders of the early Christian Church, and on the works of Aristotle. It sought to bridge the gap between religion and reason." (Encarta).

Schoolmen: generally one who is trained in scholasticism.

Septuagint: [the "G" (from Greek) or "LXX"] from an alleged seventy priests of Israel who supposedly miraculously translated the OT into Greek. It is an inaccurate or paraphrase translation of the 'bible' into Greek of the OT and NT and includes many apocryphal books. It was constructed in the early post-apostolic times most likely by Origen, Symmachus, Aquilla, and a few others. Most authors define it as a B.C. translation of the OT in c. 300 B.C. in Alexandria, which cannot be demonstrated. At best, the so-called "B.C. LXX" is a few passages or 'stories' or accounts in the OT for Greek plays in B.C. Alexandria.

Tractarian: One who writies tracts supporting a belief or doctrine, right or wrong.

Transubstantiation: "the Roman Catholic and Eastern Orthodox doctrine that the bread and wine of Communion become, in substance, but not appearance, the body and blood of Jesus Christ at consecration." (Encarta).

Vernacular Translations: A translation into the ordinary language of the people in a country or region, as distinct from official or formal language (e.g. koine Greek). A dialect translation.

Visgoths: One of two East Germanic tribes of the Goths. They played a significant roll in Europe after the fall of Rome. The other tribe was call Ostrogoths (c. 400 A.D.). The Visigoths attacked and sacked Rome in 410 A.D.

Waldensians: A name given to the churches or individuals who were dissenters from Rome. They were usually sympathetic to Apostolic or Baptist principles and denied the validity of pedobaptism (baptism of babies before the age of accountability or sincere faith). They were often called by their outstanding local barbs or bearded pastors or the name of the region where they were located (e.g. Lollards, Albigensians, Novatians, Vaudois, etc.). They are called separatist separatist Anabaptists by some authors.

Yorkshire: a 'county' in (northern) Britain.

PREFACE

This work was precipitated by an interview of this author by Chris Pinto and John Doerr of Adullam Films. They were preparing an accurate account of the history of the Bible and its underlying texts that would be placed in a DVD format. In the course of preparing for and filming the interview, they had some questions concerning Dr. John de Wycliffe, his associates, and his Bible.

After some further correspondence by email, I was pricked by the conflicting reports in the literature about John de Wycliffe, the texts he used for translating, and his associates such as John Purvey, John Trevisa, and Thomas Bardwardine. Furthermore, just the conflicting information about the "poore (or pore) preachers," called the Lollards or the Wycliffites, alone could fill a book.

It seemed to this writer that the confusion should be addressed. Certainly, "crooked ways" cannot be made "straight" by this author (Psa. 125:5, Lk. 3:5), and I do not claim to absolutely resolve these problems. Some authors have spent as many as twenty-two years studying Wycliffe and his works. This work simply points out important issues for further investigation. Anyone would be troubled by the quotes in this work that contradict each other. But perhaps presenting most of the controversies in writing will help alert future students and help them focus on certain areas for study and research (Isa. 30:8, 2 Tim. 2:15).

During the time of Wycliffe there is one thing for sure, the ruling authorities were likewise guilty of God's charges against Egypt recorded by His prophet Isaiah:

> *"That this is a rebellious people, lying children, children that will not hear the law of the LORD: Which say to the seers, See not; and to the prophets, Prophesy not unto*

> *us right things, speak unto us smooth things, prophesy deceits: Get you out of the way, turn aside out of the path, cause the Holy One of Israel to cease from before us."* (*Isaiah 30:9-11*)

May God have mercy on their souls!

In this work, in order to try and make some sense of the "Wycliffe" mess that is all too apparent, chapter three lists many of the current controversies and many different quotes by various authors that pertain to them. Several quotes will be repeated because of their importance throughout this work. Chapter four is a comparison of one hundred and fifty New Testament verses in four different translations, which are the same verses listed in a book by Dr. D. A. Waite, Th.D., Ph.D., *Defending the King James Bible.* In his work, he discusses the theological difficulties exhibited by the modern 'bible' versions in comparison to the accurate and faithfully translated *King James Bible.* It would behoove a student to have his book for reference.

Most individuals will be surprised by the results of this examination. Perhaps more studies along these lines could be done in the future with other Old Testament and New Testament verses, other controversies, and additional research.

Finally, the Words of God below describe the audacious men who came against the efforts of Wycliffe and his friends far better than this author could. They are men who tried to keep the Words of God out the hands of the laity by villainy. Isaiah said:

> "For the vile person will speak villany, and his heart will work iniquity, to practise hypocrisy, and to utter error against the LORD, to make empty the soul of the hungry, and he will cause the drink of the thirsty to fail." Isaiah 32:6

The hungry and thirsty soul cannot be satisfied with the words of man. This is one concept that Wycliffe clearly understood even though far too many in his age failed to comprehend this important tenet. Today, this lack of wisdom and understanding stands as a great barrier to translating the pure Words of God accurately and faithfully into other languages. May God bless the men and women around the world who are striving to correct this most serious error. There is coming a day soon when we can all shout together:

> *"Thou hast trodden down all them that err from thy statutes: for their deceit is falsehood." (Psalms 119:118)*

During the fourteenth century, God raised up a very important man to help His people deter the enemy who had lost appreciation for "the fear of the Lord;" the Standard of God. Wycliffe was that man.

> "So shall they fear the name of the LORD from the west, and his glory from the rising of the sun. When the enemy shall come in like a flood, the Spirit of the LORD shall lift up a standard against him." (Isaiah 59:19)

God's "standard" rips holes in men's hearts and generates great fear among His enemies. May John de Wycliffe be remembered as a man who used the tools God gave him to advance the cause of the poor, the downtrodden, the brokenhearted, and those in bondage to the world. As God's "standard" was released to a starving population in the fourteenth century by Wycliffe and his associates through works containing the Words of God, the reaction of the enemy was predictable. The same phenomena occurs today in many societies such as China where any work containing God's Words is suppressed and anyone owning the works are punished. Need we even speak of the atrocities in Muslim communities and nations?

As a result of these inappropriate reactions, the enemy is able to create confusion. Great care must be exercised when examining history because of purposeful and accidental additions, subtractions, and changes in accounts. This author does not blame anyone for their unintentional statements that may be incorrect. He does abhor those who deliberately change facts to fit an agenda. The difficult job for the historian is to try and decipher the true facts.

The Lord knows this author has made many unintended errors in the books that he has written, and he is certain there are many in this one. However, in all that any of us do, may it be without vanity, collusion, or deceit; most importantly, may it be:

Sola dei Gloria! (For God's glory alone)

H. D. Williams, M.D., Ph.D.

CHAPTER 1

INTRODUCTION

How translations of the Scriptures came about is very important to students of the Bible. God gave man His inspired, perfect, pure Words in Hebrew, Aramaic, and Greek, which He has preserved (Psa. 12:6-7, Mat. 24:35, and many other places). He commanded that His Words were to be translated into the languages of the world (Rom. 16:25-26, 1 Cor. 14:21, Col. 1:5-6). The English translations of the Scripture show a progression until they culminate in "the glorious King James Bible."

Many essentials are important to proper translating. The method of translating, the art or practice of translating, the underlying texts used, the theology that guides the translators, the syntax and stability of the receptor language, and many other factors are all important. In the age of Wycliffe, the English language was continuing to develop from a mixture of Latin, Gothic, German, French, and Anglo-Saxon. The dialect preceding Wycliffe was 'old English', which grew into what is called 'middle English.'

It is critically important to Christians in the English speaking language-groups to know which texts were used to make an English translation, who were the translators, and when the translations were made. The answers to these questions are important for several reasons. (1) Our Lord Jesus Christ made it abundantly clear that if we love Him we were to guard, protect, preserve, watch over, and keep His Words (Jn. 14:15, 23, and many other places). (2) Believers in the Lord Jesus Christ should acknowledge and honor those who have gone before them that have diligently carried out God's command to:

> *"Go ye therefore, and teach all nations, baptizing them in the name of the Father, and of the Son, and of the Holy Ghost: Teaching them to observe all things whatsoever I have commanded you:…(Matthew 28:19-20),*

Dr. John de Wycliffe, his colleagues, and the "poore preachers" associated with him sought to evangelize the Welsh, Scottish, and English in the Isles of Britain. Dr. Wycliffe was even called "the fifth evangelist." Some of his students went to the continent and influenced John Huss (see below). All of them were hampered by many factors and they were at considerable risk of death and imprisonment. (3) Brothers and sisters in Christ need to be aware of the tactics of the enemy to prevent His *Gospel* from being made known to "all nations." It is sad that Dr. Wycliffe and his associates were hampered from accurately and faithfully translating the pure, preserved Words of God in Hebrew, Aramaic, and Greek into the English language according to the syntax of the language because of corrupted manuscripts (Rom. 16:25-26, 1 Cor. 14:21, Col. 1:5-6). But, they were hindered by many other factors as well, which will be addressed in this work. They used the tools available to them mightily. They were great men of superior character and courage. (4) We need to respect those whose lives, examples, and work(s) encourage us to be "steadfast" in treacherous times. (5) It is also important for the English-speaking churches to know how the inspired Words of God have been preserved, how they were placed into the hands of the laity, and how they were translated [e.g. Was accurate and faithful word-for-word or dynamic equivalent (interpretive) translating used?]. (6) Students need to be aware that the differences found in versions of the Bible in the past and present editions were often the result of differing, often corrupted, underlying manuscripts that were used to make these translation.

Many versions through the centuries are based upon a handful of corrupted texts, whereas the appropriate translations for the believer stand upon many manuscripts from many countries that are supported by vernacular translations and church elder quotes. Were the handwritten manuscripts used by Wycliffe and his associates corrupt? Were the MSS produced by Wycliffe et al influenced by the authorities of the age? Were the Wycliffe Bible translators limited by the lack of knowledge of Hebrew, Greek, and other oriental languages?

Common Problems

In the age of Wycliffe, the corruption of Latin Biblical texts was noted by Dr. Wycliffe and his followers (q.v.). Can we learn from what they faced as they used the tools, manuscripts, and talent of their age?

In today's postmodern atmosphere, we are seeing similar circumstances in society just like situations Wycliffe encountered that are bound to worsen. For example: (1) there is an obvious plan to remove the preserved Scripture from the hands of people around the world by substituting a Canon of Scripture (COS) determined by scholars or "doctors" rather than receiving the COS as accepted by sanctified churches. This began with the subtle changing of the Words in the canon but has mushroomed into a plan to remove entire books of the canon and to substitute apocryphal books. Authorities in power are determined to establish the "bible" they consider the 'world' should read.[5] (2) This is a palpable or obvious attitude among many "scholars" in many nations, which is being driven by ecumenism. Even laws are being passed in many

---

[5] H. D. Williams, M.D., Ph.D., *The Attack on the Canon of Scripture* (The Old Paths Publications, Cleveland, GA, 2008). This book presents the recent actions and criticism by scholars of the preserved Canon of Scripture.

cultures to imprison or kill "infidels" or "fundamentalists" (anywhere in the world) who speak against certain religion(s) and their leaders or their 'book' of religion or doctrine chosen by the religious leaders. The growth of the oppressors around the world is exponential. Anyone opposed to the two leading religions of the world, Islam and Catholicism, or for that matter in this day and time those who challenge any religious "faith" including evolution, are called divisive or troublemakers. Many sound Biblical students of God's Words (2 Tim 2:15) are "[s]ounding trumpets to cry alarm" and raising voices in warning to call saints everywhere to be alert (2 Chron. 13:12). Their alerts are being met with charges of heresy, apostasy and schism. The watchmen of God are accused of intolerance by the enemies 'new' definition of tolerance and of causing divisions in the church.[6] As a matter of fact, the new buzz word by the enemies of Truth is "**divisive**."

Wycliffe and his associates endured similar charges that resulted in imprisonment and often death. In response to postmodern threats, we can learn and be encouraged from Wycliffe and his associates' reactions as they dealt with horrible conditions. We can also be aware of those who denigrated them, those who still deny their importance, and those who belittle their attempt to place the Words of God into the hands of the laity, in spite of severe limitations. Without a doubt, Wycliffe and his associates were the first god-fearing English men who worked diligently at a proper translation of the ***whole*** Bible into the English of their time for the

[6] Jeffrey Khoo, "Truth or Lies?" (*The Burning Bush*, Far Eastern Bible College, Singapore, Vol. 12, Number 2, July 2006) p. 65 and many other articles in The Burning Bush over the last several years. Furthermore, this author has received personal letters at his home accusing him of being divisive for being "so adamant" about the KJB. Many of my colleagues and brothers in Christ have notified me that they have received similar charges. The internet is filled with accusations and venom against those who would defend the perfect preservation of the Words of God as He promised in many verses such as Psa. 12:6-7; Mat. 5:17-18. 24:25; 1 Pe. 1:23-25.

whole population of England. For their activities they were severely persecuted and killed.

Furthermore, many researchers have noted the altering and recording of historical events to obscure evidence in order to preserve the status quo of the rich prelates and civil authorities in the age of Wycliffe. Wycliffe and associates were severely threatened for placing works ***containing*** the Words of God into the hands of the public because God's Words undermine humanistic philosophy, doctrine, tradition, or purpose.

Conflicting Accounts

As a result of a deceitful, lying, subtle enemy, the student of Scripture and of the history of the church, particularly the history related to the early English Bible, must be careful accepting what is 'truth.' There are many contradictory reports about the era of Wycliffe, his associates, his translations, and the texts of Scripture he used for translating the whole Bible.

This work is primarily a record of the conflicting accounts that are related to John de Wycliffe and his followers. Hopefully, it will serve as a reminder to all of us to be slow to accept pronouncements or facts from scholars and authors, but **to remember there is but one Truth which can be declared with certainty**, which is the preserved inspired, inerrant, infallible, "received" Bible that can be traced to Apostolic times. It is only logical and appropriate that we must rely upon only **one** foundation, the preserved received Words of God, and the **accurate and faithful** translation of those Words (Psa. 11: 3).

Purposeful Altering of History

This study will help us recall that we must accept no author's "facts" as revelation or truth. We are all prone to error. However, what is most disconcerting is the *purposeful* altering of history for gain by some. Dr. David Brown reports:

> "The [Roman] Catholics have gone to great lengths in their efforts to revise history and claim them [as truth]."[7] [HDW, my addition for clarity].

For example, Catholic authorities admit to some of these deceptions and 'errors.' Dr. David Daniell reports:

> "Even the Catholic scholar William Lindanus (born 1529) wrote of 'the errors, vices, corruptions, additions, detractions, mutations, uncertainties, obscurities, pollutions, barbarism and solecisms of the vulgar Latin translation.'"[8]

However, not only is the trail of Jerome's Latin Vulgate used by the Roman Catholic Church obscured for the sake of "tradition;" the history of those associated with it is also "played down" in order to white-wash the modern Catholic text placed before approximately 1 billion baptized Roman Catholics.[9] This author is certain that this tendency to

---

[7] David L. Brown, Ph.D., *The Incomparable Book—The Holy Bible, The History of the English Bible* (David L. Brown, Ph. D. Oak Creek WI, Pastor, First Baptist Church, Oak Creek, WI. email: drbookman@yahoo.com) p. 54. This is the best history of the English Bible that this author has discovered.

[8] David Daniell, *The Bible in English, Its History and Influence* (Yale University Press, New Haven and London, 2003) p. 12

[9] "The Roman Catholic Church - the largest branch of Christianity - says there are a total of 1.086 billion baptized members around the globe. This figure is

obscure history, to corrupt documents, and to favor the tradition or authority of those in control has helped create some of the "Wycliffe Controversies" addressed in this work.

The Arrival of Scriptures in England

That being said, let us look briefly at what is recorded concerning the arrival of the Scriptures in England, those who brought them, and the history of the English translations as it leads up to the time of the venerable Dr. Wycliffe.

There is frequent mention of a legendary account of Joseph of Aramethea bringing the *Gospel* to the isle of Great Britain in the immediate post-apostolic times. Without a doubt, the story was embellished over the years in order to sell opportunities to view factitious artifacts of his alleged journey. This kind of fraud is an appalling act that is still being used by some factions, which usurps proper spiritual worship and dupes individuals out of their hard earned money.[10]

> "The Apocryphal legend, however, supplies us with the rest of his story by claiming that Joseph [of

---

expected to exceed 1.1 billion in 2005, with rapid growth in Africa and Asia. However, there are no reliable figures for the number of practicing Catholics worldwide." From an article in April, 2005 accessed 6/2008 from http://news.bbc.co.uk/1/hi/world/4243727.stm

[10] See http://exposingchineseancestorworship.blogspot.com/2008/04/western-museums-with-chinese-artifacts.html and http://www.tpub.com/content/religion/14229/css/14229_109.htm (worship of Buddha) and http://pow.reonline.org.uk/christianity.htm and black Roman Catholic worship of artifacts http://www.americancatholicpress.org/Bishop_%20Perry_Black_Catholic_Worship.html and Mary Worship of apparitions, icons, and idols, see http://www.marypages.com/

Aremethia] accompanied the Apostle Philip, Lazarus, Mary Magdalene & others on a preaching mission to Gaul. Lazarus & Mary stayed in Marseilles, while the others travelled north. At the English Channel, St.Philip sent Joseph, with twelve disciples, to establish Christianity in the most far-flung corner of the Roman Empire: the Island of Britain. The year AD 63 is commonly given for this "event", with AD 37 sometimes being put forth as an alternative. It was said that Joseph achieved his wealth in the metals trade, and in the course of conducting his business, he probably became acquainted with Britain, at least the south-western parts of it. Cornwall was a chief mining district and well-known in the Roman empire for its tin. Somerset was renowned for its high quality lead. Some have even said that Joseph was the uncle of the Virgin Mary and therefore of Jesus, and that he may have brought the young boy along on one of his business trips to the island. Hence the words of Blake's famous hymn, Jerusalem:

And did those feet, in ancient time, Walk upon England's mountains green?

"It was only natural, then, that Joseph should have been chosen for the first mission to Britain, and appropriate that he should come first to Glastonbury, that gravitational center for legendary activity in the West Country. Local legend has it that Joseph sailed around Land's End and headed for his old lead mining haunts. Here his boat ran ashore in the Glastonbury Marshes and, together with his followers, he climbed a nearby hill to survey the surrounding land. Having brought with him a staff grown from Christ's Holy Crown of Thorns, he thrust it into the ground and announced that he and his twelve companions were "Weary All." The thorn staff immediately took miraculous root, and it can be seen there still on Wearyall Hill. Joseph met with the local ruler, Arviragus, and soon secured himself twelve hides of land at Glastonbury on which to build the first monastery in Britain. From here he became the country's evangelist.

"Much more was added to Joseph's legend during the Middle Ages. He was gradually inflated into a major saint and cult hero, as well as the supposed

> ancestor of many British monarchs. He is said to have brought with him to Britain a cup, said to have been used at the Last Supper and also used to catch the blood dripping from Christ as he hung on the Cross. A variation of this story is that Joseph brought with him two cruets, one containing the blood and the other, the sweat of Christ. Either of these items are known as The Holy Grail, and were the object(s) of the quests of the Knights of King Arthur's Round Table. One legend goes on to suggest that Joseph hid the "Grail" in Chalice Well at Glastonbury for safe-keeping
>
> "There is a wide variance of scholarly opinion on this subject, however, and a good deal of doubt exists as to whether Joseph ever came to Britain at all, for any purpose."[11]

And so, we begin this journey with an interesting, but most likely an embellished account. However, there is significant factual information concerning missionaries who brought the *Gospel* into Britain very early. Dr. David Brown reports:

> "Christianity was introduced early into England. "There is evidence that evangelists from the East had penetrated to Britain by the middle of the second century; as not long after Tertullian (197 AD) writes— "*There are places of the Britons, which were unaccessible to the Romans, but yet subdued to Christ.*"[12]

Someone had to bring the Gospel to Britain. Was it Joseph of Arimathea? We will never know the answer to this question with certainty. However, there is information concerning the early arrival of the *Gospel* in Britain.

---

[11] http://www.britannia.com/history/biographies/joseph.html.

[12] David L. Brown, Ph.D., *The Incomparable Book—The Holy Bible, The History of the English Bible* (David L. Brown, Ph. D. Oak Creek WI, email: drbookman@yahoo.com) p. 47. This is the best history of the English Bible that this author has discovered.

A Brief Account of Early Britain

Dr. Daniell also references Tertullian and adds a comment by Origen:

> "Tertullian, 'the father of Latin Theology', writing from Carthage around AD200, made the point that Christianity was by then established in the remoter fringes of the Roman Empire including even *Britannorum inaccessa Romanis loca* ('places of the British not approached by the Romans'). In Alexandria at about the same time, Origen celebrated the fact that Christianity was by then firmly found at the very ends of the world, *quae mundi limites tenent,* regions which include *Britannia* or *terra Britanniae.*"[13]

The Romans left Britain in 410 A.D., after ruling the island for 355 years. As a result, the vacuum of power created by the Roman legions leaving the isle of Britannia precipitated a series of pagan Saxon invasions, which caused most of the southern part of Britain to turn to idolatry.

The Influence of Ulphilas

However, waiting in the wings in the land of the Visigoths[14] was a godly man, Ulphilas (4th century A.D.), whose influence would affect Britain from the land of the Goths. The Roman Ulphilas had been captured by the Goths to act as servant to the Gothic people. It is widely

---

[13] Daniell, p. 28 (*The Bible in English*).

[14] One of two East Germanic tribes of the Goths. They played a significant roll in Europe after the fall of Rome. The other tribe was call Ostrogoths (c. 400 A.D.). The Visigoths attacked and sacked Rome in 410 A.D.

reported that Ulphilas (Ulfilas, Ulfila, or Wulfila) became a Gothic evangelist and translated the Bible into the Gothic language in the mid-4th century.[15] He was a 'bishop' among the Goths.

> "Among those who took part in the council at Constantinople (381 A.D.) was Ulphilas, a Bishop of the Goths."[16] (HDW, my addition).

He was knowledgeable in the Latin, Greek, and Goth languages. Samuel Eliot said:

> "Ulphilas undertook labors which no other Goth had ever attempted. Endeavoring to raise the character of his race, he began with changing the sources of its inspirations. The Emperor to whom he first presented himself in behalf of his flock, called him" the Moses of the age..."The Greek, the Latin and the Gothic language," according to one of his disciples, could henceforth be used together "in the Church of Christ.""'[17]

As the influence of the Gothic language spread to regions of Germany, France, and finally Britain, his Bible came with it. Rev. Joseph Bosworth, D.D., Professor of Anglo-Saxon, at Oxford said in one of his works:

> "The present volume contains four translations of the Gospels. These translations were made by the leading men,-the intellectual aristocracy of their day. **The first version is the Gothic by Ulphilas, in the 4th century**. What vigour and decision of mind,-what a clear

[15] Brown, p. 47-49 (*The Incomparable Book*).
[16] Samuel Eliot, *History of Liberty, Part II, The Early Christians* (Little Brown and Company, Boston, 1853) p. 109.
[17] Ibid. p. 158 (Eliot, *History of Liberty*).

> view of the future extension and influence of the Germanic race, must Ulphilas have had to induce him to translate the Scriptures into the vulgar 'tongue of his people, in an age when Greek and Latin were the only languages employed for literary purposes! **Ulphilas deeply felt, from His own experience, that the power of the word of God to convince the understanding and to influence the conduct would be limited, unless it was not only preached, but read in the mother tongue, through which the best affections of the heart are most easily touched.** These remarks are equally applicable to the translation of the Gospels in the 8th or 10th century from the Vetus Italica into Anglo-Saxon, and to the Wycliffe version of the whole Bible from the Vulgate into English in the 14th century, which was the dawn of that scriptural light that preceded the Reformation."[18]

Surely, Ulphilas' influence through his translation spread with the language. The seed planted by him to place the Words of God into the hands of the common people would influence godly men in the future such as Wycliffe and Tyndale. *"He that goeth forth and weepeth, bearing precious seed, shall doubtless come again with rejoicing, bringing his sheaves with him."* (Psalms 126:6) Hearts would be pricked by the Holy Spirit to give their very lives for that purpose: 'planting the seed' of God. Oh! how many of us hope and pray that hearts will be stirred in these last days to defend the preserved Words of God as He promised to preserve Them and either assist others to place Them into hands of the many language groups of the world or to go themselves.

As the Gothic language spread to the German low country, it was mixed with the Norman French "lingua franca." In a few years, the local

---

[18] Rev. Joseph Bosworth, D.D., Professor of Anglo-Saxon, Oxford, *The Gothic and Anglo-Saxon Gospels in Parallel Columns with the Versions of Wycliffe and Tyndale Arranged with Preface and Notes* (Joseph Russell Smith, London, 2nd edition, 1874) p. ii.

common language became the Anglo-Saxon, which spread to England with the Saxon invasions. As the Anglo-Saxon was effected by the local dialects in England, it became the "old English" and finally the "middle English" language. The middle English is said to have developed by the twelfth century.[19] Middle English would be the dialect Wycliffe used to translate the Latin 'biblical' texts into English. The question is: "Which Latin texts did he use?" This is a recurring question in the postmodern age and will be addressed in this work (see below).

The Continuing Influence of Christianity

Christianity continued to have a place in Britain over the centuries, in spite of the pagan invasions and other influences throughout the years. Many outstanding God-fearing men were involved in the isle's of Britannia. Dr. Brown mentions Maewyn Succat, better known as St. Patrick (c. 430A.D.), Colum Cille (or Columba) (c. born 521 or 522 A.D.)[20], and Caedmon (c. 650 A.D. paraphrase). The first translators were Aldhelm and Guthlac the Hermit (c. 706 A.D., a literal translation of the Psalms). Later glosses[21] and translations appeared by British Christians such as the Lindisfarne Gospels (also known as St. Cuthberts's Gospels or the Book of Durham), Bede's Gospel (735 A.D.), Alcuin of York's five

[19] Dr. Jack Moorman, *Forever Settled* (Dean Burgon Society Press, Collingswood, NJ, 1999) p. 185.

[20] Dr. Brown mentions there is much "tainted material" concerning Columba, particularly the association with a "monastery" of Roman Catholic association. See Brown, p. 54 (*The History of the English Bible).*

[21] A gloss is word-for-word translating between a text without regard to syntax.

books of the OT (late 700's), Alfred the Great's contribution (mid 800's, Decalogue, Ex, 21, 22 and 23) and several others.[22] .

Extant Portions of English Scriptures

These following translations and paraphrases of **portions** of the Anglo-Saxon Bible are extant:

> 1. Pentateuch, Joshua, Judges, and Ester, paraphrased by Aelfric, in the latter part of the tenth century.
> 2. Some of the History of the Kings, and perhaps Jos., by the same.
> 3. The Ten Commandments in Exodus xx, and parts of the three following chapters, by King Alfred, in the latter part of the ninth century.
> 4. The Book of Psalms; two versions in the beginning of the eighth century by Aldhelm and Guthlac.
> 5. The same book, as found in manuscripts of the eleventh century.
> 6. Part of the Proverbs, translated probably in the close of the ninth century.
> 7. The Gospel of John, by the Venerable Bede in the eighth century.
> 8. The four Gospels by Aldred, probably in the end of the ninth century.
> 9. The Gospel of Matthew by Farmen, probably in the tenth century.
> 10. The Gospels of Mark, Luke, and John, by Owen, about the same period.
> 11. The Four Gospels somewhat later. [The published translation.]
> 12. And, again, the Four Gospels in the Anglo-Norman Dialect.
> 13. [The non-canonical Apocryphal Books of Judith and the Maccabees, by Aelfric in the latter part of the ninth century, which are not considered Scripture.]"[23]

---

[22] Brown, p. 50-61 (*History of the English Bible)*..

One author reports:

> "A manuscript copy of the Latin Gospels, a Saxon version, interlined, known by the name of the Durham Book, is attributed on probable evidence to about the time of Alfred. We possess another Latin transcript of the Gospels, with a Saxon translation, introduced after the same manner, known by the name of the Rushworth Gloss. This manuscript appears to be a production of the tenth century.' Among the valuable manuscripts of Benet College, Cambridge, is a third copy of the Gospels in the Saxon tongue, written a little before the Conquest. And a fourth belonging to the same period, and which appears to have been copied from the former, may be seen in the Bodleian Library. But an ecclesiastic, who did more than all his brethren towards supplying his countrymen with instruction from the Scriptures in their own language, was Elfric."[24]

The Old Latin Manuscripts in England

Here is a significant fact that many fail to notice. Before circa 600 A.D. the manuscripts used by these various translators were Old Latin manuscripts. Until about 200 A.D., Greek was the language of nations. Afterward, Latin began to supplant Greek in many areas of the Roman Empire, even though koine Greek continued to be the primary language in Byzantium.[25] Old Latin manuscripts from primarily North Africa,

---

[23] Samuel Bagster, *The English Hexapla* (Samuel Bagster and Sons, Paternoster, 1841) p. 4.

[24] The Rev. Robert Vaughan, *Tracts and Treatises of John de Wycliffe, D.D., Selections and Translations from his manuscripts and Latin Works* (The Wycliffe Society, Blackburn and Pardon, Hatton Garden, London, 1845) p. lviii.

[25] The continued use of Greek in the Byzantine empire emanating from Constantinople help preserved the Greek texts recorded by the Apostles and Prophets. When the Turks invaded Constantinople in 1453, the texts were

Northern Italy, and other parts of the empire are extant. As Latin developed, Pope Damasus I commissioned Jerome to make a new translation of the Bible into Latin about 400 A.D., but he used corrupted Alexandrian-type Greek manuscripts.[26] It was not until later in England that Benedict Biscop, founder of Northumbria[27] and the monasteries at Monkwearmouth in 674 and Jarrow in 681, brought many Latin books to Britain from **Rome**.[28] Without a doubt, the Latin Vulgate came with these books. (see the charts, Latin Translations and English Scriptures, in the Appendix). This author has no knowledge of the Latin Vulgate in England before this period of time.

Vulgar (Common) Translations

It seems appropriate to this author to place before the reader the brief account of translations of the Scripture over the centuries noted by the King James Bible Translators' "Preface" in the 1611 edition. One of the

---

brought into many areas of Europe. "Most importantly, the fall of Constantinople accelerated the scholarly exodus of Byzantine Greeks which caused the influx of Classical Greek Studies into the European Renaissance" along with copies of the "Received Texts" of the Bible. (see http://en.wikipedia.org/wiki/Fall_of_Constantinople)

[26] David Cloud, "Jerome and the Latin Vulgate" (Way of Life Literature, FBIS, Port Huron, MI, 2001) "Modern textual critic Bruce Metzger admits that the Greek manuscripts used by Jerome "Apparently belong to the Alexandrian type of text" (Metzger, The Text of the New Testament, p. 76). This means they were in the same family as those underlying the modern versions."

[27] Northumbria (sometimes spelled Northhumbria) is primarily the name of both a medieval petty kingdom of Angles, in what is now north east England and southern Scotland, and of the earldom which succeeded it when a united Anglo-Saxon kingdom became England. The name reflects the approximate southern limit to the kingdom's territory: the Humber estuary. Northumbria was formed in central Great Britain in Anglo-Saxon times

[28] Daniell, p. 32 (*The Bible in English*).

significant reasons for placing it here is to emphasize the support for the preservation of Scripture by our Lord through "vulgar" (common language) translations. The account by these excellent scholars in the sixteenth century is important to this discussion since they are only 300 years removed from John de Wycliffe's age and they are fellow countrymen. Please notice the mention of John Trevisa, a colleague of John Wycliffe at Oxford, as a translator of the Gospels in item number 18 below. He is an important person in the discussion about the controversies surrounding Wycliffe. Please note that Jerome (S. Hierome) (c. 340-420 A.D.) favored the texts of the church historian Eusebius (c. 265-c. 340). Jerome considered the "received" text manuscripts as corrupted by someone (i.e. *Lucian* **or** *Hesychius*), because they were so different from the Alexandrian text-types. Of course, Jerome was wrong. Also, notice the mention of "Beda" (Bede), "Ulpilas" (Ulphilas) and others who are important in the discussion concerning the arrival of Scripture in Britain.

The Translating of the Scripture into the Vulgar Tongues. (From the Preface of the King James Bible)

> • 1 Now though the Church were thus furnished with *Greek* and *Latin* translations, even before the faith of **CHRIST** was generally embraced in the Empire: [S.Hieronym. Marcell, Zosim.] (for the learned know that even in *S.Hierome's* time the Consul of *Rome* and his wife were both Ethnicks, and about the same time the greatest part of the Senate also) yet for all that the godly-learned were not content to have the Scriptures in the language which themselves understood, *Greek* and *Latin*, (as the good lepers [2King.7:9] were not content to fare well themselves, but acquainted their neighbours with the store that God had sent, that they also might

provide for themselves) but also for the behoof and edifying of the unlearned which hungered and thirsted after righteousness, and had souls to be saved as well as they, they provided translations into the vulgar for their countrymen, insomuch that most nations under heaven did shortly after their conversion hear **CHRIST** speaking unto them in their mother tongue, not by the voice of their minister only, but also by the written word translated.

• 2 If any doubt hereof, he may be satisfied by examples enough, if enough will serve the turn.

• 3 First, *S.Hierome* [S.Hieron. præf. in 4. Evangel.] saith, M*ultarum gentium linguis Scriptura ante translata, docet falsa esse quæ addita sunt*, etc., i.e. *The Scripture being translated before in the languages of many nations, doth shew that those things that were added* (by *Lucian* or *Hesychius*) *are false*.

• 4 The same Hierome elsewhere [S.Hieron. Sophronio.] affirmeth that he, the time was, had set forth the translation of the *Seventy, suæ linguæ hominibus*, i.e. for his countrymen of *Dalmatia*.

• 5 Which words not only *Erasmus* doth understand to purport, that *S.Hierome* translated the Scripture into the *Dalmatian* tongue, but also *Sixtus Senensis*, [Six. Sen. lib. 4. Alphon à Castro lib. 1. ca. 23.] and *Alphonsus à Castro*, (that we speak of no more) men not to be excepted against by them of *Rome*, do ingenuously confess as much.

• 6 So *S.Chrysostome*, [S.Chrysost. in Johan. cap. 1. hom. 1.] that lived in *S.Hierome's* time, giveth evidence with him: *The doctrine of S.John* (saith he) *did not in such sort* (as the philosophers did) *vanish away: but the Syrians, Egyptians, Indians, Persians, Ethiopians, and infinite other nations, being barbarous people, translated it into their (mother) tongue, and have learned to be (true) philosophers, he meaneth Christians.*

• 7 To this may be added *Theodorit*, [Theodor. 5. Therapeut.] as next unto him both for antiquity, and for learning.

• 8 His words be these, *Every country that is under the sun is full of these words* (of the Apostles and Prophets) *and the Hebrew tongue* (he meaneth the Scriptures in the *Hebrew* tongue) *is turned not only into the language of the Grecians, but also of the Romans, and Egyptians, and Persians, and Indians, and Armenians, and Scythians, and Sautomatians, and briefly into all the languages that any nation useth*. So he.

• 9 In like manner, [P.Diacon. li. 12. Isidor, in Chron. Goth. Sozom. li. 6. cap. 37.] *Ulpilas* is reported by *Paulus Diaconus* and *Isidor* (and before them by *Sozomen*) to have translated the Scriptures into the *Gothic* tongue:

• 10 *John* Bishop of *Seville* by *Vasseus*, to have turned them into *Arabic* about the year of our Lord 717: [Vaseus in Chron. Hispan.]

• 11 *Beda* by *Cistertiensis*, to have turned a great part of them into *Saxon*:

• 12 *Efnard* by *Trithemius*, to have abridged the French Psalter, as *Beda* had done the *Hebrew*, about the year 800:

• 13 King *Alured* by the said *Cistertiensis*, to have turned the Psalter into Saxon: [Polydor. Virg. 5 histor. Anglorum testatur idem de Aluredo nostro.]

• *14 Methodius* by *Aventinus* [Aventin. lib. 4.](printed at *Ingolstad*) [B. Rhenan. rerum German. lib.2.] to have turned the Scriptures into [Circa annum 900.] *Sclavonian*:

• 15 *Valdo*, Bishop of *Frising*, by *Beatus Rhenanus*, to have caused about that time the Gospels to be translated into *Dutch* rhythm, yet extant in the library of *Corbinian*:

• 16 *Valdus*, by divers, to have turned them himself, or to have gotten them turned, into *French* about the year 1160:

• 17 *Charles*, the fifth of that name, surnamed *The wise*, to have caused them to be turned into *French*, about 200 years after *Valdus's* time, of which translation there be many copies yet extant, as witnesseth *Beroaldus*. [Beroald.]

• 18 Much about that time, even in our King *Richard* the Second's days, ***John Trevisa*** translated them into *English*, and many *English* Bibles in written hand are yet to be seen with divers, translated, as it is very probable, in that age.

• 19 So the *Syrian* translation of the New Testament is in most learned men's libraries, of *Widminstadius's* setting

> forth; and the Psalter in *Arabic* is with many, of *Augustinus Nebiensis's* setting forth.
> • 20 So *Postel* affirmeth, that in his travel he saw the Gospels in the *Ethiopian* tongue; and *Ambrose Thesius* allegeth the Psalter of the *Indians*, which he testifieth to have been set forth by *Potken* in *Syrian* characters.
> • 21 So that to have the Scriptures in the mother tongue is not a quaint conceit lately taken up, either by the Lord *Cromwell* in *England*, or by the Lord *Radevil* [Thuan.] in *Polonie*, or by the Lord *Ungnadius* in the Emperor's dominion, but hath been thought upon, and put in practice of old, even from the first times of the conversion of any nation; no doubt because it was esteemed most profitable to cause faith to grow in men's hearts the sooner, and to make them to be able to say with the words of the Psalm, *As we have heard, so we have seen*. [Ps.48:8]"[29]

Please note that the phrase, "John Trevisa translated **them** into English" in item number 18 refers back to a translation of the *Gospels* in item number 15. Some writers quote item 18 out of context to make it seem to refer to a translation of the 'whole' Bible, something that cannot be sustained. The antecedent of "them" is the *Gospels*. For example, the following quote is guilty of this indiscretion:

> So what is the truth? Was John Wycliffe "first"? If so, in what sense was he first? First at what? And why is *he* remembered whereas others, apparently, are not?... There were *English* translations of the Scriptures before John Wycliffe came along... As all these nations were certainly converted by the Roman Catholic Church, for there was then no other to send missionaries to convert anybody, this is really a valuable admission. The Translators of 1611 [again, i.e., the translators of the "King James" Version--JAH], then, after enumerating many converted nations that had the Vernacular

[29] Preface to the 1611 King James Bible from http://m2.aol.com/AVBibleTAB/av/KJVpre.htm.

> Scriptures, come to the case of England, and include it among the others. 'Much about that time,' they say (1360), 'even in our King Richard the Second's days, John Trevisa translated them into English, and many English Bibles in written hand are yet to be seen that divers translated, as it is very probable, in that age. ... So that, to have the Scriptures in the mother tongue is not a quaint conceit lately taken up, either by the Lord Cromwell in England [or others] ... but hath been thought upon, and put in practice of old, even from the first times of the conversion of any nation.' his testimony, from the Preface, (too little known) of their own Authorized Bible, ought surely to carry some weight with well disposed Protestant...So why did anyone begin to suggest that John Wycliffe was "first"? Perhaps he was first in producing an *un*authorized English translation?"[30]

The facts do not line up with the quote above. The Roman Church did not authorize any translations to be used except the Latin Vulgate translation of the whole Bible and a few portions of Scripture such as the Psalter by "lay" persons. The Latin Vulgate Bible was only to be used by the prelates (priests), monks, and friars; not the laymen. The Scriptures were never authorized by the Roman Catholic Church for the laity or "lunch-box" workers until the 20th century. Rome wanted to keep the Scriptures out of the hands of the common people.

> "For 600 years the Roman Catholic Church attempted to keep vernacular translations of the Bible out of the hands of the people. The Council of Toulouse, in 1229, decreed that "the laity" could not possess the books of the Old and New Testament "in the vulgar tongue." Waldensian and other Bible-believing people were mercilessly persecuted and their Scriptures destroyed. The Council of Trent, in 1546, claimed that the indiscriminate distribution of the Scriptures caused

[30] http://johnscorner.blogspot.com/2006/11/bible-translation-3-john-wycliffe.html.

> more evil than good and forbade the people to possess the Bible without a written license. Those who possessed Bibles without a license were commanded to deliver them up to the Catholic authorities under threat of inquisition terrors. Booksellers were forbidden to sell any Bibles except to people who possessed a license from the Catholic church. Huge quantities of Scriptures in English, Germany, Italian, French, Spanish, and in other languages, were confiscated and destroyed throughout the 13th to the 19th centuries. Bible translators and distributors were imprisoned and burned."[31]

The Roman Church only tolerated some translations of parts of the Scripture into a vulgar tongue such as the Psalter or Proverbs.

The Definition of "Bible" in the Middle Ages

Furthermore, the term "Bible" was used for **parts** of the Scripture in the middle ages; not the 'whole' Bible. Dr. Daniell said:

> "Care is needed, moreover, not to mis-understand what is meant by 'Bible'. For many centuries, copies of any Latin Bible in Europe that were complete (known as **'pandects'** from the Roman word for complete bodies of law) were so rare as to be remarkable. A more usual reference is that given by Gregory of Tours in his Historia Francorum of about 576, noting of a Bible that 'three volumes had been place upon the altar; then specifying that these were the Prophets, the Epistles and the Gospels."[32] (HDW, my emphais).

---

[31] David Cloud, "Rome Destroyed Bibles" (Way of Life Literature, Port Huron, MI, 2001).

[32] Daniell, p. 30 (*The Bible in English*).

It is interesting that Wycliffe is not mentioned by the King James Bible Translators. This is in part due to the wishes of King James I at the Hampton Court proceedings where the authorization for the King James Bible was received. It is well reported that King James was opposed to the Puritan concept of presbytery (elder) form of church government. Rather King James preferred the Bishop type rule because of sedition worries. Subsequently, Dr. John Rainolds, a Puritan leader, recommended that:

> "unlawful and seditious books be suppressed"[33]

We suspect that Wycliffe was still an anathema in England because of the hate for him spewed out by Roman authorities. As a matter of fact, Wycliffe's works were neglected by scholars until the eighteen hundreds (q.v.) and venom was still being spewed against him and his associates in the nineteen sixties.

> "That the last handing on of the baton, taken as read by earlier historians, was denied from the 1960s, when Wyclif was derided and Lollardy (which was said to have had no connection) was 'seen as an incoherent and inchoate assembly of eccentrics, mostly of little education, expressing views which have economic rather than academic roots."[34]

The fact remains that Wycliffe was greatly involved in translation work and opposition to Rome. He and his associates were first class scholars (q.v.). A more appropriate question to address by the enemies of Wycliffe would be: "By whom and when was a complete translation of the Bible placed before the people of England and where is the manuscript?"

---

[33] Laurence M. Vance, *King James His Bible and Its Translators* (Vance Publications, Pensacola, FL, 2006) p. 19.
[34] Daniell, p. 76 (*The Bible in English*).

Conflicting Accounts

There is conflicting information in the literature concerning when and how much of the Bible was translated. There are some authors who would claim the whole Bible was translated into English for the laity before Wycliffe. William Addis and Thomas Arnold said:

> "It is certain the Bible was familiar to laymen in the fourteenth century, and **that the whole of the N.T. at least could be read in translations**. Blessed Thomas Moore distinctly says: "**The whole Bible long before Wycliffe's days by virtuous and well-learned men translated into the English tongue**, and by good and godly people with devotion and soberness well and reverently read....Myself can read and show you Bibles fair and old written in English, which have been known and seen by the Bishop of the diocese and left in layman's hands to such as he knew for good and Catholic folk that used it with devotion and discretion." "Some exaggeration indeed of what Wycliffe did ," says Gaintner, "appears to have prevailed even from an early period. It has been a common belief that he was the first to translate the Bible into English, and that it was the whole Bible that he himself translated. Both of these must be considered questionable; the latter extremely so...What Master Wycliffe translated and vulgarized, Knighton tells us 'was the gospel that Christ committed to the clergy and the doctors of the church'; and the 'Gospel' here cannot be understood as more than the four Gospels at the utmost. It may, in fact, be less. (Lollardy and the Reformation in Europe" p. 102)"[35]

And so the controversies begin. **First**, it is claimed in the quote above that Wycliffe only translated the Gospels. Yet, many complete

---

[35] William E. Addis, Thomas Arnold, *A Catholic Dictionary Containing Some Account of the Doctrine, Disciplines, Rites, Ceremonies, Councils, and Religious Orders of the Catholic Church, Part II* (Kessinger Publishing, 2004, originally published, 1916, 9th Edition, London) p. 874

Bibles exist claiming to be Wycliffe's translation. Furthermore, Wycliffe himself claimed that he translated the Bible. Dr. Cloud reports:

> "When Wycliffe began the translation work, the Pope in Rome issued "bulls" against him. Wycliffe's reply was as follows:
>
> "You say it is heresy to speak of the Holy Scriptures in English. **You call me a heretic because I have translated the Bible into the common tongue of the people**. Do you know whom you blaspheme?"...(Fountain, *John Wycliffe,* pp. 45-47)[36]

Second, it is claimed the **whole** Bible was available **in English** for the laymen long before Wycliffe. If this is true, where are the translations? This reminds one of the controversy concerning the Septuagint (also called "The LXX" or "The G"[37]) which is a translation of the "whole" Old Testament (OT) into Greek containing the apocrypha. Some claim a 300 B.C. Greek translation of the "G" in Alexandria, Egypt, was made whereas others claim the "G" was an A.D. translation. But no B.C. Greek translation of the entire OT can be demonstrated; only a few "parts" of several OT books are available in Greek. Furthermore, they are translations that are very poor paraphrases. Those **few** Greek MSS of the OT that were discovered in the Dead Sea Caves (Qumran) are probably A.D. manuscripts in light of other A.D. manuscripts found in the same caves with them that are dated c. 132 A.D.[38]

---

[36] David Cloud, D.D., "John Wycliffe: The Father of the English Bible" (Way of Life Literature, FBIS, 2001) p. 3. Dr. Cloud is quoting David Fountain.
[37] H. D. Williams, M.D., Ph.D. "The Character of God's Words is Not Found in the 'G' But is Found in the Ancient Landmarks" (*Dean Burgon Society Message Book*, #15, Dean Burgon Society, Collingswood, NJ, 2005) p. 24.
[38] Karen H. Jobes and Moises Silva, *Invitation to The Septuagint* (Baker Academic, Grand Rapids, MI, 2000) p. 57, 74, 168, 171-172.

Similar to the "G" difficulties and confusion, there is great confusion concerning specific unaltered editions of Wycliffe's Bibles. Exact copies are impossible to find because: (1) they were handmade copies, (2) the editions were progressively translated and improved (see chapter 3), (3) portions of the translations were passed among the populace as chapters as books were translated. Andrew Miller said:

> "As soon as the translation of a portion was finished, the labor of the copyists began, and the Bible was ere long widely circulated wither wholly or in parts. The effect of this bringing home the word of God to the unlearned—to citizens, soldiers, and the lower classes—is beyond human power to estimate. "Wycliffe" said one of his adversaries, "has made the gospel common, and no more open to laymen and to women who can read than it is wont to be to clerks well leaned and of good understanding; so that the pearl of the gospel is scattered and is trodden under foot of swine."[39]

(4) In addition, the English language was still in development, which makes the translations difficult to read. The spelling was being progressively changed even at that time. A study of 150 verses or passages in chapter four of this work shows that words were spelled differently by different scribes in the two editions of the EV quoted. Also, more than one scribe worked on each manuscript because the spelling for the same word changed within the work, and sometimes within the same verse. (5) Furthermore, people desperate for Truth hand copied passages or portions of the Wycliffe Bible very poorly. Some of these portions are extant. (6) Lastly, the Roman Catholic church had developed a strangle hold on most nations and their people. "Rome ruled England and Europe

[39] Andrew Miller, *Church History* (Way of Life Literature electronic edition, Port Huron, WI, May 2003, Chapter 30, John Wycliffe) p. 7 of chapter 7.

with an iron fist"[40] and controlled what was allowed into the hands of people.

Wycliffe's Influence

In contrast to this age, people were so desperate for Truth in Wycliffe's time that they would pay large sums of money to have a few hours with the Book as it was being translated and revised.[41] The influence of Wycliffe, his translation work, and his associates was so significant that a contemporary would state derogatorily that "every second man that you meet is a Lollard"[42] in England. Others said they were as numerous as the "sands of the sea." Miller said:

> "Wycliffe had organized no sect during his life, but the power of his teaching was manifested in the number and zeal of his disciples after his death. From the hut of the peasant to the palace of royalty, they were to be found everywhere under the vague name of "Lollards."[43]

Another author wrote:

> "Lollardy was the political and religious movement of the Lollards from the mid-14th century to the English Reformation. Lollardy was supposed to have evolved from the teachings of John Wycliffe, a prominent theologian at the University of Oxford beginning in the 1350s - however, it is possible that the Lollards actually

[40] Cloud, p. 2 ("John Wycliffe, The Father of the English Bible").
[41] Williams, p. 133 (*The Lie*).
[42] The Bible Museum, www.greatsite.com/timeline-english-bible-history/john-wycliffe.html, accessed 04/15/2008.
[43] Miller, p. 9 (*Church History,* Chapter 30).

predated Wycliffe. Its demands were primarily for reform of the Roman Catholic Church. It taught that piety was a requirement for a priest to be a "true" priest or to perform the sacraments, and that a pious layman had power to perform those same rites, believing that religious power and authority came through piety and not through the Church hierarchy. Similarly, Lollardy emphasized the authority of the Scriptures over the authority of priests. It taught the concept of the "Church of the Saved", meaning that Christ's true Church was the community of the faithful, which overlapped with but was not the same as the official Church of Rome. It taught a form of predestination. It advocated apostolic poverty and taxation of Church properties. It also denied transubstantiation in favour of consubstantiation ...*Lollard*, *Lollardi* or *Loller* was the popular derogatory nickname given to those without an academic background, educated if at all only in English, who were reputed to follow the teachings of John Wycliffe in particular, and were certainly considerably energized by the translation of the Bible into the English language. By the mid-15th century the term *lollard* had come to mean a 'heretic' in general. The alternative, *Wycliffite*, is generally accepted to be a more neutral term covering those of similar opinions, but having an academic background."[44]

Wycliffe and Follower's Works Precipitate Fear

These factors caused the ungodly in power in the fourteenth century to fear the populace and to instigate investigations and accusations. Therefore, much of Wycliffe's work by his associates was done in secrecy. Names were not placed on written works (see below).

[44] http://www.answers.com/topic/lollardy. Accessed 05/2008.

Why Were Wycliffe Bible Revisions Made?

As a result of these conditions and others related to the need for concealment during a time of persecution, the handwritten "Wycliffe Bibles" demonstrate that the editions of 1380-1395 were continuously in revision. So, one has to ask, who was editing and for what purpose? Furthermore, one has to ask if the revisions or different editions are linked to changes in the English language, to the use of different or newly found manuscripts, or attempts to bring them in line with a certain edition of the Roman Catholic Latin version (e.g. the Latin Vulgate), which was also in a constant state of reconstruction. C. P. Hallihan wrote the following in the *Quarterly Journal* of the Trinitarian Bible Society:

> "But the text-stream of the Latin Bible was again in rapid decline. The simultaneous use of the old and new versions (of the Latin Vulgate) led to great corruptions of both, and various 'merged' texts were formed according to the taste or judgment of scribes; and the rent was made worse! Textual instability is a great hindrance. By the mid 8th century the Latin Bible called the Vulgate was in use in handwritten copies through Western Europe; Jerome's they called it, but few if any copies would agree with the 405 Bethlehem copy. Some attempts to tidy the text did stand out—Cassiodorus in 6th century south Italy, Alcuin of York with Charlemagne's patronage in 800, Theodolph of Orleans about the same time. A group of Paris scholars effected a revision in the 13th century—the one which first divided the Bible into chapters—which was to be the basis of the early printed editions. For us, the outstanding fruit of the Medieval Latin Bible tradition is the use that Wycliffe made of it to produce an English language Bible, still a version of an uneven version, but

> hastening the Reformation and its outstanding Bible work in England."[45] (HDW, my addition)

In light of the above, all of the issues surrounding why the Wycliffe Bible editions were made is daunting. Were they made for linguistic purposes (smoothing of the English), translation reasons (better words and progressive translating), or because superior manuscripts were found or both? Furthermore, any "old" editions of the Wycliffe Bibles for comparison purposes are very expensive. One website reports the following about the Wycliffe Bibles:

> "TRY to find this spiritual and Biblical masterpiece anywhere else and you will discover that you cannot. This is a chance to own one of the most important literary works of the entire Medieval period. You will not find this edition anywhere else in this format and at this price. Portions of Wycliffe's Bible have recently sold for $100's of dollars, and a printing from 1731 of the New Testament alone is currently listed on the open-market at $89,500. The only complete handwritten copy of the Wycliffe Bible on the open-market in 2007 is listed at $2,750,000."[46]

So, you are probably asking why Dr. Wycliffe and his translations are so important to us in the history of the Bible 600+ years later. It is hard for individuals today to realize the extreme difficulties during Wycliffe's time. Once these difficulties are apprehended and appreciated, one has greater respect for the man and his heartfelt desire to honor the doctrines of Scripture and for the movement that he help **continue** and promulgate at great risks, called Lollardy (q.v.). Understanding the battles Wycliffe and his associates encountered encourages us to continue the

---

[45] C.P. Hallihan, "The Latin Vulgate" (*Quarterly Journal*, Trinitarian Bible Society, issue 579, April-June, 2007) pp. 11-12.

[46] http://www.rasitesbooks.com/Wycliffe.html

fight for the Words of God and the doctrines based upon them with the same determination.

May all of us be warriors like Wycliffe and his followers and use the tools the Lord has allowed us in this age. Let us not grow weary; let us not faint; let us not quit until every nation and language-group has the Words of the Saviour in their possession in their dialect. In spite of the increasing difficulties encountered in modern times by opponents to God's promises revealed in His preserved, inerrant, infallible, pure, perfect inspired Words, we must defend Truth and the Captain of our Faith.

The 'postmodern' age exhibits some of the same characteristics Wycliffe faced such as (1) corrupt editions or versions of God's Words, (2) attempts to direct attention to false traditions, ceremonies, sacramentalism, and pronouncements of fraudulent religious leaders (3) claims that only the message brought by "doctors" of the church should be accepted as guiding light, rather than written, preserved, inerrant, infallible, inspired Words of God, (4) false doctrines, (5) false philosophies, such as postmodernism, (6) falsely organized and administrated churches, (7) worship of relics, images, and artifacts, (8) many modern false Gnostic-like claims such as the claims of inspiration or "truth" of Apocryphal and pseudoepigraphal books,[47] and (9) the attempt to bring all people into unity under the same earthly human church authority (ecumenism).

Let us learn from Wycliffe and his works, even if his Bibles were based primarily upon the wrong (Latin) texts and contain apocryphal books. He used the tools available to him, just as we are required to do today.

---

[47] H. D. Williams, M.D., Ph.D., *The Attack on the Canon of Scripture* (The Old Paths Publications, Cleveland, GA, 2008). The entire work is devoted to the attack on the books of the Bible.

CHAPTER 2

THE MAN, WYCLIFFE

"The Morning Star of the Reformation"
"The Father of the English Bible"
"The Man of the Age"
"Doctor Evangelicus"
"The Fifth Evangelist"
"The English Reformer"
"The Father of the English Bible-Translation"
"The First Protestant"
"The Great Master at Oxford"
"The Princely Yorkshireman"
"The Pure-hearted Pastor of Lutterworth"

A Brief Look at Wycliffe's Life

Dr. Wycliffe (1320-1384 A.D.; or 1324-1384; or 1327-1384, or 1330-1384) is a daunting figure in history. In 1856, Mrs. Conant said of Wycliffe:

"But the poor, unlettered, unarmed populace gained nothing by this triumph of their masters. Their only hope, though they knew it not, was in the restoration of what will ever be **the only Magna Charta of the weak—The Holy Scriptures**.

Then arose **the Man of the Age**. Among the brilliant and imposing forms that crowd the arena of that stirring time—the magnificent Edward III, and his chivalrous son,[48] the martial barons, the gorgeous array of ecclesiastical dignitaries—stands alone and preeminent the apostolic form of John Wyckliffe, Rector of Lutterworth.

We call him **the man of the age**, who into a dead Past drops the seed of a living Future; who infuses into the social mass leavening ideas, which, sooner or later, by their inherent quickening energy, work essential changes in the inner and outer life of society. This John Wickliffe did. The supreme and binding authority of the Holy Scriptures as the guide of Christian faith and life; the right of all men, without distinction, to the possession of the Scriptures; these are the living thoughts which Wickliffe cast into the soil of the fourteenth century. They inspired the labors of his active years; they culminated in that great gift to the Anglo-Saxon race, the Holy Bible in the common tongue."[49]

He was called "the fifth evangelist"[50] in Bohemia:

"Across the seas in Bohemia, where the views of Wyclif were transplanted, they took deeper root than in England, and assumed an organized form. There, the English Reformer was called **the fifth evangelist** and, in

[48] King Edward III reigned for fifty years from 1327 – 1377. He is noted for setting off the 100 year war against France. He turned the kingdom over to Edward the Black Prince (because of the armor he wore). The Black Prince died in 1376 before his father, Edward the III. The Black Prince's son, Richard II became King. However, the Black Prince's brother, John of Gaunt (1340-1399) would become the effective ruler because of Richard's youthfulness. John of Gaunt would often be Wycliffe's protector.

[49] Mrs. H. O. Conant, *The English Bible* (Sheldon, Blakeman & Co., New York, 1856, J. J. Reed printers) p. 17.

[50] "Fifth Evangelist" most likely refers to the penchant of Wycliffe and others such as Augustine to call the men who recorded the Gospels of Matthew, Mark, Luke, and John, "evangelists." See Ian Christopher Levy, *John Wyclif On the Truth of Holy Scripture,* (Medieval Institute Publications, Western Michigan University, Kalamazoo, Michigan, 2001) p. 54, 82, etc.

> its earlier stages, the movement went by the name of Wycliffism."[51]

He is called "The Morning Star of the Reformation" and "The First Protestant" by historians looking back at his accomplishments. Dr. Brown said:

> "How were Wycliffe's Catholic views changed so drastically that he has been called "**The First Protestant"** and **"The Morning Star of the Reformation?"** The answer is really very simple. He began to study the Bible."[52] (HDW, amen; not my emphasis).

He was called the "evangelical doctor" (Doctor Evangelicus) by his contemporaries.

From Student to Priest to Professor to Protestant

He was an outstanding student at Merton Hall, Oxford, where he received his Bachelor of Arts in 1356 in philosophical studies. Later, he became a professor and eventually master (or head) of Balliol College, Oxford around 1360 (the date is obscure). He received his B.A. in Theology in 1369 and his Doctorate in Theology in 1372.

---

[51] Phillip Schaff, *History of the Christian Church, Vol. 6* (Master's Christian Library, Ages Software, Albany, OR, 1997) p. 268. Johann Sebastian Bach (d. 1750), the famous and great musician, was also called "the fifth evangelist." This author is not certain how the term arose; perhaps it alludes to the four Gospels; the fifth would be a living 'fifth evangelist."

[52] David L. Brown, Th.M., *Our English Bible Heritage* (David L. Brown, Oak Creek, WI) p. 3.

He was appointed to several rectorships (parishes). He was at Fillingham, Lincolnshire as rector from 1361 to 1368; the rectorship at Lutterworth was his final home until his death in 1384.

> "John Wyclif, called **the Morning Star of the Reformation**, and, at the time of his death, in England and in Bohemia **the Evangelical doctor**, was born about 1324 near the village of Wyclif, Yorkshire, in the diocese of Durham. His own writings give scarcely a clew to the events of his career, and little can be gathered from his immediate contemporaries. He was of Saxon blood. His studies were pursued at Oxford, which had six colleges. He was a student at Balliol and master of that hall in 1361. He was also connected with Merton and Queen's, and was probably master of Canterbury Hall, founded by Archbishop Islip. He was appointed in succession to the livings of Fillingham, 1363, Ludgershall, 1368, and by the king's appointment, to Lutterworth, 1374. The living of Lutterworth was valued at £26 a year."[53]

In 1860, Samuel Howard Ford said the following about Wycliffe and his final rectory at Lutterworth:

> "Lutterworth! Associations cluster round it more potent in their influence than the clash of armies or the fall of kings. The lone voice that went forth from it, the light that gleamed from it in the fourteenth century are heard and felt still, must echo and beam through all time, and all eternity. It was the voice and light of truth, truth which once generated is immortal. **Chains can not bind it; time can not weaken it.** Eternal is its nature; eternity is its guardian. (Bancroft) John De Wickliffe, rector of Lutterworth, was the chosen instrument to announce that truth, and bear aloft that flame-torch through the world's valley of the shadow of death. On the banks of the Tee, in Yorkshire, John Wickliffe was born, in 1324. With

[53] Schaff, p. 237. Also see, Fox's *Book of the Martyrs*, Vol. 7, "Persecution of John Wyckliffe", p. 183. £26/year in today's dollar equivalent is $52.00/year.

> Bradwordine (sic), and Occan, and Dunn, and Scotus, the luminaries of the age, he passed his early manhood in Oxford University. He entered the clerical order, and beheld before him the highest honors in the "Church." But, like Luther, God's Word had found entrance into his soul, and, in obedience to its teaching he tore away from his heart the webs and wrappages of error which incased and deadened it. On, step by step, he struggled into light, until on the Bible and the Bible alone, he took his lone and defiant position. Among the principles he advocated were, that the church consisted only of believers, the saved; that baptism was a "sign of grace received before," and consequently should be administered to those only who professed to have received "grace."[54] (HDW, my emphasis)

Canterbury Hall Debacle

Early in Wycliffe's life at about the age of forty, he was appointed as one of eleven scholars to Canterbury Hall (College) at Oxford, which was established by Archbishop Islip (bishop from 1349-1366); but his appointment was withdrawn by Archbishop Stephen Langham (bishop from 1366-1368, and again in 1374). He was appointed to Canterbury in 1365 as a professor, but was continuously associated with turmoil and strife. The Benedictines caused his ejection from his post in 1371. Wycliffe appealed to the pope, but was brushed aside because he supported King Edward III's refusal to pay a tribute promised by King John (1164-1216) to the pope. Church historian Andrew Miller said:

> "The submission of [King] John to Innocent III, was the turning-point in the history of the papacy in this country. In the humiliation of the sovereign the whole

---

[54] Samuel Howard Ford, *The Origin of the Baptists: Traced Back by Milestones on the Track of Time* (Way of Life Literature, Port Huron, MI, FBIS, 2003, Chapter V, "Century Fourteen: Wickliffe and the Lollards") p. 1.

> nation felt itself to be degraded. England never could forget such abject prostration on the part of its king at the feet of a foreign priest. From that hour a spirit of disaffection towards Rome grew up in the minds of the English people...About the year 1366 a controversy had arisen between Urban V and Edward III in consequence of the renewed demand of an annual tribute of one thousand marks, which King John had bound himself to pay to the Roman see, as an acknowledgement of the feudal superiority of the Roman pontiff over the kingdoms of England and Ireland."[55]

Perhaps in response to the mayhem at Canterbury, the "Great Schism" and demand for taxes from Rome (see below), he wrote *"On the Divine Dominion"* in 1373-74 and shortly thereafter in 1375, *"On the Divine Commandments."* By 1379, he had completed a commentary on the **entire** Bible:

> "which students were already regarding as a standard reference."[56]

He was forced completely out of the Oxford University and Canterbury Hall (college) by 1381, but not before accomplishing a feat wrought with danger; the English translation of the Bible by 1380.

Wycliffe's Major Contributions

This great man's importance lies in two major accomplishments:

---

[55] Andrew Miller, *Church History* (Way of Life Literature electronic edition, May 2003, Chapter 30, John Wycliffe) p. 3-4.
[56] Ian Christopher Levy, *John Wycliffe, On the Truth of Holy Scripture, Translated with an Introduction and Notes* (Medieval Institute Publications, Western Michigan University, Kalamazoo, MI, 2001) p. 5.

(1) He was responsible for placing an English version of the ***whole*** Bible **containing** the Words of God into the hands of the commoners. Wycliffe said:

> "The sacred Scriptures be the property of the people, and one which no party should be allowed to wrest from them."[57]

And he said:

> "If God's Word is the life of the world, and every word of God is the life of the human soul, how may any Antichrist, for dread of God, take it away from us that be Christian men, and thus to suffer the people to die for hunger in heresy and blasphemy of men's laws, that corrupteth and slayeth the soul."[58] Wycliffe, *The Wicket,* as quoted in Final Authority, p. 123.

Even so, Wycliffe's Bible was translated from Jerome's Latin Vulgate, which was based upon corrupted Alexandrian MSS. As we shall see, Wycliffe and his associates discovered that the Latin Vulgate MSS commonly available during the fourteenth century were corrupted. Wycliffe and his associates revised the text they used back toward Jerome's translation made in the early fifth century. According to some authors, he used "Old Latin" MSS, also. The translation was accomplished in spite of great opposition from Rome in the late fourteenth century.

---

[57] David Cloud, "John Wycliffe and the Lollards" (FBIS, March 17, 2000).
[58] Bill Grady, *Final Authority* ( ) p. 123.

(2) He opposed Roman Catholicism's "killing fields,"[59] as the first English reformer. Rome's "killing fields" destroyed many people spiritually and physically throughout Europe during the "Dark Ages," which lasted until about 1000 A.D. The persecutions persisted on the Continent until the 16th century. In England the 'fields' were killing the spirit of men, but murder had not arrived. But soon, the declaration of Archbishop Thomas Arundel to burn anyone caught translating, owning, or reading "the Book" would intercede. He said in 1408:

> "WE THEREFORE DECREE AND ORDAIN THAT NO MAN SHALL, HEREAFTER, BY HIS OWN AUTHORITY, TRANSLATE ANY TEXT OF THE SCRIPTURE INTO ENGLISH, OR ANY OTHER TONGUE, by way of a book, libel, or treatise, now lately set forth in the time of John Wyckliff, or since, or hereafter to be set forth, in part or whole, privily or apertly, **upon pain of greater excommunication**, until said translation be allowed by ordinary of the place, or, if the case so require, by the council provincial (Edie, I, p. 89)...This pestilential and most wretched John Wycliffe of damnable memory, a child of the old devil, and himself a child or pupil of Anti-Christ, who while he lived, walking in the vanity of his mind...crowned his wickedness by translating the Scriptures into the mother tongue" (Fountain, *John Wycliffe,* p. 45)"[60]

---

[59] "Killing Fields" is a term that has crept into the English language from the 'killing fields' of the Khmer Rough of Cambodia around 1975. Now, we see 'killing fields' all over the world, as murdering leaders attempt to ethnically cleanse nations or regions (e.g. Bosnia, Iraq, Zimbabwe). Before or during Dr. Wycliffe's life, the Roman Catholic church was involved in crusades, even children's crusades, and inquisitions against the dissenters from Rome, leaving literally millions dead; therefore, the "killing fields" is a very appropriate term. Furthermore, the "killing fields" of Rome suppressed Biblical spiritual growth, knowledge of God's Words and their authority, in favor of human philosophy and papal authority, a major problem in Wycliffe's time.

[60] David Cloud, "John Wycliffe and the Lollards" (Way of Life Literature, Port Huron, WI, 2000 from the book *Rome and the Bible: Tracing the History*

And finally, the English legislature followed suit by passing an Act that required the English sheriffs to take an oath to persecute the Lollards (q.v.). Soon after, another Act was passed affirming the penalty of death:

> In 1414, the English legislature under Henry V (1413-22), joined in asking for harder measures against the Lollards. 'After a suspected rising of the Lollards, a law was passed, declaring that ALL WHO READ THE SCRIPTURES IN THE MOTHER TONGUE SHOULD 'FOREIT LAND, CATEL, LIF, AND GOODS, FROM THEYR HEYRES [THEIR HEIRS] FOR EVER'"[61]

Many of the Lollards went to prison or to their deaths in the "killing fields" of Rome in England.

In spite of the persecutions and continuing to follow Wycliffe's lead, other dissenters from Rome in the years immediately before or during the Reformation, were John Huss (1369-1415), Desiderous Erasmus (1466-1537), Martin Luther (1483-1546), Philip Melancthon (1497-1560), Jacques Lefevre D'Etaples (1455-1560), William Farel (1489-1565), John Calvin (1509-1564), and William Tyndale (1484-1536).

As the "morning star" (usually considered the planet Venus) shines the brightest just before dawn, Dr. Wycliffe is called the "morning star of the Reformation." He is the Englishman who is alleged by many to be the first to bring the light of all the Scriptures to the English-speaking world. But, is he? Some authorities close to Romanism flatly deny this (see below). One thing for sure, he is the unbelievably spiritual, godly man who is most identified with the spark that lighted the fire of reform that led nations and people out of the "Dark Age." He was ordained a Roman Catholic priest in 1351 (before his B.A.), but he and his followers were also

---

of the Roman Catholic Church and its Persecutions of the Bible and of Bible Believers) p.10.

[61] Ibid. p. 11 (Cloud, "John Wycliffe and the Lollards").

called Baptists, Anabaptists, and Protestants by some authors because of his teaching, preaching, and writings.[62] However, the Baptists (or Waldensians or Lollards) preceded him in England as evidenced by an old Baptist chapel uncovered by archaeological digs at Hill Cliffe near Warrington on the borders of Lancashire in a secluded part of Cheshire. A tombstone there has the date 1357, "the time when Wycliffe was still a Fellow at Merton College, Oxford."[63] Without a doubt, however, Wycliffe was a reformer who lead many out of darkness and into being protestants against Rome. He would send his students at Oxford and his followers called "poore preachers" around Britain. They simply presented the gospel in the earliest stages of Wycliffism. Initially, they did not become involved in political matters.

Rome's "Universal" Presence in the 13th Century

It is a fact that essentially all were Roman Catholics in the days of Wycliffe. Many individuals in the populace and in the civil government of England objected to the dominance of the Roman Church over civil matters and religious affairs. But, as the years passed by, and even though he was a Catholic priest, Dr. Wycliffe became very outspoken concerning

---

[62] Joseph Ivemy, *A History of the English Baptists* (Way of Life electronic edition, Port Huron, MI, printed in London, 1811, Vol. 1,) Chapter 2, p. 13. Also, J. M. Cramp, *Baptist History* (Way of Life electronic edition, first published in 1869) The Revival Period, Chapter V, p. 2. Also, Samuel Howard Ford, *The Origin of the Baptists* (Way of Life electronic edition, Port Huron, MI, first published 1860, Chapter V) Century Fourteen, Wickliffe and the Lollards, p. 2. See Thomas Armitage, *A H*[63] J.J. Goadby, *Bye-Paths in Papist History* (Way of life electronic edition, 2003, first published by Elliot Stock, London, 1871, Chapter II, Ancient Baptist Churches in England) p. 1

his rejection of Roman Catholic doctrine. He rejected (1) papal authority over and against the Scriptures, (2) transubstantiation, (3) indulgences, (4) Rome's organization and administration of the church, (5) idol worship, and (6) corruption in the ranks of Catholic prelates, monks, and friars. The church historian, Andrew Miller said of Wycliffe:

> "But that which brought him such fame and popularity at Oxford, was his defense of the university against the encroachments of the mendicant friars. He fearlessly and unsparingly attacked these orders, which he declared to be the great evil of Christendom. They were now four in number—Dominicans, Minorities or Franciscans, Augustinians, Carmelites—and swarmed in all the best parts of Europe. They strove hard in Oxford, as heretofore in Paris, to obtain the ascendancy. They took every opportunity of enticing the students into their convents, who, without the consent of their parents, were enlisted into the mendicant orders."[64]

The Pope's Army

The Roman authorities were classified as: (1) the pope's (rich) prelates, who were high ranking members of the clergy such as an abbot, bishop, or cardinal. They made up the 'secular clergy' who were more involved with political than religious concerns. (2) Included in the pope's army were the wealthy monks or 'regular clergy' and (3) the friars or Mendicant[65] Orders who feigned poverty.[66] "Soul freedom" was disdained

---

[64] Andrew Miller, *Church History* (Way of Life Literature electronic edition, May 2003, Chapter 30, John Wycliffe) p. 3.

[65] Mendicant means "begging for and living on money given by strangers in the street" or "a member of a religious order such as the Franciscans, Dominicans, Carmelites, or Augustinians that forbids the ownership of property and encourages working or begging for a living" (Encarta).

by the pope and his emissaries in Wycliffe's age. Anyone expressing freedom from Rome's oppressive policies was hunted down and silenced by these three branches of the pope's army. Furthermore, significant evidence exists that the pope's army was infected by "criminals" who committed unspeakable crimes, such as murder, robbery, and fornication, even though they were "churchmen." Many of them were alcoholics. These atrocities went on for hundreds of years and as we know, they continue to exist today (e.g. pedophilia).

> "It is publicly stated to Henry (II) by his judges, that during the first ten years of his reign, more than a hundred murders had been committed by clergymen, besides thefts, robberies, and other crimes, for which they could not punish them."[67] (HDW, my addition)

Furthermore, the pope's emissaries were often successful in convincing government leaders that opposition to Roman Catholic authority and leadership of the populace would result in the rebellion of the masses against the authority of kings and regional princes. The "Peasant Revolt" (also called Tyler's Rising or the Great Rising) of 1381 was attributed to Wycliffe and his followers by Rome. However, Wycliffe had nothing to do with it. He dispised violence (q.v.). However, it is suspected that his long term friend and curate, John Purvey was involved in several revolts against Rome.[68]

---

[66] Hannah O'Brien Chaplin Conant, *The English History of the Translation of the Holy Scriptures into the English Tongue with Specimens of the Old English Versions* (Sheldon, Blakeman, and Company, New York, 1856) p. 19-39.

[67] Conant, p. 20. (*The English Bible,* quoted from Henry's History, vol. vi, pl. 59). King Henry II's reign was March 31, 1519 – July 10, 1559

[68] Maureen Jurkowski, "New Light on John Purvey", (*The English Historical Review,* Vol. 110, No. 439, Nov. 1995) pp. 1180-1190. Jurkowski is at the University of Keele, North Midlands, UK; and see Schaff, p. 241.

The *Encyclopedia Britannia* reports that "the archbishop of Canterbury, Simon of Sudbury, was murdered in the revolt," called the Peasant's Revolt. Obviously, this precipitated great opposition by Rome against anyone who may have been even remotely associated with the event.

The revolt gave support to Rome's claims that rebellion against Rome's rule would by extension lead to insurrection and rejection of all authority; in other words anarchy. Subsequently, the kings and princes of those days in many nations would be convinced of "danger" and would often join forces with the Roman Church to imprison or kill leaders of any opposition to Rome's policies.

Popes, Kings, and Taxes

However, kings often found themselves obligated to the pope's taxes and decrees far beyond their heart's desire. This created great tension between the "state-church" and the government in many regions of the empire. England was at the heart of many disagreements with the pope. The allegiance of England's monarchs to Rome waxed hot and cold. Wycliffe was a great defender of the "rights" of Kings over the pope.

Wycliffe would travel to Brugs, France at the request of the King of England, Edward III (1312-1377) and parliament in 1374 to defend England's refusal to pay a levy or tax upon the nation to the pope. King John (1164-1216) had agreed to pay a heavy tax thirty-three years earlier. It is here at Brugs that we find the first mention of John of Gaunt (1340-1399), King Edward's favorite son and Duke of Lancaster. The Duke was the effective ruler of England during Richard II reign.[69] He was also the

[69] Daniell, p. 71.

brother of the "black prince," (1330-1376), so named because of the black armor he wore. The Black Prince would never become King and would die before his father, King Edward III.

Wycliffe's Significant Protectors

John of Gaunt would be Wycliffe's protector for many years against many adversaries and the "wiles" of Rome. Wycliffe was also protected by two Queens, Queen Joan and Queen Anne:

> "One of these [protectors] was JOHN OF GAUNT, the Duke of Lancaster, who protected Wycliffe for many years. John was a large man and a bold warrior. His armor, which is displayed today in the Tower of London, is 6 foot 9 inches. Another protector was QUEEN JOAN (1328-85). She was the wife of Edward... (1360-76), also known as the Black Prince (so named because of his black armor). When Edward died in 1376, she became the Queen Mother to her son Richard II. In 1378, the enemies of Wycliffe called him to stand before a tribunal of bishops in Lambeth Palace. Wycliffe was accused of spreading heresies, but the bishops were frustrated in carrying out any sentence. "...Sir Richard Clifford entered with a message from the Queen Mother, the widow of the Black Prince, forbidding them to pass sentence upon Wycliffe" (Fountain, *John Wycliffe*, p. 33). QUEEN ANNE, the wife of Richard II (1367-1400), also assisted Wycliffe."[70] [HDW, my addition]

A person not commonly mentioned as a protector of Wycliffe by authors is Lord Henry Percy (c. 1377), Marshall of England. Andrew Miller said:

---

[70] http://lifegivingword.googlepages.com/john

> "Wycliffe answered to the citation and proceeded to St. Paul's Cathedral, but not alone. He was accompanied by John of Gaunt, duke of Lancaster, and Lord Percy, marshal of England. The motives of these great personages were no doubt political, and added no real honor to the name or to the cause of Wycliffe."[71]

Obviously, God was at work protecting Wycliffe. Even though John of Gaunt did not support Wycliffe during the charges over 'transubstantiation' (see below), after Wycliffe's death in 1384, John of Gaunt would defend him again. Miller, perhaps speaking of Wycliffe's English gloss of all the Scriptures for a commentary for teaching, said that in 1390 after Wycliffe's death in 1384:

> "In the year 1380 the English Bible was complete. In 1390 the bishops attempted to get the version condemned by Parliament, lest it should become an occasion of heresies; but John of Gaunt declared that the English would not submit to the degradation of being denied a vernacular Bible."[72]

The Great Schism

Wycliffe's efforts for England and against the Roman Church doctrine and papal authority occurred as a result of papal political schemes and overt "papal" sin. Political popery would lead to two, and eventually three popes. One pope was located at Avignon, France, and another in Rome, and yet another in Piza.[73] One pope would settle in

---

[71] Andrew Miller, *Church History* (Way of Life Literature electronic edition, May 2003, Chapter 30, John Wycliffe) p. 5

[72] Ibid. p. 7 (Miller, *Church History*).

[73] The following website is an interesting account of the schism: http://www.mostholyfamilymonastery.com/Great_Western_Schism.html

Spain. The split is called the "Great Schism," which began in 1378 and lasted for nearly forty years, until 1417"[74] Phillip Schaff reports:

> "The papal schism, occurring in the midst of his (Wycliffe's) public career, had an important bearing on his views of papal authority."[75] (HDW, my addition).

In another passage, Schaff reports on the schism, saying:

> "Incensed at the attack made upon their habits and perquisites, and upon their national sympathies, the French cardinals, giving the heat of the city as the pretext, removed one by one to Anagni, while Urban (V) took up his summer residence at Tivoli. His Italian colleagues followed him, but they also went over to the French. No pope had ever been left more alone. Forming a compact body, the French members of the curia demanded the pope's resignation. The Italians, who at first proposed the calling of a council, acquiesced. The French seceders then issued a declaration, dated Aug. 2, in which Urban was denounced as an apostate, and his election declared void in view of the duress under which it was accomplished. It asserted that the cardinals at the time were in mortal terror from the Romans. Now that he would not resign, they anathematized him. Urban replied in a document called the *Factum*, insisting upon the validity of his election. Retiring to Fondi, in Neapolitan territory, the French cardinals proceeded to a new election, Sept. 20, 1378, the choice falling upon one of their number, Robert of Geneva, the son of Amadeus, count of Geneva. He was one of those who, four months before, had pointed out Tebaldeschi to the Roman mob. The three Italian cardinals, though they did not actively participate in the election, offered no resistance. Urban is said to have received the news with tears, and to have expressed regret for his untactful and self-willed course.

---

[74] Daniell, p. 71. However, the split of the Greek Orthodox Church from Roman Church in the 11th century (1054) was also called the "Great Schism."

[75] Schaff, p. 238.

> Perhaps he recalled the fate of his fellow-Neapolitan, Peter of Murrhone, whose lack of worldly wisdom a hundred years before had lost him the papal crown. To establish himself on the papal throne, he appointed 29 cardinals. But it was too late to prevent the schism which Gregory XI had feared and a wise ruler would have averted. Robert of Geneva, at the time of his election 36 years old, came to the papal honor with his hands red from the bloody massacre of Cesena. He had the reputation of being a politician and a fast liver. He was consecrated Oct. 31 under the name of Clement VII. It was a foregone conclusion that he would remove the papal seat back to Avignon. He first attempted to overthrow Urban on his own soil, but the attempt failed. Rome resisted, and the castle of St. Angelo, which was in the hands of his supporters, he lost, but not until its venerable walls were demolished, so that at a later time the very goats clambered over the stones."[76] (HDW, my addition).

The following three significant events in Wycliffe's life precipitated his preaching, teaching, and writing against Rome: (1) The clamorous events that occurred in Avignon related to defending the King against paying tribute (taxes) to Rome by Wycliffe, (2) the "Great Schism" in 1378, and (3) his removal from Canterbury in 1381 year, Wycliffe would become a champion defender against the corruption of Roman Catholicism. He despised ecclesiastical abuse.[77]

Wycliffe, the Anglo-Saxon Realist

Wycliffe was an Anglo-Saxon who:

[76] Schaff, p. 93-94.
[77] Schaff, p. 247.

> "was a moderate realist and ascribed to nominalism all theological error."[78]

Nominalism is a philosophical theory that denies the existence of universals; believes that there are no realities other than concrete individual objects. The motivation for a nominalist's beliefs flows from several concerns, the first one being where "universals" might exist. The Greek philosophers famously held that there is a realm of abstract forms or universals apart from the physical world. However, naturalists assert that nothing is outside of space and time. They asserted "names" given to universals were just "names," representing 'nothing.' Therefore a nominalist denied a word in the Bible such as olive tree, fig tree, Ephraim, etc. could stand for anything other than a real "object." A nominalist is a naturalist who denies anything exists out side of physical objects in space and time as we know it. They were the early existentialists. In the middle ages, several men were prominent nominalists: William of Ockham, Roscelin, and P. Abelard. Early nominalists were Aquinas and Augustine.[79]

Wycliffe, the English Tractarian

As a result of these theological travesties, political and religious turmoil, and many short-comings of the prelates, monks, and friars mentioned above, Wycliffe began to write many "tracts" against the atrocities occurring in and by the Roman Church. Wycliffe was terse in his criticism of Rome. Dr. Schaff writes again:

[78] Schaff, p. 245.
[79] See HighBeam Research.

> "The divine claims of the papacy itself began to be a matter of doubt. Writers like Wyclif made demands upon the pope to return to Apostolic simplicity of manners in sharp language such as no one had ever dared to use before."[80]

Fortunately, he was initially protected by the King(s) of England, parliament, John of Gaunt (Duke of Lancaster), the English queens, and the masses who loved him. It was claimed by his adversaries that every other person on the streets of England were Wycliffites or Lollards.

Even so, the danger and the stress on Wycliffe was great. His physical appearance betrayed the spiritual warfare and jeopardy on every side.

> "William Thorpe, a young contemporary standing in the court of Archbishop Arundel, bore testimony that "he (Wycliffe) was emaciated in body and well-nigh destitute of strength, and in conduct most innocent. Very many of the chief men of England conferred with him, loved him dearly, wrote down his sayings and followed his manner of life."[81] (HDW, my addition).

His most important tract (treatise), called the *Trialogus*, was written in response (1) to the mass amount of money collected in England and (2) to the indulgences offered for the crusaders by pope Urban VI when he was warring with the pope(s) at Avignon, France and Spain during the "Great Schism."

> "The most important of Wyclif's theological treatises, the Trialogus, was written in this period. It lays down the principle that, where the Bible and the Church do not agree, **we must obey the Bible, and, where**

[80] Ibid. p. 95. (Schaff, *History of the Christian Church*).

[81] Ibid. p. 243 (Schaff).

> **conscience and human authority are in conflict, we must follow conscience."**[82]

As Wycliffe's wisdom grew and as he was persecuted, he wrote profusely. He was responsible for writing many "tracts," but those **against** Rome came in his latter years. Incidentally, Wycliffe's arguments against the pope in favor of England's leaders in the thirteen hundreds was undoubtedly the fountainhead of ideas in the early 16th century (1) for supremacy of the King of England over the pope, (2) for King Henry VIII's (1491-1547) divorce from Queen Catherine of Aragon and marriage to Anne Boleyn, (3) for Archbishop of Canterbury, Thomas Cranmer's (1489–1556) declaration in favor of the King, that resulted in the beginning of the Anglican Church. [83] However, a few centuries later another change in course for England was promoted when many tracts would be written **in favor of** Rome by the "Tractarians" or "Puseyites" of the Oxford Movement in the latter half of the eighteen hundreds who were trying to (re)turn England to Rome.

> "In sermons, tracts and larger writings, Wyclif brought Scripture and common sense to bear. His pen was as keen as a Damascus blade. Irony and invective, of which he was the master, he did not hesitate to use. The directness and pertinency of his appeals brought them easily within the comprehension of the popular mind. He wrote not only in Latin but in English. His conviction was as deep and his passion as fiery as Luther's, but on the one hand, Wyclif's style betrays less of the vivid illustrative power of the great German and little of his sympathetic warmth, while on the other, less of his unfortunate coarseness. As Luther is the most vigorous tract writer that Germany has produced, so Wyclif is the foremost religious pamphleteer that has arisen in England; and the impression made by his clear

[82] Schaff, p. 243.

[83] http://www.allsaintsjakarta.org/anghist.htm#51.

> and stinging thrusts may be contrasted in contents and audience with the scholarly and finished tracts of the Oxford movement led by Pusey, Keble and Newman, the one reaching the conscience, the other appealing to the aesthetic tastes; the one adapted to break down priestly pretension, the other to foster it."[84]

The success and persistence of popery through the centuries is best characterized as:

> "the masterpiece of Satan"[85]

The Great Preacher: Wycliffe

Many of Wycliffe's sermons are extant ("294 of his English sermons and 224 of his Latin sermons have been preserved"[86]) He was the great preacher of his age and Schaff notes:

> "His work, *The Pastoral Office*, which is devoted to the duties of the faithful minister, and his sermons lay stress upon preaching as the minister's proper duty. Preaching he declared the "highest service,"[87]

His preaching was founded upon his beliefs concerning Truth, the church, and literal interpretation of Scripture. He defined the "church" as the body of the elect whose head is Christ.

> "The Church was defined in (Wycliffe's) *Civil Lordship* to be the body of the elect,— living, dead and

[84] Schaff, p. 240.
[85] Jones, *History of the Waldenses* (Way of Life Literature, Port Huron, MI, published in 1816 as found in Sismondi's *History of the Crusades Against the Albigenses,* quoted by Cramp) see chap. V., sect. 6).
[86] Schaff, p. 246.
[87] Schaff, p. 247.

not yet born,—whose head is Christ. Scarcely a writing has come down to us from Wyclif's pen in which he does not treat the subject, and in his special treatise on the Church, written probably in 1378, it is defined more briefly as the body of all the elect—*congregatio omnium predestinatorum*. Of this body, Christ alone is the head."[88] (HDW, my addition)

He also lashed out at "confessionalism" (confession to a priest):

"The rule of auricular confession Wyclif also disparaged."[89]

Wycliffe's View of Scripture

Toward the end of his life, Wycliffe arrived at the true end point of fundamental exegesis of the Scripture–literal interpretation. Schaff reports:

"Wyclif devotes much time to the principles of biblical exposition and brushes away the false principles of the Fathers and Schoolmen by pronouncing the "literal verbal sense" the true one. On occasion, in his sermons, he himself used the other senses, but his sound judgment led him again and again to lay emphasis upon the etymological meaning of words as final. The topological, anagogical and allegorical meanings, if drawn at all, must be based upon the literal meaning. Wyclif confessed his former mistake of striving to distinguish them with strict precision. There is, in fact, only one sense of Scripture, the one God himself has placed in it as the book of life for the wayfaring man."[90]

Wycliffe said:

---

[88] Schaff, p. 248.
[89] Schaff, p. 250
[90] Schaff, p. 255.

> "This is why I am accustomed to say that each part of Holy Scripture is true according to the divinely intended literal sense (*de virtute sermonis divini*)."[91]

And Wycliffe said that he and others disregarded interpretation **contrary** to the literal sense. He said:

> "For this reason the doctors often counsel that a sense which is contrary to the intended sense of the author should be dismissed."[92]

And concerning Scripture, Levy, a translator of Wycliffe's Latin works, said this about Wycliffe's approach to Scripture:

> "And nothing can be allowed to cast doubt upon the truthfulness of the Holy Spirit and the words of the Savior."[93]

As his beliefs about Scripture evolved, it caused him to desire the Words of Scripture (as opposed to a "doctors" interpretation) to be in the hands of the people, and his translation was begun. Much of the translation work probably proceeded from his commentaries on the Bible used at Oxford for teaching his students:[94]

---

[91] Levy, p. 93 (from his translation of Wycliffe's *De veritae sacrae scripturae*)..

[92] Ibid. p. 93 (Levy, from his translation of Wycliffe's *De veritae sacrae scripturae*).

[93] Ibid. p. 18.

[94] "Columbia Encyclopedia reports: "As far as the New Testament is concerned, Wyclif's authorship of the Early Version is based on his authorship of the "Commentary on the Gospels" from http://www.newadvent.org/cathen/15367a.htm. Other authors report Wycliffe commented on the "whole" Bible.

> "The New Testament was completed in 1380 and the Old Testament in 1382, just two years before he died."[95]

Certainly, John de Wycliffe's involvement in translating for the laity precipitated many of the attacks upon him, but he was harassed for many other reasons mentioned throughout this work (q.v.).

Wycliffe's Friends and Influences

Before addressing the controversies and in order to present a clear picture of Wycliffe's life, it behooves us to mention influential men who preceded his time and those who influenced him during his training. In his early career, Professor Wycliffe was known as a superior scholar of scholastics and debates. He was obviously influenced by the following men:

> "The chief survivors of the dialectical Schoolmen were Durandus and William Ockam. Gabriel Biel of Tübingen, who died just before the close of the fifteenth century, is usually called the last of the Schoolmen. Such men as D'Ailly, Gerson and Wyclif, sometimes included under the head of mediaeval scholastics, evidently belong to another class. A characteristic feature of the scholasticism of Durandus and Ockam is the sharper distinction they made between reason and revelation. Following Duns Scotus, they declared that doctrines peculiar to revealed theology are not susceptible of proof by pure reason. The body of dogmatic truth, as accepted by the Church, they did not question."[96]

---

[95] http://lifegivingword.googlepages.com/john
[96] Ibid. p. 143 (Schaff).

However, as Wycliffe grew in wisdom and understanding of God's Words, his interest in scholasticism waned and his focus shifted to "the sword of the Lord." He subsequently continued his education by obtaining his B.A. in theology and receiving his doctorate in 1372 as previously mentioned. He was influenced greatly by the Waldensians or Lollards from the county of Herefordshire. Nicholas of Hereford (from Herefordshire) was Wycliffe's "principle supporter in Oxford" and a colleague, although Nicholas was excommunicated and eventually became a monk (q.v.). Wycliffe was not excommunicated until probably 1395 after his death in 1384 .[97]

Professor Thomas Bradwardine (c. 1290–August 26, 1349), the '*doctor profundus*' at Oxford, who had been influenced by the Lollards in his home county of birth, Sussex, was one of Wycliffe's teachers at Oxford.[98]

> "Bradwardine enjoyed such an enviable reputation that Wyclif and other English contemporaries gave him the title, the Profound Doctor—*doctor profundus*. In his chief work on grace and freewill, delivered as a series of lectures at Merton, he declared that the Church was running after Pelagius."[99]

What were the beliefs that the Lollards presented to the English people that frightened the Roman authorities? A summary was presented to the English parliament in 1395. Whether they emanated from Wycliffe

---

[97] Daniell, 73.

[98] See the map in the appendix by G.M. Trevelyan found in *England in the Age of Wycliffe* (London: Longmans, Green, 1909). From: http://www.lollardsociety.org/map.html.

[99] Schaff, p. 233 (*Hisotry of the Chruch, Vol. 6*). Pelagius, a British or Irish monk who denied the doctrines of original sin and predestination and defended human goodness and free will; his views were declared heretical by the Council of Ephesus in 431 (circa 360-418) (http://dictionary.reference.com/search?q=Pelagius)

or whether they were incorporated by Wycliffe in his teachings cannot be determined for certain, although they most likely were from the Waldensian connection to the Lollards. What is certain is the spirit of their claims that go back many centuries. The Encyclopedia Britannica gives a summary of their *"Twelve Conclusions"* presented to parliament:

> They began by stating that the church in England had become subservient to her "stepmother the great church of Rome." The present priesthood was not the one ordained by Christ, while the Roman ritual of ordination had no warrant in Scripture. Clerical celibacy occasioned unnatural lust, while the "feigned miracle" of transubstantiation led men into idolatry. The hallowing of wine, bread, altars, vestments, and so forth was related to necromancy. Prelates should not be temporal judges and rulers, for no man can serve two masters. The *Conclusions* also condemned special prayers for the dead, pilgrimages, and offerings to images, and they declared confession to a priest unnecessary for salvation. Warfare was contrary to the New Testament, and vows of chastity by nuns led to the horrors of abortion and child murder. Finally, the multitude of unnecessary arts and crafts pursued in the church encouraged "waste, curiosity, and disguising." The *Twelve Conclusions* covered all the main Lollard doctrines except two: that the prime duty of priests is to preach and that all men should have free access to the Scriptures in their own language. The Lollards were responsible for a translation of the Bible into English, by Nicholas of Hereford, and later revised by Wycliffe's secretary, John Purvey."[100]

Because of Wycliffe's outstanding leadership and sound opposition to Rome, he gathered around him many followers who were scattered throughout England and even on the continent. Among his

100 Lollard. (2008). In Encyclopædia Britannica. Retrieved May 29, 2008, from Encyclopædia Britannica Online: http://www.britannica.com/EBchecked/topic/346626/Lollards.

supporters and students were the "pore preachers" who took his message around England, including John Huss of Bohemia (Czechoslovakia), a Roman Catholic priest of Hussite fame, and his supporter Jerome of Prague. All of his supporters were called Wycliffites in the literature. His supporters were also composed of graduates from Oxford, of laymen, and of Lollards.

> "Wyclif, at Oxford, and John Huss in Bohemia, attracted great attention by their sermons and brought down upon themselves ecclesiastical condemnation. Huss was one of a number of Bohemian preachers of eminence. Wyclif sought to promote preaching by sending out a special class of men, his 'pore preachers.'"[101] "These "pore priests," as they were called, were taken from the list of Oxford graduates, and seem also to have included laymen."[102]

Wycliffe's Friend, Chaucer

Geoffrey Chaucer (1343 – 1400?), was called "the father of English literature." He was a contemporary and friend of Wycliffe. In *The Canterbury Tales,* the 'pore preacher' was probably Wycliffe. He said of him:

"A good man was there of religioun
That was a pore Persone of a town;
But rich he was of holy thought and werk;
He was also a lerned man, a clerk,
That Christes gospel trewly wolde preche.
* * * * * * *
This noble ensample to his shepe he gaf,
That first he wrought and after that he taught.

---

[101] Ibid. p.170 (Schaff).
[102] Ibid. p. 240 (Schaff).

* * * * * * *

A better priest I trow that nowhere non is,
He waited after no pompe ne reverence;
Ne maked him no spiced conscience,
But Christes lore and his apostles twelve
He taught, but first he folwed it himselve."
CHAUCER.[103]

Rome Attacks Wycliffe

John de Wycliffe's outrage against Rome eventually drew the ire of the church and he was summoned to a synod in 1377:

> "before the tribunal of William Courtenay, bishop of London, at St. Paul's, where the proceedings opened with a violent altercation between the bishop and the duke (John of Gaunt, Duke of Lancaster)."[104] (HDW, my addition).

Eventually, his writings were confiscated and destroyed primarily because he refuted transubstantiation and placed the Scriptures in English into the hands of the people.

> "Rigid inquisition was made for copies of the condemned teacher's writings and those of (Nicholas of) Hereford."[105] (HDW, my addition).

[103] Schaff, p. 236-237.
[104] Schaff, p. 238
[105] Schaff, p. 242.

Recall, Nicholas of Hereford was one of his supporters. Finally, Wycliffe was even prohibited from preaching; so, instead he wrote.

> "Wyclif was inhibited from preaching, and retired to his rectory at Lutterworth. Hereford, Repyngdon, Aston and Bedeman, his supporters, recanted. The whole party received a staggering blow and with it liberty of teaching at Oxford. Confined to Lutterworth, Wyclif continued his labors on the translation of the Bible, and sent forth polemic tracts, including the *Cruciata,* vigorous condemnation of the crusade which the bishop of Norwich, Henry de Spenser, was preparing in support of Urban VI. against the Avignon pope, Clement VII."[106]

Wycliffe Called a Heretic

Because of Wycliffe's public preaching, tracts, and translation work, he was called every derisory word available by the pope, such as terrible devil—*horrendus diabolus*,[107] heretic, Lollard (a derisory name in that age). Wycliffe shot back at the pope calling him "anti-Christ."

He eventually succumbed to a stroke (cerebrovascular accident) which left him impaired physically. He died in 1384. Even in death, he was not left at peace:

> By the decree of (Archbishop) Arundel, **Wyclif's writings were suppressed**, and it was so effective that Caxton and the first English printers issued no one of them from the press. The Lateran decree[108] of February, 1413, **ordered his books burnt**, and the Council of Constance, from whose members, such as Gerson and

[106] Schaff, p. 242-243.
[107] Schaff, p. 249
[108] Decrees issued from the Lateran Palace in Rome where many councils were held in 649, 823, 864, 900, 1102, 1105, 1110, 1111, 1112, and 1116 1123, 1139, 1179, 1215, 1512-1517.

D'Ailly, we might have expected tolerant treatment, formally condemned his memory and **ordered his bones exhumed** from their resting-place and 'cast at a distance from the sepulchre of the church.' The holy synod, so ran the decree, 'declares said John Wyclif to have been a notorious heretic, and excommunicates him and condemns his memory as one who died an obstinate heretic.' In 1429, at the summons of Martin IV., the decree was carried out by Flemmyng, bishop of Lincoln."[109] (HDW, my emphasis)

And

"In 1414, the reading of the English Scriptures was forbidden upon pain of forfeiture 'of land, cattle, life and goods from their heirs forever.'"[110] "During the reign of Henry V (1413-22), an Act was confirmed by which the "English sheriffs were forced to take an oath to persecute the Lollards, and the justices must deliver a relapsed heretic to be burned within ten days of his accusation. ... No mercy was shown under any circumstances" (Armitage, A History of the Baptists, 1890, I, pp. 323, 325). In 1414 the legislature under Henry V joined in asking for harder measures against the Lollards. "After a suspected rising of the Lollards, a law was passed, declaring that ALL WHO READ THE SCRIPTURES IN THE MOTHER TONGUE SHOULD 'FORFEIT LAND, CATEL, LIF, AND GOODS, FROM THEYR HEYRES [THEIR HEIRS] FOR EVER'" (Eadie, History of the English Bible, I, p. 89)."[111]

Anywhere Wycliffites were found, Rome pursued them. Eventually, secular authorities hunted them down because of the pressure and influence of the pope's armies. On the continent for the next several

---

[109] Schaff, p. 244.
[110] Schaff, p. 257.
[111] http://lifegivingword.googlepages.com/john

centuries, Wycliffites, called Hussites in Bohemia from John Huss (1369-1415), were persecuted and killed.

> "Cochlaeus (1479-1552), Archbishop of Mainz, in writing against the Hussites, went beyond all former computations and ascribed to Wyclif the plump sum of 303 heresies, surely enough to have forever covered the Reformer's memory with obloquy."[112] (HDW, my addition, the Hussites, from John Huss of Bohemia, were like the Wycliffites)

Horrible Persecutions

J. M. Cramp establishes that the beginnings of burnings of dissenters from Rome began prior to Wycliffe's time. He said:

> "Fearful scenes were enacted. The human bloodhounds were at work in all directions. "This year," says one of the writers of the times, speaking of the year 1233, "innumerable heretics were burned in every part of Germany." Still they were unsubdued.... Some withdrew to more friendly lands."[113]

Prior to Wycliffe's age, England was the only country in Christendom that did not have a law for burning of heretics. Miller said:

> "Down to the beginning of the fifteenth century there had been no statue law in England for the burning of heretics. In all other parts of Christendom the magistrate, as under the old Roman imperial law, had obeyed the mandate of the bishops. England stood alone: without legal warrant no officer would have

---

[112] Schaff, p. 248.

[113] J. M. Cramp, *Baptist History* (Way of Life electronic edition, Port Huron, MI, chapter III, from "The History of the General Baptists" by Adam Taylor) p. 2.

> executed the ecclesiastical criminal. "In all other countries," says Milman, "the secular arm received the delinquent against the law of the church...." The obsequious Henry, to gratify the archbishop, issued a royal edict, ordering every incorrigible heretic to be burnt alive. The lying tongues of the priests and friars had so industriously circulated reports of the wild and revolutionary purposes of the Lollards, that Parliament became alarmed and sanctioned the King's decree."[114]

As the persecutions in England became severe, some of the early reformers associated with Wycliffe recanted their "alleged" heresies. This should not be held against them because the torture was severe and their families were threatened. We should have compassion. Few men can withstand watching their loved ones abused and battered although we should be steadfast *"unto death"* (Isa. 53:12, 2 Cor. 4:11, Phil. 2:30, Rev. 2:10). Many were branded or sent to the fires.

> "Many Lollards were branded and otherwise marked: Many were marked for life as "heretics" by branding or by being forced to wear special clothes. Some were forced to wear a depiction of a fiery torch on their clothes during the rest of their lives as a reminder "that they deserved burning" and as a continual warning to others of the potential price of standing upon the Bible and rejecting Roman Catholic authority. To go into the public without this garment or with it covered meant death. "And, indeed, to poor people it was true,--put it off, and be burned; keep it on, and be starved: seeing none generally would set them on work that carried that badge about them" (Evans, Early English Baptists, I, p. 23, f1)."[115] "The most prominent personages connected with the earliest period of Wycliffism, Philip Repyngdon, John Ashton, Nicolas Hereford and John Purvey, all recanted. The last three and Wyclif are associated by Knighton as the four arch-heretics. Repyngdon, who had

[114] Miller, p. 9-10 (Miller, *Church History,* chapter 30).
[115] http://lifegivingword.googlepages.com/john

> boldly declared himself at Oxford for Wyclif and his view of the sacrament, made a full recantation, 1382. Subsequently he was in high favor, became chancellor of Oxford, bishop of Lincoln and a cardinal, 1408. He showed the ardor of his zeal by treating with severity the sect whose views he had once espoused."[116]

It is well known that Purvey and other Wycliffites suffered greatly in prison.

> "It is probable that Purvey died in prison in miserable straits for his faith in the Word of God sometime during or after 1427. We are told he "endured great suffering in Saltwood Castle"[117] (Eadie, *History of the English Bible*, I, p. 65)."[118] (HDW, remember Wycliffe's bones were removed from his grave and burned in 1428 or 1429 secondary to 'hate').

Wycliffe's Curate: John Purvey "The Library of the Lollards" "Wycliffe's Glosser" "Doctor Eximius"

John Purvey is intimately associated with Wycliffe and with the Lollard movement in England in the thirteen hundreds. He was known as Wycliffe's roommate at Oxford and his curate or secretary at Lutterworth. When Wycliffe retired to Lutterworth from Oxford as a result of official discipline, but also as a gift from the King and legislature, John Purvey

[116] Schaff, p. 263-264.

[117] **Saltwood Castle** is a castle in Saltwood village— which derives its name from the Castle— 1 mile (2 km) north of Hythe, Kent, England.

[118] http://lifegivingword.googlepages.com/john

went with him. As we shall see below, Purvey was a scholar. Dr. Brown reports:

> "With the help of his personal secretary, John Purvey, Wycliffe translated the New Testament from Latin into Middle English in 1380 and the first English manuscript New Testament appeared. Two years later (1382), again with the help of Nicholas of Herford and John Purvey the Old Testament was completed and the entire hand scribed Bible was issued."[119]

Although many have deflated John Purvey's reputation, such as the "evidence presented by Professor Anne Hudson,"[120] Purvey's standing continues to (re)build, which may help restore some if not a lot of his reputation. The information about Purvey that is particularly attacked and denied is the account in the literature that he wrote the *Prologue* to the Purvey edition (LV) of the Wycliffe Bible, which was edited after Wycliffe's death from 1388 until 1395 when it was published.

Maureen Jurkowski reports:

> "New discoveries among Public Record Office sources can now, however, solve some of the mysteries of Purvey's life and work."[121]

The records demonstrate beyond doubt that Purvey was a Lollard, arrested many times, participated in revolts against the King's army at St. Giles Field, and was removed from the priesthood. Jurkowski reports:

---

[119] Brown, p. 4 (Our English Bible Heritage).

[120] Anne Hudson, "John Purvey: A Reconsideration of the Evidence for his Life and Writings" (*Viator*, xii (198), pp. 355-80.

[121] Maureen Jurkowski, "New Light on John Purvey", (*The English Historical Review,* Vol. 110, No. 439, Nov. 1995) pp. 1180-1190. Jurkowski is at the University of Keele, North Midlands, UK.

> "dismissory letters for the ordination to the priesthood of a John Purvey of Lathbury, Buckinghamshire, in 1377/8."[122]

He participated in "the Oldcastle revolt"[123] (q.v.). Also, he had many Latin works in his possession at his final arrest for the revolt against the King. This indicates he was better educated than previously admitted by recent scholars and could very likely have been a translator. Although it is hard for scholars to admit Purvey's involvement, their comments suggest otherwise. Jurkowski says:

> "In sum, the contents of Purvey's collection of books are what one would expect of someone engaged in this work of redaction and indicative that he was a participant, **if not a leader**, in these endeavors. Apart from the works referred to by Netter, it remains impossible to attribute the authorship of individual works to him, particularly those which had been completed some years earlier, such as the Prologue to the Wycliffite Bible. **Nevertheless, the fact that Purvey possessed a sermon cycle of some sort, as well as several of the works commonly cited in both the Prologue and the Wycliffite gospel glosses, heightens the possibility that he had been involved in the production of some or all of these works, while his participation in the Oldcastle revolt lends circumstantial support to the case for his authorship of the Disendowment Bill.** Although in no way reinstating the enormous reputation built up over the centuries, the new information presented here at the very least corroborates **Netter's evidence and justifies his portrayal of Purvey as a 'librarius' and 'doctor eximius' of Lollardy**... Purvey was a strong advocate of the layman's right to preach, and his involvement in the revolt implies that, like his master (Wycliffe) he was willing to assign an even greater role to secular rulers in

[122] Ibid. p. 1180. (Jurkowski).
[123] Ibid. p. 1181. (Jurkowski).

> religious affairs—the leadership in the reform of the Church.."[124] (HDW, my emphasis).

There is no doubt that Purvey recanted his involvement in Lollardy under extreme persecution during his first imprisonment and subsequent trials for heresy. It is interesting that some men arrested with him at his second arrest related to the St. Giles Field incident were "executed," but he was not. Perhaps it was because he was known as an "English scholar"?

> "The first preachers of the sect (Lollards), Hereford, Purvey, Aston and Brute, had been **scholars and theologians**; but more and more as time went on the priests were simple, poor men, and no great Lollard divine succeeded Wycliffe.[125] (HDW, my addition and emphasis)

Columbia Encyclopedia reports:

> "Purvey, John, c.1354–c.1421, **English scholar**, who in support of the Lollardy movement completed the first thorough translation of the Bible into English. Becoming associated with John Wyclif at Oxford, he accompanied the Lollard leader to Lutterworth in 1382 and there perhaps finished a faulty translation of the Bible previously begun by others under Wyclif's inspiration. He completed (c.1395) a careful and **scholarly translation** entirely his own. These two versions were erroneously attributed to Wyclif himself until modern times. The second shows a prose style better than that of Wyclif's writings; portions of it were later used by the translators of the King James Version.

---

[124] Ibid. p. 1189-1190. (Jurkowski)

[125] George Macaulay Trevelyan, *England in the Age of Wycliffe* (Longmans, Green, and Company, New York, London, and Bombay, 1900) p. 339.

> Purvey continued active as a Lollard until his arrest in 1401."[126]

He was given a rectory at "West Hyde , near archbishop Arundel's palace at Saltwood" after recanting on his arrest and trial for heresy in 1401, but the records show he did not stay there very long; he rejoined the fight against Rome's emissaries.[127] In 1414 he was rearrested for the Oldcastle revolt.

Wycliffe's Associate: Nicholas of Hereford

Nicholas of Hereford, Wycliffe's colleague and supporter at Oxford, recanted and became a Carthusian Monk because of the Roman Catholic persecution.[128]

> "Hereford, Wyclif's fellow-translator, appealed to Rome, was condemned there and cast into prison. After two years of confinement, he escaped to England and, after being again imprisoned, made his peace with the Church and died a Carthusian."[129]

Wycliffe's Enemy: Thomas Arundel

Soon after Wycliffe's death, dissenters from Rome and the followers of Wycliffe in England by order of Archbishop Arundel were not

---

[126] See http://www.answers.com/topic/john-purvey.

[127] Ibid. p. 1181. (Jurkowski).

[128] A Carthusian is a member of a monastic order founded by St. Bruno in 1086 near Grenoble, France. [Origin: 1520–30; < ML *Cartusiānus,* by metathesis from *Catursiānus,* after *Catursiānī* (*montés*) district in Dauphiné where the order was founded]
http://dictionary.reference.com/search?q=Carthusian

[129] Reference lost.

only imprisoned in horrible conditions, but were also sent to the fires for their religious beliefs.

> "The Constitutions of Thomas Arundel: In 1408 Thomas Arundel, Archbishop of Canterbury, at the Synod of Oxford, made a constitution which rendered it illegal to read any of Wycliffe's writings or translations within the province of Canterbury. "Detected copies of the Bible, or of any of its component books, would consequently be destroyed" (H.W. Hoare, *Our English Bible: The Story of Its Origin and Growth*, 1901, p. 100). The *Constitutions of Thomas Arundel* made this brash demand: "WE THEREFORE DECREE AND ORDAIN THAT NO MAN SHALL, HEREAFTER, BY HIS OWN AUTHORITY, TRANSLATE ANY TEXT OF THE SCRIPTURE INTO ENGLISH, OR ANY OTHER TONGUE, by way of a book, libel, or treatise, now lately set forth in the time of John Wyckliff, or since, or hereafter to be set forth, in part or in whole, privily or apertly, upon pain of greater excommunication, until the said translation be allowed by the ordinary of the place, or, if the case so require, by the council provincial" (Eadie, I, p. 89). This was the first English statute for the burning of heretics (though Bible-believing Christians had been burned before this), and it was not repealed until 1677, or 276 [sic. 269] years later. This is Arundel's estimation of the Bible translator: "This pestilential and most wretched John Wycliffe of damnable memory, a child of the old devil, and himself a child or pupil of Anti-Christ, who while he lived, walking in the vanity of his mind ... crowned his wickedness by translating the Scriptures into the mother tongue" (Fountain, *John Wycliffe*, p. 45)."[130] [HDW, my addition]

---

130 http://lifegivingword.googlepages.com/john

Lollard Tower (Prison)

Wycliffe's Follower: Sir John Oldcastle

One of the great accounts during the age of Wycliffe is the description of the persecution and martyrdom of a Wycliffe follower (called a Wycliffite), Sir John Oldcastle, a Lollard, who refused to recant. He was held in the infamous Lollard Tower at Lambeth where Purvey and Hereford were held.

> "With Sir John Oldcastle, otherwise known as Lord Cobham from his marriage with the heiress of the Cobham estate, it was different. He held firm to the end, encouraged the new preachers on his estates in Kent, and condemned the mass, auricular confession and the worship of images. Arundel's court, before which he appeared after repeated citations, turned him over to the secular arm "to do him to death." Oldcastle was imprisoned in the Tower,[131] but made his escape and was at large for four years. In 1414, he was charged with being a party to an uprising of 20,000 Lollards against the king. Declared an outlaw, he fled to Wales, where he was seized three years later and taken to London to be hanged and burnt as a traitor and heretic, Dec. 15, 1417. John Foxe saw in him "the blessed martyr of Christ, the good Lord Cobham."[132]

[131] The "Tower" was the infamous Lollard Tower at Lambeth where dissidents were imprisoned. "Lambeth Palace, the London headquarters of the Archbishop of Canterbury, was named Lollard's Tower." http://lifegivingword.googlepages.com/john

[132] Schaff, p. 265.

The Lollard prison (the "tower") is infamous. Scrawled on its walls are these words:

"Jesus amor meus (Jesus is my love)"[133]

More than a few Wycliffite "pore preachers," and Lollards followed Oldcastle into the flames and were "burnt." Almost 200 years later in 1523, Wycliffe continued to be blamed for causing men to fall into heresy.

> "Writing in 1523 to Erasmus, Tonstall, bishop of London, said of Lutheranism that "it was not a question of some pernicious novelty, but only that new arms were being added to the great band of Wycliffite heretics."[134]

Wycliffe Honored by the Populace

Although Wycliffe was despised by the prelates, friars, and monks, he was adored by many of the inhabitants in England in his day and in the centuries to come even to the present day. The author of this work is among them.

> "In the popular judgment of the English people, John Wyclif, in company with John Latimer and John Wesley, probably represents more fully than any other English religious leader, independence of thought, devotion to conscience, solid religious common sense, and the sound exposition of the Gospel. In the history of the intellectual and moral progress of his people, he was the leading Englishman of the Middle Ages."[135]

---

[133] K. Connolly, *The Indestructible Book* (Baker Books, Grand Rapids, NY, 1996) p. 80.
[134] Schaff, p. 268.
[135] Schaff, p. 244.

Wycliffism Spreads Across the English Channel

In 1559, the legislation aimed at Lollards was repealed. But not before Wycliffism (Lollardism) had gained a firm foot in surrounding nations, particularly Bohemia. This came about as a result of John Huss and Jerome of Prague. Jerome had studied at Oxford and was influenced by Wycliffe. Furthermore, Queen Anne, King Richard II's wife, was from the royal family in Bohemia and was taught by Wycliffe before he died. When the Queen passed away in England, her Bohemian attendants returned to their native land and brought Wycliffe's writings to Bohemia.[136] The following quote is repeated from earlier in this work with additional information.

> One of these was JOHN OF GAUNT, the Duke of Lancaster, who protected Wycliffe for many years. John was a large man and a bold warrior. His armor, which is displayed today in the Tower of London, is 6 foot 9 inches. Another protector was QUEEN JOAN (1328-85). She was the wife of Edward III (1360-76), also known as the Black Prince (so named because of his black armor). When Edward died in 1376, she became the Queen Mother to her son Richard II. In 1378, the enemies of Wycliffe called him to stand before a tribunal of bishops in Lambeth Palace. Wycliffe was accused of spreading heresies, but the bishops were frustrated in carrying out any sentence. "...Sir Richard Clifford entered with a message from the Queen Mother, the widow of the Black Prince, forbidding them to pass sentence upon Wycliffe" (Fountain, *John Wycliffe*, p. 33). The trial ceased. QUEEN ANNE, the wife of Richard II (1367-1400), also assisted Wycliffe. She was daughter to the Roman emperor Charles IV and sister of Wenceslaus, king of Bohemia. Anne was only a teenager when she was brought to England to wed

[136] H. D. Williams, M.D., Ph.D., *The Lie That Changed the Modern World* (Bible For Today Press, Collingswood, NJ, 2004) p. 134.

> Richard. She brought versions of Scriptures in German, Bohemian, and Latin with her into England. She loved Wickliffe's doctrine and sent copies of Wycliffe's books into Bohemia by her attendants (Ivimey, I, p. 69). The godly queen died in June 1394, at the age of twenty-seven."[137]

All of these things, under the watchful eye of an Almighty God, insured that the flames of reformation and rejection of Rome's false doctrines would spread.[138]

> "Across the seas in Bohemia, where the views of Wyclif were transplanted, they took deeper root than in England, and assumed an organized form. There, the English Reformer was called the fifth evangelist and, in its earlier stages, the movement went by the name of Wycliffism. It was only in the later periods that the names Hussites and Hussitism were substituted for Wycliffites and Wycliffism. Its chief spokesmen were John Huss and Jerome of Prague, who died at the stake at Constance for their avowed allegiance to Wyclif."[139]

It was in Bohemia that we see the launching point of some of the worst feats of the Jesuits, called the Society of Jesus Christ, which was the army of the Black Pope. Recall that eventually the Jesuits' presence would be felt more in England than anywhere else.[140] However, "the gates of

---

[137] http://lifegivingword.googlepages.com/john

[138] See Williams, p. 134-167 (*The Lie*) and Schaff, p. 269. Also, please remember that the Baptists were not "Reformers." They were the descendants of the Biblical churches from Apostolic times. We like to say, "Baptists came around the Reformation."

[139] Schaff, p. 268

[140] There were more secretive Jesuits in England than any other country. See Williams, *"The Lie"*, p. 73. Dr. Desanctis was a high ranking Jesuit in Rome who left the Roman Church. He said: "…it is no wonder therefore, if a Jesuit should feign himself a Protestant, for the conversion of Protestants."

hell" could not hold back the spread of doctrine based upon the preserved Words of God.

The desire of the English pioneer of reform, Wycliffe, would soon place the Scripture into the hands of the laity. It would begin succeeding beyond all expectations.

> "For hundreds of years no eminent teacher had emphasized the right of the laity to the Word of God. It was regarded as a book for the clergy, and the interpretation of its meaning was assumed to rest largely with the decretists and the pope. The Council of Toulouse, 1229, had forbidden the use of the Bible to laymen. The condemned sects of the 12th and 13th centuries, especially the Waldenses, had adopted another rule, but their assailants, such as Alanus ab Insulis, had shown how dangerous their principle was. Wyclif stood forth as the champion of an open Bible. It was a book to be studied by all Christians, for "it is the whole truth." Because it was given to the Church, its teachings are free to every one, even as is Christ himself."[141]

Wycliffe's views are said to have been conveyed around the world by the ashes of his burnt bones that were scattered in the stream Swift near his final rectory and burial place, Lutterworth.

> "[Thomas] Fuller says, [thus this brook the Swift] has conveyed his ashes into the Avon, Avon into the Severn, Severn into the narrow seas, they to the main ocean. And thus the ashes of Wycliffe are the emblem of his doctrine, which now is dispersed all over the world."[142] [HDW, my addition]

---

141 Schaff, p. 255.

142 Fuller, as quoted by Westcott, p. 309 (*Quarterly Review*, "The English Bible). Also, See Alexander McClure, "The Glorious History of the English Bible" (Preface to *Translators Revived,* Way of Life Literature, FBIS, c. 1850) preface.

We recoil at this scene 30 years after Wycliffe's death. We disdain the fact that Archbishop Chicheley of Canterbury went down to Lutterworth, removed Wycliffe's bones, burned, and scattered them. However, Thomas Armitage appropriately indicated it was used of God to breathe new life into "the great preacher's" sermons. He said:

> "...Chicheley, Archbishop of Canterbury, went down in state to Lutterworth to give new life to the venerable rector and to set him preaching again. A great body of solemn clergy went with him to enforce the grim sentence, and somehow managed to keep straight faces while they went through the pious farce of dragging the ghastly Yorkshire frame from the tomb. The little sanctuary stood on a hill, and when they had sated their ghostly ire at the charnel-house they drew the skeleton to the tiny river Swift, consumed it with dry fagots and threw the ashes into the generous stream. Every atom of his dust rested on a softer, purer bosom that day than Chicheley had ever known. Such a treasure had never floated on the laughing brook before, so it divided his holy ashes with the Severn and the sea. Little Lutterworth was too small either for his Bible or his bones, and now they are welcomed by the wide world."[143]

Our sovereign God was able to use this evil for His purposes. This little drama called attention to Wycliffe's efforts to place the Scripture into the hands of the laity and to his opposition to Rome. The account would become well known. The English reformer's aspirations would be followed in the years to come by men like William Tyndale and John Rogers.

---

[143] Thomas Armitage, *A History of the Baptists* (Way of Life electronic edition, Port Huron, MI, May 2003, chapter "Post-Apostolic Times, the Bohemian Brethren and the Lollards", first published 1819) p. 3.

Wycliffe's Titles

The titles at the beginning of this chapter attributed to this God fearing man during his age and over the centuries reveal not only very appropriate praise of him, but they also suggest his "reformation" activities and desires during a time of great darkness, evil, persecution, and suppression of the *Truth*. He "overcame" great obstacles. During Wycliffe's time, information could not be disseminated rapidly. There were no printing presses, telephones, computers, satellites, or other means of rapid communication. Manuscripts were copied by hand. His enemies in the Roman Catholic Church were not deterred from pursuing him by the English authorities.

Furthermore, papal revisionists were scattered throughout the known world, who changed or destroyed historical records and documents. As a result of these and other conditions, such as the Black (Bubonic) Plague or Black Death that caused millions of deaths throughout Europe and England from 1347 – 1351, historical records are sparse. Wycliffe's accomplishments are obscured. Subsequently, controversies about Wycliffe, his associates, and his translations of the Bible have arisen. Over the last two recent decades, debates are surfacing concerning Dr. John de Wycliffe and his associates such as John Trevisa, Nicholas of Hereford, and particularly John Purvey, the Lollards or Wycliffites[144] and the various translations or editions known as the Wycliffe Bibles.

---

[144] Some authors consider only Oxford graduates and collegues of Wycliffe at Oxford and elsewhere as Wycliffites, excluding the Lollards.

Name Changes For the Wycliffe Bibles

Until recent times, the version(s) of the whole Bible attributed to Wycliffe, which was translated between 1380 -84, has typically been known as the edition translated by Wycliffe with the help of Nicholas of Hereford and some authors include John Purvey. But, because of questions concerning whether Wycliffe actually performed very much of the translation work, the 1380-1384 edition is called the Early Version (EV) by **modern** scholars. This author believes this is wrong (q.v.). Furthermore, the later edition(s) of 1388-1395, which were allegedly edited by John Purvey or John Trevisa after Dr. Wycliffe's death, was called into question also and was therefore named the Late Version(s) (LV) instead of the Purvey edition of the Wycliffe Bible.

William E. Nix said:

> "The theology of Wycliffe was not reflected in the Wycliffe translations so much as in his tracts, treatises, and sermons, such as *The Last Age of the Church* (1356), *The Schism of the Popes* (1378), and *The Truth of Scripture* (1379. He was not guilty of spreading Protestantism as such, but was involved with placing the Scriptures into the vernacular and distributing them, but this in itself became a basic tenet of Protestantism. His probable translation principle is set forth in the *English Hexapla,* which makes the following observation: "...In translating from the Vulgate, Wycliffe has most faithfully adhered to that version; he seems to have adopted Hampoles's principle: "In this work y seke no straunge englishe, bot esiest and communeste, and siche that is moost lyche to the latyne, so that their knoweth not the latyne by the englishe may come to many latyne wordis.'" He adhered to this principle to such an extent that "the earlier Wycliffite version is an extremely literal rendering of the Latin original. Latin construction and Latin word-order are preserved even when they conflict

> with English idiom." The latter Wycliffite version is credited to his secretary, John Purvey (ca. 1354- 1428), who replaced many of the Latinate constructions with the native English idiom, with the net result being a tendency to drift away from the liturgical Latin, and consequently to weaken papal influence over the English people. In addition, Jerome's prefaces were replaced by a general prologue."[145]

There are 250 extant manuscripts of portions or of 'whole' Wycliffe Bibles:

> "about twenty surviving manuscripts of the 1380s are of the whole Bible, almost ninety of the whole New Testament." .[146]

Two Controversies: The Tip of the Iceberg

These two controversies: (1) did Wycliffe translate the EV, and (2) who edited or translated the LV after his death are the tip of the iceberg. Without a doubt, the modern controversies have arisen primarily from the lingering effects of the severe persecutions instigated by the Roman Catholic "Church" during Wycliffe's era. As a result, as mentioned before, written works lack proper identification of their sources and authors because of fear of imprisonment or death by those found translating them or even owning them.

In addition, if the works could be found by the Roman or political authorities, they were destroyed. The owners of Wycliffe manuscripts

---

[145] William E. Nix, "Theological Presuppositions and Sixteenth Century English Bible Translation, Part 1" (*Bibliotheca Sacra*, Dallas Theological Seminary, Vol. 124, Jan. 67) p.44.

[146] Dr. Jack Moorman, *Forever Settled, A Survey of the Documents and History of the Bible* (Dean Burgon Society Press, Collingswood, NJ, 1999, ISBN 1-888328-06-1, DBS #1428) P. 149.

were severely punished or killed by the cruel and painful means of being tied to a stake and burned. Most of us in modern times forget the sacrifices of those who went before us to place the Scripture into our hands. We have also not appropriated Jesus' commandment: *"If you love me, keep* (guard, protect, preserve, watch over) *my commandments"* (Jn. 14:15). Many modern "saints" do not understand the meaing of the commandment. Furthermore, most present day 'bible' sellers and promoters do not have the interests of the church of the Living God at heart; rather, their own "bellies."

Dr. John de Wycliffe did not shirk his responsibilities. Wycliffe and his followers clearly understood their duties as servants and watchmen of a Holy God, even if it meant "brynning." This is the primary significance and importance of studying Wycliffe and his followers, so that we may be encouraged to defend and preserve the Words of God. Certainly, the men before and during Wycliffe's age were hampered by suppression of manuscripts and loss of *"liberty which we have in Christ Jesus, that they might bring us into bondage"* (Gal. 2:4).

This work has briefly examined Wycliffe's life and will enumerate some of the controversies in the chapters to follow. More confusion seems to arise each year. Several charts covering significant events in Wycliffe's life are attached to the rear of this work for correlation of dates and events.

As Wycliffe grew in "wisdom," "understanding," and "the fear of the Lord," he was repelled by the actions of Roman authorities and drew progressively further and further away from Roman Catholic doctrine. Some authors report that during the Black Plaque, Wycliffe spent a considerable amount of time in his room praying and reading the Scripture. It was during these years that his focus on the Truth emerged and he began to preach and write against false teachings. He wrote many tracts against false doctrines as he spiritually developed and comprehended how wrong Rome was in the administration and organization of the Church. As he learned, he revealed Rome's errors to the people of Britain. Rome's anger grew progressively until it was no longer tolerant of him in any way.

Why Rome Hated Wycliffe

The following reasons are why Rome hated Wycliffe. The reasons are from David Cloud's "John Wycliffe: The Father of the English Bible:"

1. "He taught that the apostolic churches have only elders and deacons 'and declared his conviction that all orders above these had been introduced by Caesarean pride' (Shelton, II, p. 415)."
2. "Wycliffe believed the Bible to be the Word of God without error from beginning to end. He testified, 'It is impossible for any part of the Holy Scriptures to be wrong. In Holy Scripture is all the truth; one part of Scripture explains another' [(David) Fountain, *John Wycliffe*, p. 48]." (HDW, my addition).
3. "Wycliffe's foundational doctrine was that the Bible is the sole authority for faith and practice and that men had the right to interpret Scripture for themselves before the Lord. He said, 'Believers should ascertain for themselves what are true matters of their faith, by having the Scriptures in a language which all may understand.'"
4. "Wycliffe was very bold against the pope, contending that 'it is blasphemy to call any head of the church, save Christ alone' (Thomas Crosby, *History of the English Baptist,* I, 1740, p. 7)." He also said:

a. "It is supposed and with much probability, that the Roman pontiff is the great Antichrist."
b. "How then shall any sinful wretch, who knows not whether he be damned or saved, constrain men to believe that he is head of holy Church?" (Shelton, II, p. 415)."
c. "Antichrist puts many thousand lives in danger for his own wretched life. Why, is he not a fiend stained foul with homicide who, though a priest, 'fisths in such a cuase?'"

5. "Wycliffe taught that men have the right to have the Bible in their own languages and was willing to endure the wrath of the Catholic authorities by translating the Scriptures into English."
6. "There is some evidence that Wycliffe rejected infant baptism, at least toward the end of his life. There is evidence of this from his own writings. Wycliffe taught that 'baptism doth not confer, but only signify grace, which was given before'. This principle undermines the doctrine of infant baptism. The *Martyrs Mirror*, first published in Dutch in 1660, states that in 1370 Wycliffe issued an article 'declared to militate against infant baptism' (p. 322)."[147]

These are some of the reasons Wycliffe was so disliked by the Roman prelates and their supporters. The main thrust of Roman Catholicism's attack began 150 years before Wycliffe. Christopher Anderson said:

> "That it was not only unlawful, but injurious, for the people at large to read the Scriptures, had, indeed, for ages, been regarded as an axiom, by all these

[147] Cloud, p. 3-5 ("John Wycliffe: The Father of the English Bible").

> nations. Nor was this idea left to pass merely as a received opinion. Not to mention other proofs, more than a hundred and fifty years before Wycliffe had finished his determined purpose, or in the year 1229, at the Council of Toulouse, when forty-five canons were passed and issued for the extinction of heresy and the establishment of peace, what were two of those canons? One involved the first court of inquisition, and another the first canon which forbade the Scriptures to the laity, or the translation of any portion of them into the vulgar tongue. The latter was expressed in very pointed terms: "We also forbid the laity to posses any of the books of the Old and New Testament, except, perhaps, the Psalter or Breviary for the Divine Offices, or the Hours of the Blessed Virgin, which some, out of devotion, wish to have; but having any of these books translated into the vulgar tongue, we strictly forbid."[148]

Perhaps these glimpses of the man Wycliffe show why his works were burned by Rome, why he was persecuted, why his followers were persecuted, and why many of the records concerning him are lost. As a result scholars have debated many issues for the last several decades.

Some of the Issues Raised

Among the issues or questions raised secondary to past and recent scholarship are:

1. Was John de Wycliffe born in Hipswell, Ipswell, or Wycliffe-on-Tees or Wycliffe-on-Wye? (One location may be more important for contact with Lollards)?
2. Was he born in 1320, 1324, 1327, or 1330.

[148] Christopher Anderson, *The Annals of the English Bible* (from www.williamtyndale.com/0johnwycliffe.htm, accessed 02/2008) p. 60.

3. Did Dr. Wycliffe do any of the translation of the Latin manuscripts (MSS) of the Bible into English? If he did, what portion did he do?
4. Is the Early Version (EV) of the Wycliffe Bible translated from Rome's Latin Vulgate MSS, which is the work of Sophronius Eusebius Hieronymus (who is called Jerome) from Hebrew and Greek MSS? Did Dr. Wycliffe use the "vulgar" or "old" Latin MSS often used by the Waldensian church leaders in Northern Italy and the piedmont (valley) areas of France and Spain?
5. Is the EV the first English translation of the Bible?
6. Did translators who were associated with Dr. Wycliffe revise the EV "back" to the Latin Vulgate after his death, which is called the Late Version (LV)?
7. Was John Purvey, Wycliffe's personal secretary, one of the translators of the EV or was he a 'simply' a copyist?[149]
8. Was John Purvey the person who caused the LV to be a more idiomatic English translation and more aligned with the Latin Vulgate?
9. Did Rev. Josiah Forshall and Sir Frederic Madden, the authors of the splendid 4 volume work on Wycliffe translations published in 1850, incorrectly attribute the LV to Purvey in their preface?
10. Was John Trevisa or John Purvey the "J" in the Cambridge MS (Ee.1.10) of the MSS of Wycliffe's translations, since

[149] Remember, there were no printing press until Johannes Gensfleisch zur Laden zum Gutenberg's (c. 1400 – February 3, 1468) in the 1430's. During Wycliffe's time all works were handwritten and copied. Even so, some copies of Wycliffe's Bibles produced by hand are exquisite and demonstrate advanced lithographic techniques.

only two names, Nicholas of Hereford, and one of "J" are mentioned in the 250 extant MSS?

11. Are the EV and LV really separate translations or **a** translation in progress (i.e. retranslation, revision, improvement)?
12. If Dr. Wycliffe was the most outstanding "scholastic" scholar of the "schoolmen" at Oxford in the thirteen hundreds, would he be unfamiliar with Greek, since many classics used for 'scholasticism' were written in Greek and some were translated into Latin?
13. Was Dr. Wycliffe a Lollard? Did "Lollardy" (from mutterers, mumblers, tares, lullaby, or Walter Lollard, see below) arise as a Wycliffian sect or did they predate Wycliffe (i.e. were they Waldensians from Germany or France and subsequently Herefordshire)?
14. Did the KJB translators use Wycliffian phraseology, or earlier English works, or Tyndale's (alternate spelling, Tindale) phraseology?
15. Did the martyr John Huss study under Wycliffe at Oxford or did Queen Ann's attendants from Bohemia bring Wycliffe's writings to Huss after her death?
16. Did Wycliffe ever propose a *sola scriptura* "theory"?[150] (*Truth*, p. 19)

---

[150] Levy said: "...Wycliffe never proposed a *sola scriptura* theory..." because he never "precluded the Church fathers as inspired interpreters of the Bible" [and] "Wycliffe was not opposed in principle to canon law, therefore, only the notion that papal statutes could be put on a par with Scripture." (Levy, p. 19 preface to his translation of "*On the Truth of Holy Scripture*). In light of Wycliffe's life and writings, it is beyond this author's understanding how anyone could not conclude Wycliffe put Scripture above all (q.v.).

CHAPTER 3

CONTROVERSIES

The "Ban" on Wycliffe and His Works

Before proceeding, a comment needs to be made concerning the difficulty researchers share concerning the details of events surrounding John de Wycliffe's life. Dr. Wycliffe was born and lived during a difficult time. Severe persecutions and tumultuous events such as the "Great Schism" and the "Peasant's Revolt" described above were occurring.

MAGNA CARTA
1297 A.D.

Furthermore, the barons already had their "Magna Carta,"[151] but the poor peasants didn't have any document defending their "freedom." Because of Wycliffe's dream to place the Magna Carta of the poor, the Holy Bible, into the hands of the common people, his works were banned by the ecclesiastical prelates in England and

---

[151] *Magna Carta, 1297: "Widely viewed as one of the most important legal documents in the history of democracy..."* http://www.archives.gov/exhibits/featured_documents/magna_carta/

in Rome and for a while by England's government. Furthermore, the clerics and authorities condemned his tracks, sermons, and translation work to the flames.

Even so, many of Wycliffe's works are extant. But, as a result of (1) the widespread destruction of his works, (2) the fear of accurately recording the names of his followers on works secondary to the persecutions, and (3) the tampering with his works by his opponents, many facts concerning Wycliffe and his works are unresolved.

In addition, many of the works, which came about because of Wycliffe's tenacity, bravery, and faith, remained **unprinted** for many years because of fear of retribution. There was a ban on his works. As a matter of fact, his edition of the Scriptures was not **printed** until Forshall and Madden's four volume work in 1850 that placed the Wycliffe (EV) translation of the New Testament in 1380 and the Old Testament in 1382 beside the Purvey (LV) edition (1388-1395) in parallel columns. Forshall and Madden spent twenty-two years preparing their work.

Dr. Schaff describes the results and reason for the "ban," saying:

> "In his *prologue*, Purvey makes express mention of the "English Bible late translated," and affirms that the Latin copies had more need of being corrected than it. One hundred and seventy copies of these two English bibles are extant, and it seems strange that, until the edition issued by Forshall and Madden in 1850, they remained unprinted. The reason for their not being struck off on the presses of Caxton and other early English printers, who issued the *Golden Legend*, with its fantastic and often gruesome religious tales, was that Wyclif had been pronounced a heretic and his version of the Scriptures placed under the ban by the religious authorities in England."[152]

[152] Schaff, p. 256.

Also, as previously mentioned, this may be the reason the KJB translators do not mention Wycliffe in their Preface in 1611.

The Latin Question

Please note the reference to the Latin copies in the quote above. Was the writer of the preface referring to the Latin Vulgate, which "had more need of being corrected" or to other "Old Latin" MSS?

The Latin Vulgate's origin can be traced to Jerome. He used Alexandrian text-types that many scholars believe emanated from Origen's pen. Origen's works, in particular his *Hexapla*, were taken to Caesarea where Pamphilius, Origen's student, placed them in a library used by the church historian Eusebius to produced the Bibles ordered by Emperor Constantine. It is believed by many excellent scholars that Jerome used the Greek and Hebrew texts "revised" by Origen.

The Old Latin (OL) MSS are closer to the Received Hebrew Masoretic and Greek Texts than the work of Jerome. The OL MSS were used by Waldensian type churches in Northern Italy. Also, several OL MSS exist from several areas of the empire, particularly Northern Egypt.

Much Research Needed

There is much research that needs to be done concerning Wycliffe and his works because of the ban and neglect of them for so many years. "It is a source of scholarly shame..."[153] Many debates surround this great man, "the fifth evangelist." The remainder of this work will briefly review some of the controversies surrounding him, his works, and his associates.

---

[153] Daniell, p. 78

It is almost a miracle that any of his works survived unto the present day because of the wholesale destruction of Wycliffe's and the Lollards' works by the papal 'blood thirsty wolves'. It is not this authors intention to resolve the issues; rather, simply to enumerate them and to call attention to them.

Controversy #1

How is his name spelled?

Even the spelling of his name is controversial. It has been spelled differently in various countries and well as by various authors. Phillip Schaff said:

> Wyclif's name is spelled in more than **twenty different ways**, as Wiclif, accepted by Lechler, Loserth, Buddensieg and German scholars generally; Wiclef, Wicliffe, Wicleff, Wycleff. Wycliffe, adopted by Foxe, Milman, Poole, Stubbs, Rashdall, Bigg; Wyclif preferred by Shirley, Matthew, Sergeant, the Wyclif Society, the Early English Text Society, etc. The form Wyclif is found in a diocesan register of 1361, when the Reformer was warden of Balliol College. The earliest mention in an official state document, July 26, 1374, gives it Wiclif.[154] [HDW, my emphasis]

In this work, we will follow Foxe's spelling of Wycliffe's name. His name is often seen as John de Wycliffe after the custom of assuming names from the village, town, or city where a family lived. It is a Biblical custom, also. For example, "Elimelech,...Ephrathites of Beth-lehem-judah" (Ruth 1:2).

---

[154] Phillip Schaff, *History of the Christian Church, Vol. 6* (Master's Christian Library, Ages Software, Albany, OR, 1997) p. 622.

Controversy #2

Where and when was he born? Does where he was born make a difference?

His birth place and the date of his birth (1320, 1324, 1328, or 1330) are disputed facts. Some claim that Wycliffe was born in Hipswell (or Ipswell or Spresswell), West Yorkshire, near Richmond or Wyclif-on-Tees, South Yorkshire. They are located further apart on current maps than previously claimed.

> "Leland, our first authority for the place of birth, mentions Spresswell (Hipswell) and Wyclif-on-Tees, places a half a mile apart...On Wyclif's birthplace, see Shirley, *Fasciculi*, p. x sqq."[155]

The "Tees" is a river. The village of "Wyclif" was located on its banks. The significance is related to the traveling poor Lollard Waldensian) preachers who had a significant influence on Wycliffe and Wycliffe on them, particularly those coming out of Herefordshire in the thirteen hundreds.

Wyclif-on-Tees would be easier to reach by foot or horse than Richmond (Hipswell) and would be nearer Herefordshire. The importance is the possible influence of Welsh Baptists and Waldensians in England, who seemed to concentrate in a deep valley near Olchon in or near Hereford in the county of Herefordshire, UK. It is protected by some steep terrain. The villages of Herefordshire and the surrounding counties were frequented by the Baptist preachers or Waldensians coming out of Olchon. They avoided the areas where there was a significant presence of the pope's armies (see the map in the appendix). It would include the

[155] Ibid. (Schaff, History of the Christian Church).

areas or counties that bordered the valley surrounded by 'mountains' that extended North and South out of Herefordshire.

> "Joshua Thomas, in his *History of the Welsh Baptists*, describes some Baptists who lived in the 14th century **in Olchon in Herefordshire**, and he believes **Wycliffe "received much of his light in the gospel" from these separatist believers** (Ivimey, Vol. I, pp. 65-67)."[156]

In spite of the attempts of the authorities to suppress Lollardy, it continued to spread and by the sixteenth century had many adherents in many locations (see the map in the appendix).

Some authors report Wycliffe was born in Richmond or in Hipswell, Yorkshire in various years from 1320 to 1330:

> Wycliffe was born about the year 1330 at Hipswell, Yorkshire, to a farming family who owned tracts of land, centered in the town of Wycliffe-on-Tees.[157]

Another said:

> "The 'Morning Star' of the Reformation (the phrase is John Bale's in 1548) was born near Richmond in Yorkshire in 1324."[158]

William E. Nix said:

> "It was in his recoil from the spiritual apathy and moral degeneracy of the clergy that John Wycliffe (ca.

---

[156] Subir Balasundaram, "John Wycliffe, the Father of the English Bible", http://lifegivingword.googlepages.com/john, accessed 04/2008.
[157] Wards Book of Days, "On This Day in History, http://www.wardsbookofdays.com/31december.htm, accessed 04/2008.
[158] Daniell, 70.

1328-1384) was thrust into the limelight, and the first complete Bible was translated into English."[159]

Brooke Foss Westcott said:

> "Wycliffe was born in 1324, in the parish of Wye-cliffe, situated on the banks of the river Wye, in Yorkshire."[160]

Others report:

> John Wycliffe was born around 1330, the son of the lord of the manor of Wycliffe-on-Tees, a small village near Richmond in Yorkshire.[161]

Another says:

> "John Wycliffe (1320-1384) was a theologian and early proponent of reform in the Roman Catholic Church during the 14th century.... Wycliffe was born at Ipreswell, (modern Hipswell), Yorkshire, England, between 1320 and 1330;"[162]

Controversy #3

Was Dr. Wycliffe the progenitor of Lollardism or was the doctrine he preached and taught similar; therefore Lollardism

---

[159] William E. Nix, "Theological Presuppositions and Sixteenth Century English Bible Translation, Part 1" (*Bibliotheca Sacra*, Dallas Theological Seminary, Vol. 124, Jan. 1967) p. 43.
[160] Brooke Foss Westcott, "The English Bible" (*Quarterly Review*, John Murray, London, Jan & April, 1870, printed by William Clowes & sons) p. 323.
[161] http://www.crosbyheritage.co.uk/blog/entry/colins-little-known-facts-john-wycliffe-and-lutterworth/ accessed 04/15/2008.
[162] The Bible Museum, www.greatsite.com/timeline-english-bible-history/john-wycliffe.html, accessed 04/15/2008.

was associated with Wycliffe, but predated him? Were the Lollards actually Waldensians? How did the "Lollard" name arise? Was it from Walter Lollard? Does "Lollard" mean mutterers (mumblers) or something else?

Dr. Wycliffe's followers were called Wycliffites and Lollards by many authors. His doctrine was called Lollardism or Wycliffism. Christopher Anderson wrote:

> "Any influential connection, however, between the Waldensians or Vaudois and Wycliffe has never been clearly proved, and probably never will. At all events, before he could be stimulated by their example, he seems to have taken his ground, as it is only in his latest compositions that a few slight references to them are to be found, as to a people with whose sufferings he sympathized. He was on the Continent, at Bruges, it is true, from 1374 to 1376, but he had commenced, and must have been far advanced in his undertaking, long before then. In short, as far as the term can be applied to any human being, the claims of Wycliffe to originality have now come to be better understood, and every Christian will recognize the "Secret Mover" (i.e., the sovereign hand of God)."[163]

Dr. Schaff seems to favor the origin of the doctrines of Lollardism from Holland and France, but contrary to many others he denies that the name originated from Walter Lollard. He said:

> "Although the impulse which Wyclif started in England did not issue there in a compact or permanent organization, it was felt for more than a century. **Those who adopted his views were known as Wycliffites or Lollards,** the Lollards being associated with the

---

[163] Christopher Anderson, *The Annals of the English Bible* (William Pickering, London, 1845) p. 61.

> Reformer's name by the contemporary chroniclers, Knighton and Walsingham, and by Walden. The former term gradually gave way to the latter, which was used to embrace all heretics in England. The term Lollards was transplanted to England from Holland and the region around Cologne (France). As early as 1300 Lollard heretics were classed by the authorities with the Beghards, Beguines, Fratricelli, Swestriones and even the Flagellants, as under the Church's ban. The origin of the word, like the term Huguenots, is a matter of dispute. **The derivation from the Hollander, "Walter Lollard," who was burnt in Cologne, 1322, IS NOW ABANDONED** [Fredericq, I. 172. A certain Matthew, whose bones were exhumed and burnt, is called Mattaeus Lollaert. Fred., I. 250. For documents associating the Lollards with other sectarists, see Fred., I. 228, II. 132, 133, III. 46, etc.][164] (HDW, my addition and emphasis).

Dr. Schaff indicates in the previous quote that he believed the Lollard movement in England originated in Holland. Others report France or Germany as the origin of Lollardy (Waldensians). Joseph Milner reports a connection between Wycliffe and the Waldensians through Raynard Lollard mentioned above from Cologne, France, and other Waldensians from across the English Channel. Was "Raynard" Lollard the same as "Walter" Lollard (see below)? Catholic writers also report the connection:

> "Anglican historian Joseph Milner notes the possible connection between the Waldensians and John Wycliffe: "The connection between France and England, during the whole reign of Edward III, was so great, that it is by no means improbable, that Wickliffe himself derived his first impressions of religion from [Raynard] Lollard [a Bible-believing Waldensian leader who was burned at the stake at Cologne]" (Milner, *The History of the Church*

[164] Schaff, p. 262.

> *of Christ*, 1819, III, p. 509). Catholic writers connected Wycliffe with the Waldenses. "Thomas Walden, who wrote against Wickliff, says, that the doctrine of Peter Waldo was conveyed from France into England—and that among others Wickliff received it. In this opinion he is joined by Alphonsus de Castro, who says that Wickliff only brought to light again the errors of the Waldenses. Cardinal Bellarmine, also, is pleased to say that 'Wickliff could add nothing to the heresy of the Waldenses'" (Jones, A History of the Christian Church, II, p. 91)."[165]

This author does not believe that the name "Waldensians" derived from the Waldensian pastor, Peter Waldo. The term refers to "the people of the valley"[166]. Samuel Howard Ford said:

> "Now Mosheim, with whom there is a general agreement among historians, states that "Walter, a Dutchman of remarkable eloquence, and famous for his writings who came from Mentz to Cologne, was burned there in 1322." (History, p. 356) Fuller and Perrin state that he came to England in the reign of Edward III "from the Waldenses, among whom he was a great barb or pastor." That this man's name was Walter Reynard is most evident, and, "Lollard," a term of reproach, was given to him and his brethren because they were accustomed to sing psalms and hymns. Abelly says the word is derived from loben, "to praise," and herr, "Lord." But, however this may be, the fact is unchallenged, that Walter the Lollard, a shining light in the midnight of Papal darkness, after passing from country to country, lifting his eloquent voice and scattering over the winter seed-fields the germs of truth, passed trough (sic) England to build up the scattered flock of Christ there, and then breathed out his great soul amid the fires of

[165] http://lifegivingword.googlepages.com/john

[166] H. D. Williams, M.D., *The Lie That Changed the Modern World* (Bible For Today Press, Collingswood, NJ, 2004) p. 122-124.

> martyrdom, before John Wickliffe was born...He came from the Waldensian Baptists to England."[167]

Samuel Ford also said:

> "That this Walter Lollard was a Baptist is unquestionable. He came from the Waldensian Baptists to England, and found Baptists there, who welcomed this eloquent teacher among them, may be traced to a still higher date....In Gascony the heretics, says the old monkish historian, Sir William Newbury, *"were as numerous as the sands of the sea."* **A company of these Baptists were found in England in the tenth century**, and is thus described by Henry in his history of Great Britain, which in substance, corresponds with Napier, Collier, and Lyttleton."[168]

Other authors report that Wycliffe **founded** the Lollards. Dr. R. C. Wetzel said:

> "JOHN WYCLIFFE, the "Morning Star of the Reformation," **founded the Lollards** and published his English New Testament, the first complete manuscript. He was expelled from Oxford University for insisting Christ and not the Pope was head of the church, that the Bible instead of the church was the sole authority for the believer, and opposing the dogma of transubstantiation...JOHN WYCLIFFE died. NICHOLAS of Hereford completed the translation of the Old Testament into English."[169] (HDW, my emphasis).

---

[167] Samuel Howard Ford, *The Origin of the Baptists: Traced Back by Milestones on the Track of Time* (Way of Life Literature, Port Huron, MI, FBIS, 2003, Chapter V, "Century Fourteen: Wickliffe and the Lollards") p. 4.

[168] Ibid. p. 4 (Ford, *The Origin of the Baptists*).

[169] Dr. R. C. Wetzel, *A Chronology of Biblical Christianity* (Books For The Ages, Ages Software, 1995) p. 140-141.

The *Encyclopedia Britannica* subtly indicates under the topic "Translation of the Bible" the postmodern seeds of controversy surrounding Wycliffe and his followers.:

> "From August 1380 until the summer of 1381, Wycliffe was in his rooms at Queen's College, busy with his plans for a translation of the Bible and an order of Poor Preachers who would take Bible truth to the people. (His mind was too much shaped by Scholasticism, the medieval system of learning, to do the latter himself.) There were two translations made at his instigation, one more idiomatic than the other. The most likely explanation of his considerable toil is that the Bible became a necessity in his theories to replace the discredited authority of the church and to make the law of God available to every man who could read. This, allied to a belief in the effectiveness of preaching, led to the formation of the Lollards. **The precise extent to which Wycliffe was involved in the creation of the Lollards is uncertain.** What is beyond doubt is that they propagated his controversial views.
>
> "In 1381, the year when Wycliffe finally retired to Lutterworth, the discontent of the labouring classes erupted in the Peasants' Revolt. His social teaching was not a significant cause of the uprising because it was known only to the learned, but there is no doubt where his sympathies lay. He had a constant affection for the deserving poor. The archbishop of Canterbury, Simon of Sudbury, was murdered in the revolt, and his successor, William Courtenay (1347–96), a more vigorous man, moved against Wycliffe. Many of his works were condemned at the synod held at Blackfriars, London, in May 1382; and at Oxford his followers capitulated, and all his writings were banned. That year, Wycliffe suffered his first stroke at Lutterworth; but he continued to write prolifically until he died from a further stroke in December 1384. **Assessment** "It is no wonder that such a controversial figure produced—and still produces—a wide variety of reactions. The monks and friars retaliated, immediately and fiercely, against his denunciations of them, but such criticism grew less as

> the Reformation approached. Most of Wycliffe's post-Reformation, Protestant biographers see him as the first Reformer, fighting almost alone the hosts of medieval wickedness. **There has now been a reaction to this, and some modern scholars have attacked this view as the delusion of uncritical admirers.** The question "Which is the real John Wycliffe?" is almost certainly unanswerable after 600 years."[170]

The English historian, Joseph Ivimey, believed that the Lollards sprung from Walter Lollard, a Waldensian. He believed they were the first reformers against "Popish darkness" long before Luther, Erasmus, and other reformers. Certainly, the Waldensians had a great influence on Wycliffe, "the morning star of the reformation." Please note Ivimey's connection of the Lollards or Waldensians with Herefordshire and with the seed of reformation that began there. Ivimey said:

> "There seems to me to be reason to believe that the Lollards in England were of similar sentiments on this subject [baptism]. **Walter Lollard from whom they sprung, was a Waldensian barb**;...These it is likely, were the first public opposers of the corruptions of the church of Rome in England, after the massacre of the ancient British Christians under the direction of the pope...It might be presumed that some of their descendants, wither in **Wales**, or upon the borders of it, that is to say, in **Herefordshire** and the adjoining counties, would for some age maintain the same principles with themselves. This presumption accords with fact; for the most early and most eminent Christians in England, after the conquest, are said to have been born in this part of the island, These were Bradwardine, Brute, Sir John Oldcastle, Tyndal, Penry, and others...[T]he Baptist church of Olcon, and Chapel-y-ffin,...Olchon is a deep narrow valley, under the black

[170] John Wycliffe. (2008). In *Encyclopædia Britannica.* Retrieved May 29, 2008, from Encyclopædia Britannica Online: http://www.britannica.com/EBchecked/topic/650168/John-Wycliffe

mountain, in the parish of Cludock, and properly in Herefordshire... **It is my opinion that the first open struggle of Protestant light against Popish darkness, among our countrymen, began at or near Olchon; and that long before the appellation of Protestant was known even in Germany."**[171]

Incidentally, other authors report Thomas Bardwardine, Wycliffe's professor at Oxford, was born in Sussex, south of London, rather than Herefordshire that is west of London near Wales (see below). Wherever he was born and raised, he certainly influenced Wycliffe. Andrew Miller, the church historian, said:

> "John Wycliffe found his way to Oxford. He was admitted a student of Queen's College, but soon removed to Merton College, the oldest, the wealthiest, and most famous of the Oxford foundations. It is supposed that he was privileged to attend the lectures of the very pious and profound Thomas Bradwardine, and from his works he derived his first views of the freeness of grace, and the utter worthlessness of all human merit, in the matter of salvation. From Grotete's writings he first caught the idea of the pope being antichrist."[172]

The accounts recorded above allow us to conclude that the Waldensians had a great influence in England. Authors who wrote not long after that period of time, report Walter Lollard was a Waldensian preacher who had great influence on England (q.v.). The Waldensian or Lollard influence spread primarily from the county of Herefordshire and the protection afforded by the deep valley of Olchon. Their influence

---

[171] Joseph Ivimey, *A History of the English Baptists* (Way of Life Electronic Edition, Port Huron, MI, 1811) p. 5-6.
[172] Andrew Miller, *Church History* (Way of Life Literature electronic edition, May 2003, Chapter 30, John Wycliffe) p. 3.

spread to all of England. Their adversaries admitted that they were as numerous as the sand of the sea.

It was typical of Waldensians or the people of the valleys to seek shelter in the piedmont or valley at the foot of mountains in many countries. It is also the custom of God-fearing churches from the earliest post-Apostolic times to name their flocks after the most prominent barb (bearded pastor or preacher). Thus, the name of the Waldensians in Herefordshire, Lollards, should not surprise anyone. Joseph Ivemy relates the belief of the great chronology scholar, James Ussher (1581-1656). He said:

> "[A]rchbishop Ussher says, from Matthew Paris, 'the orders of the Friars Minorites came into England to suppress this Waldensian heresy.' And in the reign of Edward II, about the year 1315, Fuller informs us, in his ecclesiastical history, that '**WALTER LOLLARD**, that German preacher, or, (as Perrin calls him in his history of the Waldenses,) **one of their barbs, came into England, a man in great renown among them;** and who was so eminent in England that, as in France, they were called *Berengarians* from Berengarius, and *Petrobrusians* from Peter Bruis, and in Italy and Flanders, *Arnoldist,*, from the famous Arnold of Brescia; so did the Waldensian Christian from many generations after bear the name of this worthy man, being *Lollards.*" (HDW, not my emphasis)."[173]

Men who were Waldensians or Lollards or were influenced by them would have a great influence spiritually and doctrinally on Dr. Wycliffe. He would in turn greatly influence them. Bardwardine, whether he was from Sussex or Herefordshire, and many other men of renown such as "a group of knights who formed part of the kings court" were influence greatly by Waldensian doctrines.

---

[173] Ibid. p. 3 (*Ivimey, History of the English Baptists*)

> "The Lollards who followed Wyclif, often called "mumblers" (probably reflecting their scriptural based worship) represented a general, but very limited, minority theological reform movement. **The most important Lollards were a group of knights who formed part of the king's court**. These included Sir William Neville, Sir John Montague and Sir William Beachamp who enjoyed sympathetic support and active protection from the Black Prince and Gaunt, at least from 1371 to 1382."[174]

The quote above states the Lollard movement represented a "minority theological reform" faction. The Waldensians were not a small group of churches; rather, they were widely scattered over the known world and were slaughtered by the thousands through the years because of their beliefs and rejection of Roman Catholicism.[175] George Trevelyan wrote in 1900:

> "There seems to be no longer any doubt that there were ' Poor Priests' perambulating the country **before** 1380, though the degree of their Connection with Wycliffe and Wycliffism differed in different cases. (a) They were accused of playing a part in the organization of the Rising of 1381 (Wright's *Pol. Poems,* R.S., 285-6, and *Rot. Parl.,* iii. 124-5). They must have been working some time and have obtained some influence in order to incur the charge. **<u>There is no proof that Wycliffe himself commissioned or sent out any of his own friends before 1881</u>**, but some of his doctrines were being preached by irresponsible individuals, *e.g.* John Ball was accused of preaching against Transubstantiation in 1380."[176]

The Lollards were Waldensians. Frederick Nolan concurs.

---

[174] http://www.bbc.co.uk/history/british/middle_ages/richardii_reign_07.shtml
[175] See Foxe's *Book of the Martyrs* and *The Martyrs Mirror.*
[176] Trevelyan, p. 363 (England in the Age of Wycliffe).

> "Frederick Nolan, who diligently pursued the history of the transmission of the biblical text, says that the Lollards were disciples of the Waldenses (Nolan, *Inquiry into the Integrity of the Received Text*, 1815, p. xix, footnote 1)."[177]

The movement did not begin with or start after Wycliffe's departure to his home in heaven as claimed in the following two quotes. Dale Irvin and Scott Sunquist conclude:

> "The supporters went on **after** Wycliffe's death in 1384 to organize a movement called the Lollards or Mumblers, supposedly so called because of their public preaching."[178]

Levy said:

> "That he (Wycliffe) can be credited as being the progenitor of the Lollard movement, however, is much more certain."[179]

The overwhelming evidence supports the conclusion that the "movement" started by the Waldensians and can be traced back to 120 A. D. according to Theodore Beza and Reinerius Saccho.[180] When it was brought into England, it became known as Lollardy.

> "It is important to understand that there were already Waldensian, or separatist Anabaptist Christians, in England during the days of Wycliffe...Waldensians

---

[177] http://lifegivingword.googlepages.com/john

[178] Dale T. Irvin and Scott T. Sunquist, *History of the World Christian Movement, Vol. 1, Earliest Christianity to 1453* (Orbis Group, Maryknoll, NY. Continuum International Group, 2001, ISBN:0567088669) p. 488.

[179] Levy, p. 3 (*John Wycliffe On the Truth of Holy Scripture).*

[180] Williams, p. 123-124 (*The Lie)*

came to England in the 11th, 12th, 13th, and 14th centuries."[181]

Many books and authors such as *The Martyrs Mirror*, Joseph Milner's *The History of the Church of Christ*, and Frederick Nolan's *Inquiry into the Integrity of the Received Text* report on the existence of the Waldensians and thus the Lollards before Wycliffe.[182] Nolan said:

> "that the Lollards were disciples of the Waldenses (Nolan, *Inquiry into the Integrity of the Received Text,* 1815, p. xix, footnote I)."[183]

Even some Catholic authorities make the same claim.

> "Thomas Walden, who wrote *against Wycliffe*, says, that the doctrine of Peter Waldo was conveyed from France into England—and that among others Wickliff received it. In this opinion he is joined by Alphonsus de Castro, who says that Wickliff only brought to light again the errors of the Waldenses. Cardinal Bellarmine, also, is pleased to say that 'Wickliff could add nothing to the heresy of the Waldenses'" (Jones, *A History of the Christian Church, II, p. 91)"*[184]

Wycliffe's doctrine or Wycliffism simply picked up where previous martyrs left off. Lollardism, Wycliffism, Waldensianism, or whatever you would like to call it began with the doctrine of the Apostles (Acts 2:42). Thomas Armitage said the following about the Lollards and Wycliffe:

---

[181] Cloud, p. 4 (John Wycliffe: The Father of the English Bible").
[182] Ibid. p. 5.
[183] Ibid. p. 5.
[184] Ibid. p. 4.

> "The Lollards form an important link in this chain of events. The followers of Wycliff were early known by this name; but some trace their origin to Walter Lollard, who was burnt at Cologne about A.D. 1322. The term was applied at Antwerp to a society formed in 1300 for ministering to the sick—it is supposed from the Dutch *lullen*—to sing in a low tone, as at funerals, where they soothed by slowly sung dirges. But it soon became a term of reproach, by an ingenious twist, as if it were derived from *lolim* (darnel), tares amongst wheat. Wickliff was regarded as the father of the Lollards, but whether his followers assumed that name, or it was pinned to them, in stigma, is uncertain. During his lifetime Wickliff sent out great numbers of itinerant preachers, who preached in market-places, moors, commons, and wherever they could find hearers. They increased so rapidly that Pope Martin raved against them in the most vulgar manner, and Archbishop Courtenay spent five months in purging Oxford University of their presence. **The underlying spirit of Lollardism sought the right of unfettered thought, the free interpretation of the Bible as the rule of faith, and the apostolic simplicity of the ordinances."**[185]

However, much like any family or Christian name today, the word can be traced to several possible linguistic origins.

The Linguistic Meaning of "Lollard"

One source reports the name came from four possible starting points:

> "The origin of the term is uncertain, but four possibilities suggest themselves:

[185] Thomas Armitage, *A History of the Baptists* (Way of Life electronic edition, 2003, from the chapter "Post-Apostolic Times: The Bohemian Brethren and the Lollards") p. 10.

1. the Dutch word, *lollaerd*, meaning someone who mutters, a mumbler. This is also related to the Dutch word, *lull* or *lollen*, as in "a mother lulls her child to sleep", or "to sing or chant";

2. the Latin *lolium*, tares (mingled with the Catholic wheat);

3. after the Franciscan, Lolhard, who converted to the Waldensian way, becoming eminent as a preacher in Guienne. That part of France was then under English domination, influencing lay English piety. He was burned at Cologne in the 1370s;

4. the Middle-English *loller*, "a lazy vagabond, an idler, a fraudulent beggar", likely a later usage; influenced (spuriously?) by Chaucer's use of the term in *The Canterbury Tales.*

The Dutch derivation is the most likely, due to the influence on Lollardy of the informal lay communities, originating in Deventer in Overijssel around the teaching of Gerhard Groote, in the last two decades of the fourteenth century; but the Latin *lolium* (tares) is an interesting alternative, supported by Chaucer's Epilogue to the Man of Law's Tale, in his description of the Poor Parson's preaching:

"And he'll go starting up some heresy
And sow his tares in our clean corn, perchance."[186]

Dr. Schaff said:

"Contemporaries derived it from *lolium*,—tares,—and referred it to the false doctrine these sectarists were sowing, as does Knighton, and probably also Chaucer, or, with reference to their habit of song, from the Latin word *laudare*, to praise. The most natural derivation is from the Low German, *lullen* or *einlullen* to sing to sleep, whence our English lullaby. None of the Lollard songs have come down to us. Scarcely a decade after Wyclif's death a bull was issued by Boniface IX.,

[186] http://www.answers.com/topic/lollardy

> 1396, against the "Lullards or Beghards" of the Low Countries."[187]

Controversy #4

Did Dr. Wycliffe do any of the translating of Latin Bibles into English?

Dr. Schaff believes Wycliffe translated a part of "some of the Scriptures," but that it was poorly done. He said:

> "The plain meaning of this statement [to follow by Knighton] seems to be that **Wyclif translated at least some of the Scriptures**, that the translation was a novelty, and that the English was not a proper language for the embodiment of the sacred Word. It was a cleric's book, and profane temerity, by putting it within the reach of the laity, had vulgarized it."[188] (HDW, my addition).

Tom MacArthur in an article about John Wycliffe in the Concise Oxford Companion of the English Language said:

> "Wycliffe's own share in the translations bearing his name is uncertain, but was probably considerable."[189]

Bishop Brook Foss Westcott (1825–1901) seems to attribute Wycliffe's translation to him and MANY others scattered throughout England. He said:

---

[187] Schaff, p. 262.
[188] Schaff, p. 257
[189] Tom MacArthur, *Concise Oxford Companion to the English Language* (Oxford University Press, 1998) paragraph: John Wycliffe.

> "While Wycliffe was engaged in his translation others were prosecuting **a similar work** in different parts of England. There is a manuscript translation of portions of the Epistles, the Acts of the Apostles, and the Gospel of Matthew, in the library of Corpus Christi College, Cambridge. It is in the western dialect. In the same library is a complete version of Paul's Epistles. The authors are unknown, and probably they concealed their names for the purpose of escaping persecution."[190] (HDW, my emphasis)

The Encyclopedia Britannica appears to claim that Wycliffe had little to do with the translation of the Bible and credits Wycliffe's translation to another Lollard, Nicholas of Hereford, and later revised by Wycliffe's secretary, John Purvey. The encyclopedia states:

> The Lollards were responsible for a translation of the Bible into English, by Nicholas of Hereford, and later revised by Wycliffe's secretary, John Purvey."[191]

However, Dr. Schaff reports that Henry Knighton (died c. 1396), an English historian and an Augustinian canon at the abbey of St. Mary of the Meadows, Leicester, England, believed Wycliffe translated the Bible. He reports:

> "To follow the description given by Knighton in his Chronicle, the gift of the English Bible was regarded by Wyclif's contemporaries as both a novel act and an act of desecration. The irreverence and profanation of offering such a translation was likened to the casting of

[190] Westcott, p. 326 (*Quarterly Review,* "The English Bible").
[191] Lollard. (2008). In Encyclopædia Britannica. Retrieved May 29, 2008, from Encyclopædia Britannica Online: http://www.britannica.com/EBchecked/topic/346626/Lollards.

pearls before swine. The passage in Knighton, who wrote 20 years after Wyclif's death, runs thus: —

> The Gospel, which Christ bequeathed to the clergy and doctors of the Church,—as they in turn give it to lay and weaker persons,—**this Master John Wyclif translated out of the Latin into the Anglican tongue**, not the Angelic tongue, so that by him it is become common,—*vulgare*,—and more open to the lay folk and to women, knowing how to read, than it used to be to clerics of a fair amount of learning and of good minds. Thus, the Gospel pearl is cast forth and trodden under foot of swine, and what was dear to both clergy and laity is now made a subject of common jest to both, and the jewel of the clergy is turned into the sport of the laity, so that what was before to the clergy and doctors of the Church a divine gift, has been turned into a mock Gospel [or common thing]."[192]

Others deny that Wycliffe translated **any** of the Wycliffe Bible. The present day English scholar, David Daniell, writes:

> "**It seems unlikely that Wyclif himself, pen in hand, translated <u>any</u> of 'his' Bible.** But the manuscripts were the work of men close to him, influenced by him, inspired by his teaching and preaching, there can be no doubt. It is the same with the second most extensively preserved Wycliffite English text (again surviving in spite of systematic destruction of such material), the thirty-one fine manuscripts which contain a complete cycle of 294 anonymous sermons. These present a comprehensive view of Wyclif's views,

[192] Schaff, p. 257.

> theological, ecclesiastical, social and political, but are not by Wyclif."[193]

It seems obvious that David Daniell and others must have taken their cue from Abbot Gasquet, whose doubtful work was attacked by Dr Schaff. Dr. Schaff notes the probable origin of the denial of Wycliffe's translation, saying in the quote to follow that Abbot Gasquet's opinion is "unjustifiable, if not criminal." Dr. Schaff said:

> "NOTE. – THE AUTHORSHIP OF THE FIRST ENGLISH BIBLE. **Recently the priority of Wyclif's translation has been denied by Abbot Gasquet** in two elaborate essays, *The Old English Bible*, pp. 87–155. **He also pronounces it to be very doubtful if Wyclif ever translated any part of the Bible.** All that can be attempted here is a brief statement of the case. In addition to Knighton's testimony, which seems to be as plain as language could put it, **we have the testimony of John Huss in his *Reply* to the Carmelite Stokes, 1411, that Wyclif translated the whole Bible into English**. No one contends that Wyclif did as much as this, and Huss was no doubt speaking in general terms, having in mind the originator of the work and the man's name connected with it. The doubt cast upon the first proposition, the priority of Wyclif's version, is due to Sir Thomas More's statement in his *Dialogue*, 1530, *Works*, p. 233. In controverting the positions of Tyndale and the Reformers, he said, "The whole Bible was before Wyclif's days, by virtuous and well-learned men, translated into English and by good and godly people, with devotion and soberness, well and reverently read." He also says that he saw such copies. In considering this statement it seems very possible that More made a mistake

[193] David Daniell, *The Bible in English, Its History and Influence* (Yale University Press, New Haven & London, 2003, ISBN 0-300-09930-4, 2003) p. 73.

(1) because the statement is contrary to Knighton's words, taken in their natural sense and Huss' testimony.

(2) Because Wyclif's own statements exclude the existence of any English version before his own.

(3) Because the Lollards associated their Bible with Wyclif's name.

(4) Because before the era of the Reformation no English writer refers to any translating except in connection with Wyclif's name and time. Sir Thomas More was engaged in controversy and attempting to justify the position that the Catholic hierarchy had not been opposed to translations of the Scriptures nor to their circulation among proper classes of the laity. But Abbot Gasquet, after proposing a number of conjectural doubts and setting aside the natural sense of Knighton's and Arundel's statements, denies altogether the Wycliffite authorship of the Bible ascribed to him and edited by Forshall and Madden, and performs the feat of declaring this Bible one of the old translations mentioned by More. It must be stated here, a statement that will be recalled later, that Abbot Gasquet is the representative in England of the school of Janssen, which has endeavored to show that the Catholic Church was in an orderly process of development before Luther arose, and that Luther and the Reformers checked that development and also willfully misrepresented the condition of the Church of their day. Dr. Gasquet, with fewer plausible facts and less literature at command than Janssen, seeks to present the English Church's condition in the later Middle Ages as a healthy one. And this he does

(1) by referring to the existence of an English mediaeval literature, still in MSS., which he pronounces vast in its bulk;

(2) by absolutely ignoring the statements of Wyclif;

(3) by setting aside the testimonies of the English Reformers;

(4) by disparaging the Lollards as a wholly humble and illiterate folk. Against all these witnesses he sets up the single witness, Sir Thomas More.

> The second proposition advocated by Dr. Gasquet that **it is doubtful, and perhaps very improbable, that Wyclif did nothing in the way of translating the Bible, is based chiefly upon the fact that Wyclif does not refer to such a translation anywhere in his writings. If we take the abbot's own high priest among authorities, Sir Thomas More, the doubt is found to be unjustifiable, if not criminal.** More, speaking of John Hunne, who was burnt, said that he possessed a copy of the Bible which was "after a Wycliffite copy." Eadie, I. 6O sqq.; Westcott, *Hist. of the Eng. Bible.* Gairdner who discusses the subject fairly in his *Lollardy*, I. 101–117, Capes, pp. 125–128, F. D. Matthew, in *Eng. Hist. Rev.*, 1895, and Bigg, Wayside Sketches, p. 127 sq., take substantially the position taken by the author. Gasquet was preceded by Lingard, *Hist. of Eng.*, IV. 196, who laid stress upon More's testimony to offset and disparage the honor given from time immemorial to Wyclif in connection with the English Bible. How can a controversialist be deemed fair who, in a discussion of this kind, does not even once refer to Wyclif's well-known views about the value of a popular knowledge of the Scriptures, and his urgency that they be given to all the people through plain preaching and in translation? Dr. Gasquet's attitude to "the strange personality of Wyclif" may be gotten from these words, *Old Eng. Bible*, p. 88: "Whatever we may hold as Catholics as to his unsound theological opinions, about which there can be no doubt, or, as peace-loving citizens, about his wild revolutionary social theories, on which, if possible, there can be less," etc."[194]

In 1909, Rev. Samuel McComb also traced the origin of the false theory pertaining to the denial of Wycliffe's translating to "Father (now Abbot) F. A. Gasquet. He said:

> "The Wycliffite origin of the versions printed by Forshall and Madden remained unchallenged from the fourteenth century till the year 1894, when, in the July

[194] Schaff, p. 260-261.

number of the *Dublin Review* in that year, Father (now Abbot) F. A. Gasquet published an article entitled *The Pre-Reformation English Bible,* in which he propounded the theory that these were not of Wycliffite origin but were put forth semi-officially as an authorized Catholic translation. Abbot Gasquet's article is reprinted in a volume entitled *The Old Englisk (sic) Bible and Other Essays* (London, 1897). Accompanying the reprint is a reply to the criticisms which had been passed upon his theory by Mr. F. D. Matthew in the Englisk Historical Review for January, 1895, and by F. G. Kenyon in

'Our Bible and the Ancient Manuscripts (London, 1895). A thorough and painstaking review of the whole subject appeared in two articles in the Church Quarterly Review for October, 1900, and January, 1901. The result of the discussion is undoubtedly to re-establish the tradition of the Wycliffite origin of these versions."[195]

Dr. Schaff also said:

"Sir Thomas More states distinctly that there was found in the possession of John Hunne, who was afterwards burnt, a Bible **'written after Wyclif's copy and by him translated into our tongue.'"**[196]

Even Bishop B. F. Westcott believed Wycliffe translated the Scriptures. He said:

"A single sentence from one of his sermons will show his views regarding both Church and State at that period: "All truth is contained in Scripture. 'We should admit of no conclusion not approved there. There is no court besides the court of heaven. Though there were an hundred Popes, and though all the friars in the world were turned into Cardinals, yet we could learn more from the Bible than from that vast multitude.' In his quiet

---

[195] Rev. Samuel McComb, M.A., D.D., *The Making of the English Bible* (Moffat, Yard, and Co., New York, 1909) p. 133

[196] Schaff, p. 258.

parish he laboured incessantly at the translation of the Scriptures. **He completed the New Testament in 1380.** The version was not perfect. It was made from the Latin Vulgate; yet it set forth substantially the fundamental doctrines of Revelation. The printing-press was then unknown. Every copy had to be written by hand. Wycliffe appears to have employed a number of scribes, but they were not able to supply the growing demand. Foxe tells us that some of the laymen were so anxious to obtain the Word of God, that they often gave a load of hay for a few chapters of St James or St. Paul. Having completed the New Testament, Wycliffe arranged with his friend Nicholas of Hereford to undertake a translation of the Old Testament. It was at once commenced, but ere it was completed the Romish prelates were informed of the design. Nicholas was suddenly summoned before a synod of preaching friars, held in 1382, and on the 1st of July was excommunicated. He appealed to the Pope; went to Rome; was tried and imprisoned, but soon effected his escape. He does not seem to have returned to England again during the life of Wycliffe. **Wycliffe himself, therefore, took up again the work of translation,** and had the satisfaction of finishing it before his death in 1384. The manuscript of Nicholas's translation is still extant in the Bodleian Library. It ends at Baruch iii. 20, in the middle of a sentence."[197]

Most importantly, as previously stated, Wycliffe himself said that he translated the Bible:

"You say it is heresy to speak of the Holy Scriptures in English. You call me a heretic because **<u>I have translated the Bible</u>** into the common tongue of the people. Do you

[197] Westcott, p. 325 (*Quarterly Review,* "The English Bible"). Also, see Cramp, p. 5.

> know whom you blaspheme?"...(Fountain, *John Wycliffe,* pp. 45-47)[198]

The prelates of Wycliffe's time despised his efforts. Even as recent as the nineteen sixties Dr. Daniell reports comments derogative of Dr. Wycliffe (q.v.). Dr. John de Wycliffe continues to be shunned and criticized by many. The Wycliffe Society reports:

> "Some Catholic writers have been disposed to deny that there was anything original in the conception of Wycliffe, with regard to the translation of the Scriptures into the vernacular language; but the preceding statements will suffice to show in what form, and to what extent, that claim may be urged in favour of our Reformer. Knighton, a contemporary of Wycliffe, gives full expression to the different opinions which obtained in his own time on this subject. "Christ," says that historian, "delivered his doctrine to the doctors of the church, that they might administer to the laity and weaker persons according to the state of the times, and the wants of men. **But this Master John Wycliffe translated it out of Latin into English**, and thus laid it more open to the laity, and to women who could read, than it had formerly been to the most learned of the clergy, even to those of them who had the best understanding.' And in this way the Gospel pearl is cast abroad, and trodden under foot of swine; and that which was before precious to both clergy and laity, is rendered, as it were, the common jest of both. The jewel of the church is turned into the sport of the people and what was hitherto the principal gift of the clergy and divines, is made for ever common to the laity... So spoke the canon of Leicester on this matter."[199]

---

[198] David Cloud, D.D., "John Wycliffe: The Father of the English Bible" (Way of Life Literature, FBIS, 2001) p. 3. Dr. Cloud is quoting David Fountain.

[199]Vaughan, p. ix (Tracts and Treatises of John de Wycliffe, Wycliffe Society, 1855) p. ix

In 1841, Samuel Bagster reported that John Trevisa, a contemporary and colleague of Wycliffe made his own translation of the Bible just like Wycliffe. However, remember that during those times the word "Bible" could refer to a portion. It appears that Trevisa translated the *Gospels* (q.v.). Most likely, Wycliffe and associates availed themselves to any good help available at the time. This is what good translators do. But, Samuel Bagster implies Trevisa translated the 'whole' Bible, which cannot be confirmed. He said:

> "It has been positively asserted, that John de Trevisa, a native of Cornwall, who was vicar of Berkley, translated both the Old and New Testaments into English. He was cotemporary with Wiclif, though born some years before him, and also his survivor by some years...John Trevisa was no friend to the then existing state of things in the Church...Bale attributes a version of the Scriptures to Trevisa, as also Caxton seems to do; whether they had any data for their assertion is not easy to determine."[200]

Samuel Bagster proceeds to quote some verses that allegedly come from the Trevisa work according to writings by a Dr. Waterland and published by Lewis. They are all NT verses from the *Gospels*. Alexander McClure in *Translators Revived* also reports Trevisa translated the "entire Bible":

> "Contemporary with Wiclif, was John de Trevisa, born of an ancient family, at Crocadon in Cornwall. He was a secular priest, and Vicar of Berkeley. He translated several large works out of Latin into English; and chiefly **the entire Bible**, justifying himself by the example of the Venerable Bede, who had done the same thing for the Gospel of John. This great, and good,

---

[200] Bagster, p. 33 (*The English Hexapla*).

> and dangerous task he performed by commission from his noble and powerful patron and protector, Lord Thomas de Berkeley. This nobleman had the whole of the book of Revelation, in Latin and French, which latter was then generally understood by the better educated class of Englishmen, written upon the walls and ceiling of his chapel at Berkeley, where it was to be seen hundreds of years after. Trevisa, notwithstanding his translation of the Bible made him obnoxious to the persecutors of his day, lived and died unmolested, though known to be an enemy of monks and begging friars. He expired, full of honor and years, being little less than ninety years of age, in the year 1397. Little else is known of him, or of his translation, which did not supersede the labors of Wiclif."[201]

The conclusion to this subject is that the KJB translators report that only the Gospels were translated by Trevisa (q.v.). Furthermore, only quotes of the Gospels by Trevisa can be located. If other portions of the Bible can be found that were translated by Trevisa, it would be very helpful to resolve this question.

Controversy #5

Is the Early Version (EV) of the Wycliffe Bible translated from Jerome's Latin Vulgate, which contained the Aprocypha and which was corrupted according to Wycliffe and associates? Did Dr. Wycliffe use the "vulgar" (old) Latin MSS, also? Did he or his associates know Greek or Hebrew?

---

[201] Alexander McClure, "The Glorious History of the English Bible" (Way of Life Literature, Port Huron, MI, c. 1850, preface of *Translators Revived: Biographical Notes of the KJV Translators*) preface.

The Apocrypha

The Encyclopedia Britannica states:

> "The history of the Old Testament canon in the English Church has generally reflected a more restrictive viewpoint. Even though the Wycliffite Bible (14th century) included the Apocrypha, its preface made it clear that it accepted Jerome's judgment."[202]

Many authors report "Jerome's judgment," which contends that the Apocrypha was not inspired, that it was tainted and that it was only of historical interest; the apocryphal books were not inspired canonical works. Even so, Rome's Council of Trent that began in 1545 and lasted into the 1560s included them in the Canon of that church as inspired works. The significant fact is that Wycliffe and his associates accepted the early text of Jerome, the Latin Vulgate,[203] which included the apocryphal or deuterocanonical books that were eventually accepted as inspired by Rome. F. F. Bruce said:

> "The two Wycliffite versions of the complete Bible in English (1384, 1395) included the apocryphal books as a matter of course; they were part of the Vulgate, on which those versions were based. The 'General Prologue' to the second version (John Purvey's) contains a strong commendation of 'the book of Tobias' (Tobit) because of the encouragement it provides to those who are persecuted for righteousness' sake..."[204]

---

[202] Wycliffite Bible. (2008). In Encyclopædia Britannica. Retrieved May 29, 2008, from Encyclopædia Britannica Online: http://www.britannica.com/EBchecked/topic/650184/Wycliffite-Bible

[203] Levy, p. 163.

[204] F. F. Bruce, p. 100 (*The Canon of Scripture*).

Wycliffe wrongly said the following about the apocryphal books:

> "In light of this, it seems quite likely that many apocryphal books are Holy Scripture, since they are inscribed in the Book of Life. And to this extent we should trust them explicitly or implicitly, just as our canonical Scripture...from these facts I reckon that it is both foolish and pointless for us to grapple excessively over the truth or vicissitudes of the apocryphal Scripture, since we are in full possession of the Scriptures, which are sensibly authenticated for us...On this account, all meanings which are found in our sacred manuscripts should be held in grater esteem than those other pages. It is suffiecient that one generally believe every truth with love. Whereupon, if other manuscripts contain the truth let us believe it, because it abides in our own manuscripts."[205]

The Hebrew and Greek Question

Many of the apocryphal books were written in Hebrew or Greek, but translated into Latin by Jerome. Did Wycliffe and his associates use or compare the Hebrew and Greek MSS with Latin translations? Apparently they did.

Samuel Bagster reports the following in 1841 and gives a quote from the LV prologue by "John Purnay" (a.k.a. Purvey). This particular quote is not only pertinent to the question of Hebrew and Greek knowledge by Wycliffe and associates, but it is also important to the question of whether Purvey was a translator, which is denied by many recent authors. To help understand the quote below, keep in mind that in Middle English (ME), a "curate" is a priest's assistant or secretary; "mani" means "many," "loke" means "examine" or "look at," "y'" seems to stand

[205] Levy, pp. 163-164 (*On the Truth of Holy Scriptures*).

for "the," "vnderstonden" means "understood"; the rest of the words in ME should be able to be discerned. Bagster reports:

> "Who was the author of this prologue, and consequently of the version to which it belongs? It is very evident that the writer was one whose views and doctrines were similar to those of Wyclif himself; and this makes it **prima facie** probable that the translator was one whose "Lollardism" would be so notorious, that his name would be transmitted to us amongst the learned followers of Wiclif. Of these, one of the most remarkable was John Purvy, or Purnay who...appears to have lived with him and is supposed to have acted as his curate at Lutterworth. Copies of a version of the Bible into English have the name of this person written in them, and also the prologue annexed...Purnay appears, from what has been said of him by various writers, to have been very competent to the task of the translation. Walden calls him 'The Library of the Lollards, and Wiclif's glosser, an eloquent divine, and famous for his skill in the Law.'...The following account is given at the end of the prologue of the process pursued by Purnay and his assistants in preparing for, and producing their version...:
>
>> "But lloke y' he examine trulye hys latyn bible: for no doubt he shall fynde many byblis in latyne ful false, if he loke mani. And namely newe, and the commune latyne bybles haue more need to be correctyd (as many as I haue sene in my life) than hath the English bible late translated. And where the Hebru, by witness of Jerome of Lire and other expositours dyscordith fro our Latyne biblis: **I haue set in y' marggent bi manner of a glose what y' Hebreu hath and howe it is vnderstonden in some place**. And I did this most in the psalter, y' of al our bokis discordith most from Hebru. For the chirch readeth not the psalter by the laste translation out of Hebru into Latine: but an othe translacion of

> other men y' hadden mich lasse kunninge, and holiness than Jerome had."[206]

This quote indicates that John Purvey, Wycliffe's secretary, understood Hebrew, but depended upon Jerome's Latin translation and comments as a basis of translation because "other men y' hadden mich lasse kunninge, and holiness than Jerome had." Purvey was a student, companion, and secretary of Wycliffe. It seems unlikely that Wycliffe did not know any Hebrew. However, Phillip Schaff said:

> "Wyclif was the first to give the Bible to his people in their own tongue. **He knew no Hebrew and probably no Greek.** His version, which was made from the Latin Vulgate, was the outgrowth of his burning desire to make his English countrymen more religious and more Christian."[207]

Christopher Anderson said:

> "Here, it is true, was Wyclifffe, and able and acute, a zealous and determined man, and withal an excellent Latin scholar, **but of Greek or Hebrew he knew nothing**. Nor was it at all necessary that he should possess such erudition, since a translation from either Greek or Hebrew would not have harmonized with the first, or the present, intention of Divine Providence. A reason there was, and one worthy of infinite wisdom, why not only the English translation, but most of the first European versions must be made from the Latin. These nations, including our own [i.e. England], had nothing in common with the Greek community, but for ages they had been overrun with the Latin. This language, long

---

[206] Samuel Bagster, *The English Hexapla* (Samuel Bagster and Sons, London, 1841, published by Still Waters Revival Books, Edmonton, AB, Canada) p. 28-29.

[207] Schaff, p. 256.

since dead, even in Italy, had been the refuge and stronghold of their oppressor..."[208]

Dr. McComb said:

"The really notable point which emerges in the course of the debate between Abbot Gasquet and his critics is the Abbot's admission that the versions believed to be Wycliffite are **faithful renderings of the Vulgate**. This fact would account for the spread of the version among those who had no Wycliffite doctrinal leanings."[209]

And

"But in the England of the fourteenth century, Hebrew and Greek were unknown, and the Wycliffite translation was made, not from the originals, but from the current traditional and rather corrupt text of the Latin Vulgate."[210]

Andrew McClure said:

"The admirable King Alfred, who ascended the throne two hundred years after the birth of Bede, translated the Psalms into Anglo-Saxon. But the first complete translation which can be said to have been published, so as to come into extensive use, was that made by Wiclif, about the year 1380. **It was not made from the "original Hebrew and Greek of the Holy Ghost;" but from the Vulgate, a Latin version**, chiefly prepared by Jerome during the latter part of the fourth century. John Wiclif was born in Yorkshire, England, in the year 1324. He is commonly called "the morning-star of the Protestant reformation," and of the Dark Ages,

[208] Anderson, p. 63 (*The Annals of the English Bible*).
[209] McComb, p. 159 (*The Making of the English Bible*).
[210] Ibid. p. 31.

who are often spoken of as "reformers before the reformation." Like Martin Luther, his opposition to popish errors and corruptions was at first confined to a few points; but prayer, study of the Bible, and growing grace, led him on in a constant advance toward the purity of truth. He became in doctrine what would now be called a Calvinist; and in church discipline his views agreed with those which are now maintained by Congregationalists."[211]

George Trevelyan said:

"The character and quantity of religious instruction given by a parish priest to his flock must have depended to a very great degree on the priest himself, and in consequence varied greatly in different cases. **He was expected to study the Latin Bible** diligently himself, but to instruct the people in Church doctrine as exemplified by the Creed, the Ten Commandments, the Ave Maria, the Pater Noster; the six works of mercy, the seven virtues and the seven deadly sins were also usual texts for the preacher. This was the curriculum laid down by the episcopal authority. In the next generation, when the Wycliffite movement was at death-grips with the Catholic Church, the Primate actually forbade discourses on any other text or subject... It was their familiar knowledge of the **Latin Vulgate** that made it natural and possible for Wycliffe to claim for the Bible pre-eminence as a spiritual authority... In the medieval sermon equal reverence is shown for the **Vulgate** and for the Fathers. No point is held to be proved until it has been supported by quotations from both. In this traditional practice Wycliffe and his followers were contented to rest. They backed their arguments with passages from the Bible and the Fathers, with this important difference, that they regarded the former as the ultimate authority with which all Church tradition must agree, or else be of no value whatever."[212]

---

[211] McClure, preface ("The Glorious History of the English Bible")
[212] Trevelyan, p. 127, 128,129 (England in the Age of Wycliffe).

It appears that Wycliffe and his associates knew more about the original Biblical languages than previously given credit (q.v.). However, they used as the basis of their translations the Latin Vulgate. This was also expedient because of time issues and convenience concerning simply the mechanics of handwritten manuscripts. There was also the "political" issue of getting the "Bible" into the hands of the populace before Rome stopped it. If Dr. Wycliffe and associates were using Rome's Latin Vulgate, more time for the translation would be allowed before the "hammer" dropped. More about the topic of this controversy is given throughout this work.

Controversy #6

Is the EV the first English translation of the whole the Bible? (This is related to Controversy #4 and #14.)

There are several reports that Wycliffe's translation was not the first English translation of the whole Bible. *The Cambridge History of the Bible* claims Wycliffe had access to many English versions of the Bible. Apparently, Christopher De Hamel, Ph.D. Oxford reports the MS Bodley 959 Wycliffe manuscript was :

> "**copied from a text already in English.** Therefore they were not translating but transcribing."[213]

The *Encyclopedia Britannica* reports Wycliffe used:

---

[213] G. A. Riplinger. *In Awe of Thy Word.* (A.V. Publications Corp, Ararat, VA, 2003) p. 775.

> "...**already existing (English) version**, with changes when necessary, were incorporated and made use of by the translators...[and the] text of the Gospels [a translation into English Wycliffe used at Oxford] was extracted from the Commentary upon them by Wycliffe (HDW, my addition)"[214]

Even though the *Encyclopedia Britannica* reports Wycliffe translated the *Gospels,* it implies Wycliffe had little to do with translation of the Old Testament.

> "The Old Testament of the Early Version was, according to the editors (Preface, p. xvii.), taken in hand by one of Wycliffe's coadjutors, Nicholas de Hereford. The translator's original copy and a coeval transcript of it are still extant in the Bodleian library (Bodl. 959, Douce 369). Both break off abruptly at Baruch iii. 19, the latter having at this place a note inserted to the following effect: *Explicit translacionem Nicholay de herford.* There is consequently but little doubt that Nicholas de Herford took part in the translation of the Old Testament, though it is uncertain to what extent. The translator's copy is written in not less than five hands, differing in orthography and dialect. The note may therefore be taken to refer either to the portion translated by the last or fifth hand, or to the whole of the Old Testament up to Baruch iii. 19. Judging from uniformity of style and mode of translation the editors of the Bible are inclined to take the latter view; they add that the remaining part of the Old Testament was completed by a different hand, the one which also translated the New Testament. This statement is, however, not supported by sufficient evidence. In view of the magnitude of the undertaking it is on the contrary highly probable that other translators besides Wycliffe and Nicholas de Hereford took part in the work, and that already existing versions, with

[214] Riplinger, p. 775.

> changes when necessary, were incorporated or made use of by the translators."[215]

There is significant evidence that the Wycliffe Bible was a work consisting of progressive editing and frequent copying at each stage using every resource available, even Hebrew MSS from Jewish sources. Wycliffe comments on these things in his work, *On the Truth of Holy Scripture* (q.v.). G. A. Riplinger said:

> "Dates on Bibles were omitted or removed because it was illegal to have a Bible with Wycliffe's name on it or one written with a date that might imply Wycliffe's involvement. His earliest editions are given dates between 1380 and 1384; the later editions are given dates between 1388 and 1395. These, however, may not be entirely accurate. Wycliffe's Bible evolved between 1380 and 1395. Some writers have tried to assign the changes to two separate 'events,' but actual examination of the 200 or so extant editions makes it evident that polishing was progressive, with mixed texts seen in numerous editions. This somewhat thwarts the theory that John Purvey, Wycliffe's secretary, did the entire second edition on his own after Wycliffe's death (see De Hamel or *The Cambridge History of the Bible*). 'Articles,' were collected against Purvey, because, like Wycliffe, he would not obey the pope, whom he called "Antichrist, or any of his shavelings." Such priests he called, "...heretics, blasphemers, and seducers of Christian people...Satan's own stewards." Purvey said that the Catholic practice of "...auricular confession, or private penance, is a certain whispering, destroying the liberty of the gospel, and newly brought in by the pope and the clergy, to entangle the consciences of men in sin, and draw their souls into hell." For such outspoken views and for their work on the Wycliffe Bible, both Purvey and Nicholas Hereford, editor of part of the Old Testament, were imprisoned and tortured (Foxe, vol. 3,

---

[215] Anna C. Paues, "Bible, English" (Encyclopaedia Britannica, 11th Edition, 1911).

> pp. 287, 286, 289). "This John Purvey, with Hereford, a doctor of divinity, were grievously tormented and punished in the prison..." (Foxe, vol. 3, p. 285). A prison (called Lollard's Prison in Lambeth Palace in London) was built to detain Christians. It can still be seen today with the prisoner's iron rings next to writing on the wall which reads, "*Jesus amor meus* (Jesus is my love)" (*The Indestructible Book*, p. 80)."[216]

Controversy #7

Did translators associated with Dr. Wycliffe revise the EV "back" to the Latin Vulgate after his death, which is now called the Late Version (LV) instead of "the Purvey version"?

As previously mentioned above, the various stages of translation by Wycliffe, his associates, his personal secretary, and his followers show considerable variation. The exact Latin MSS used at various stages cannot be identified with certainty. In the prologue of the LV attributed to John Purvey, but lately contested (see above and below), we find claims of many corruptions of the texts used.

> "In his *prologue*, Purvey makes express mention of the "English Bible late translated," and affirms that the Latin copies had more need of being corrected than it."[217]

Dr. Bill Grady reports:

> "Although modern scholarship stresses Wycliffe's reliance upon the Vulgate's readings, a later

[216] G. A. Riplinger, *In Awe of Thy Word* (A.V. Publications Corp, Ararat, VA, 2003) p. 776-777.
[217] Schaff, p. 256.

revision of the work of John Purvey **which brought the translation back in tune with Jerome** makes it evident that Wycliff had access to some old Latin manuscripts. Purvey's later defection to Rome sheds added light on the issue."[218]

Dr. David Brown presented a picture in his book, "Our English Bible Heritage" and made this comment:

"[The] 1208 A.D. Latin Vulgate believed to be the one Wycliffe used to translate his Bible."[219]

G. A. Riplinger reports:

"Like the KJV translators, Wycliffe began his work with the foundation of preserved English scriptures. Like them, he polished it, making reference to the aforementioned manuscripts and an accessible and accurate Bible from another language group. In his case, it was the *first* century "vulgar Latin" scriptures, called the Old Latin, first heard in Acts 2. He did *not* translate directly from an uncorrected copy of Jerome's *fourth* century Latin revision, the official Catholic 'Latin Vulgate.' The myth that the Wycliffe Bible came from this 'Latin Vulgate' arose from the misleading statement "made from the Latin Vulgate" *added* to the frontice page of an 1850 printed edition of Wycliffe's Bible, edited by Frederic Madden and Josiah Forshall. The *Cambridge History of the Bible* questions whether their text gives an "accurate impression" of all Wycliffe Bibles, since Purvey may have edited the text (vol. 2, pp. 395-407). The *true* original *Prologue* to the 'Wycliffe Bible' warns of such corrupt Latin bibles, which themselves needed correction and were not used by true Christians. "...he shall find full

---

[218] William P. Grady, *Final Authority, A Christian's Guide to the King James Bible* (Grady Publications, Inc., Knoxville, TN, ISBN 0-9628809-1-4, 2001) p. 123

[219] David L. Brown, *Our English Bible Heritage* (Contact David L. Brown, P.O. Box 173, Oak Creek WI, 1997) p. 3.

many bibles in **Latin** full **false**, if he look many, namely new; and the common **Latin bible** has **more need to be corrected**, as many as I have seen in my life, **than the English bible late translated**..." (*Prologue*, p. 58)."[220]

And:

"Therefore Wycliffe and his associates relied, not on the Latin as a final authority, but on copies of it, corrected by the Greek, Hebrew, and English. *The Prologue* adds, "...[T]he church readeth **not** the Psalms by the last translation of **Jerome** out of Hebrew into Latin, but another translation of other men..." The *Prologue* says further that in "few" places, good Bibles read as the "originals of Jerome." "Jerome was not so holy as the apostles and evangelists...neither he had so high gifts of the Holy Ghost as they had; and much more the LXX translators were not so holy as Moses and the prophets...[There were] heretics, that did away many mysteries of Jesus Christ by **guileful [lying] translation**..." (*Prologue*, p. 58). Wycliffe wrote that he was not alone in his distrust of some readings in Jerome's translation, particularly the later 'editions' of it. "[O]ne need not believe that Jerome is free from error, since many other interpreters disagree with him. Indeed, in his own time he was reproached by Augustine and his other rivals...[G]iven the corruption of the modern texts we have not certified that the books which we do have were duly emended. In light of this, when it comes to those uncorrected modern manuscripts, I say that the defect can arise from sin on the [Catholic] Church's part" (*Truth*, pp. 156, 158)."[221]

However, did Wycliffe use the Greek and Hebrew texts or was he simply trying to emphasize that they used the Latin text closest to Jerome's manuscripts? Jerome translated the Old Testament from the Hebrew and some of the New Testament by him was from Greek

[220] Riplinger, p. 788-789 (*In Awe*).
[221] Riplinger, p. 789-790 (*In Awe*).

manuscripts that he revised, but other parts of Jerome's NT were simply previous books of the Bible in Greek from the Septuagint.

In light of the comments above and the confusion surrounding the subject of which manuscripts Wycliffe used, this author made a study of one hundred and fifty verses in two editions of the EV, one of the LV, the current DR, and the KJB from 1769. From this study, it is obvious, if the editions have not been altered from the originals, that Wycliffe used the Latin Vulgate as his primary text. Furthermore this author has read Wycliffe's Work, *On the Truth of Holy Scripture,* as translated by Ian Christopher Levy. Dr. Wycliffe writes in the style of a scholar skilled in scholasticism. His comments on Hebrew and Greek are not precisely clear and difficult to discern with certainty. Levy, the translator of Wycliffe, said:

> "Yet how many of these same readers then open one of Wyclif's own books on these topics? The number drops markedly, and for some good reasons....making ones' way through a volume can be hard going. ...Thus if one is looking for an exposition broken into short, conveniently labeled passages one will be disappointed. Instead, the reader is confronted with long, sometime rambling discourses, divided merely into untitled chapters..."[222]

Also, the Wycliffe EV, the first translation of the Bible into Middle English, was more of a gloss than the LV. They are both primarily from the Latin Vulgate, and the works were translations in progress.

> "Though this second version, that of Purvey (1388), is, in general, much less pedantically literal than the first, made some eight or nine years earlier, yet such words as *derknessis* and *armeris,* for the Latin plurals

[222] Levy, p. ix (*John Wycliffe On the Truth of Holy Scriptures*).

tenebrae and *arma,* illustrate the chief defect of both the Wyclifite translations, namely, a failure to attain perfect English idiom. Purvey seems to have been quite conscious of the excessive literalness of the earlier version (1380), and of the awkwardness due to the close following of Latin idiom. In his prologue, after describing how he had toiled, in association with others, to obtain a true Latin text, and to elucidate its difficulties, he proceeds to lay down important principles of Biblical translation, which have never been superseded. Among them are: First, to translate as clearly as possible according to the sense, and not merely according to the words. Secondly, to make the sentence at least as "open" in English as in Latin, that is, to have due regard to English idiom. Nevertheless, it may be affirmed that both Wyclifite versions are far inferior in ease and idiomatic character to the Old English. It cannot be said that scholars are agreed as to the influence of the Wyclifite versions upon Tindale and the *Authorized Version;* but it is pretty clear that Tindale was influenced by them to a moderate extent, and that expressions of great force and beauty have, occasionally, been appropriated from Wyclif by the *Authorized Version,* either mediately or directly."[223]

Christopher Anderson said:

"The manuscripts of Wycliffe's version complete, are numerous still; and perhaps not much less so than those of the New Testament separately, not to mention different pieces, or entire books of the translation. In examining some of these, whether in the Bodleian Library at Oxford, in the British Museum, or in private collections, we have been struck with their legibility and beauty. They have all, indiscriminately, been called Wycliffe's version, but variations of expression are to be found in a few; and it is not so generally known that we possess two distinct versions, one under Wycliffe's own

---

[223] A. W. Ward and A. R. Waller, *The Cambridge History of English Literature* (G. P. Putman and Sons, Cambridge University Press, Cambridge, England, 1910) p. 43.

> eye, and another a revision of the entire sacred text [by Wycliffe's own assistants]. By the time that Tyndale was born, indeed, it would not have been intelligible to the people at large; moreover, **it was from the Latin Vulgate**, and the period had arrived when the translation must be drawn from the original tongues."[224]

In conclusion, it seems the primary reference for Wycliffe was the earlier versions of the Latin Vulgate. It cannot be determined with certainty if he used any Old Latin (vulgar) manuscripts. Remember, Rome was ruling with an iron hand at that time to the point of even controlling the literature used. Also, some of the later versions of the Latin Vulgate were so corrupted, which Wycliffe and Purvey recognized, that they seem to indicate that they reverted to "old" English translations of portions of Scripture and earlier Latin Vulgate manuscripts. The early "old" English portions of Scripture prior to about 600 A.D. were translated into English from "Old Latin" manuscripts (q.v.). Further study in this particular area needs to be accomplished. One thing for certain, the one hundred and fifty verses from the NT of the EV and the LV in chapter four of this work line up with the Latin Vulgate. The primary variations in the NT are spelling differences.

Controversy #8

Was John Trevisa or John Purvey the "J" mentioned in the Cambridge manuscript (Ee.1.10) of the 250 MSS extant of Wycliffe's translations? Was John Purvey one of the translators of the EV? Did Rev. Josiah Forshall and Sir Frederic Madden, the authors of the splendid 3 volume work on Wyciffe

[224] Anderson, p. 68 (*The Annals*).

translations in 1850, incorrectly attribute the LV to Purvey? (and) Was John Purvey the person who caused the LV to be a more idiomatic English translation aligned with the Latin Vulgate?

Only two names, Nicholas of Hereford, and one of "J" are mentioned in the 250 manuscripts extant. David Daniell reports:

> "that in all 250 texts, we have only two names; two mentions of Nicholas of Hereford, and one of 'J'... **The silence, indeed secrecy, may show us an essential fact, that these Bibles were made in an atmosphere of danger, even fear."**[225]

Of course, this is compatible with other comments in this work that have favored "J" as John Purvey (q.v.). Purvey is considered a scholar, translator, and a reviser of Wycliffe's Bible. More recently, some scholars have accused Rev. Forshall and F. S. Madden of hastily attributing the "J" to Purvey as the source of this claim. However, it is well known that Forshall and Madden spent twenty-two years preparing their work.

Furthermore, it can be demonstrated that before Forshall and Madden proclaimed in 1850 that Purvey edited the late version (LV) there is a Scot's version of the New Testament that identifies John Purvey as the writer of a prologue of the LV.[226] The prologue to that old Scots Bible in the dialect of the Scots says:

---

[225] Daniell, 83.

[226] Thomas Graves Law, LL.D., *The New Testament in Scots being Purvey's of the Wycliffe Version turned into Scots by Murdoch Nesbit c. 1520, Vol. III* (William Blackwood and Sons, Edinburgh and London, 1905 edited from the unique MS. In the possession of Lord Amherst of Hackney).

> "The prolouug follows closely Purveys 'prolog on the Dedis of Apostlis.'"[227]

Dr. Schaff said:

> "In his task he (Wycliffe) had the aid of Nicolas Hereford, who translated the Old Testament and the Apocryphal books as far as Baruch 3:20. **A revision was made of Wyclif's Bible soon after his death, by Purvey."**[228] (HDW, my addition).

And:

> "**The copies of Wyclif's and Purvey's versions seem to have been circulated in considerable numbers in England,** and were in the possession of low and high. The Lollards cherished them."[229]

Purvey roomed with Wycliffe, was a friend, was taught by Wycliffe, and had Latin books in his possession when arrested for activities associated with Lollards. Purvey, as previously noted in this work, was called Wycliffe's curate or personal secretary.

> "A manuscript preserved in the Bodleian, Forshall and Madden affirm to be without question the original copy of Hereford himself. These editors place the dates of the versions in 1382 and 1388. **Purvey** was a Lollard, who boarded under Wyclif's roof and, **according to the contemporary [of Purvey] chronicler, Knighton, drank plentifully of his instructions.** He was imprisoned, but in 1400 recanted, and was promoted to the vicarage of Hythe. This preferment he resigned three years later. He was

---

[227] Ibid. p. 1 (Law, *The New Testament in Scots).*
[228] Schaff, p. 256.
[229] Schaff, p. 258.

imprisoned a second time by Archbishop Chichele, 1421, was alive in 1427, and perhaps died in prison."[230] [HDW, my addition for clarity]

Westcott said:

> "Wycliffe's translation was revised and much improved by others who outlived him, the most celebrated of whom was John Purvey, a clergyman, who officiated as curate at Lutterworth, and lived with Wycliffe during the closing years of his life. It is an interesting fact that Purvey's copy of Wycliffe's original translation of the New Testament is still preserved in the library of Trinity College, Dublin; and attached to it is a Prologue, in Purvey's hand, explaining fully the plan adopted by him in revising the version, and showing that his revision was very thorough."[231]

Perhaps a handwriting expert could compare the prologue handwritten document with signatures of Purvey when he was arrested for his many activities with the Lollards.

David Daniell comments on Forshall and Madden's "splendid" four volume work in 1850, which compares the Wycliffe translation with "Purvey's" revision to a more idiomatic English version in parallel columns. Daniell said:

> "Until the 1980s, the two versions were always known as 'Wycliffe' and 'Purvey', on the grounds that Wyclif commissioned, and probably wrote part of, the first, which turned out to be less than perfect; and then got John Purvey, his secretary, to put the whole thing into better English. **Recent doubts about any connection that Purvey had with Wyclif before his last day at Lutterworth, or with Bible translation,**

---

230 Schaff, p. 256.

231 Westcott, p. 326 (*Quarterly Review*, "The English Bible").

have led to his very proper dismissal from this scene. Scholars now refer to either 'EV' for Early Versions or 'LV' for Later Versions."[232]

In Daniell's footnotes for chapter five of *The Bible in English*, he strongly supports author Anne Hudson's conclusion in her work, *John Purvey: A Reconsideration of the Evidence*. He says:

> "Hudson...reviews what little contemporary, and near-contemporary, evidence there is about Purvey. **She shows clearly that his involvement in any part of the Bible versions, including the General Prologue, was a nineteenth-century invention.** Purvey was not associated with Bible translation even by Bale and Foxe, both always eager to see 'the prohibition of vernacular scriptures as one of the surest marks of the beast upon the Roman church' (102). Forshall and Madden, 1850, I, xxi, on very shaky ground (that of an admitted guess by an eighteenth-century writer, one Waterland, or Waterton), attribute not only the Later Version and other works to Purvey, but the authorship of the General Prologue (and others). This error was followed to such an extent (Deanesly, 1920, 266-7, even added *The Compendious Olde Treatis* to his list of writings) that one used to read of 'Purvey's Principles' of bible translation."[233]

Westcott said:

> "The Prologue was first printed separately **in 1536**, with the title, 'The Dore of Holy Scripture.' It is prefixed to the edition of Wycliffe Bible by Forshall and Madden. It was Purvey's revised edition of the New Testament, and not the original version of Wycliffe, which was published by Lewis in 1731, and again by Baber AD 1810, and in Bagster's 'Hexapla.' Both

[232] Daniell, 79-80.
[233] Daniell, p. 800-801.

versions are given complete for the first time in the magnificent 'Work of Forshall and Madden."[234]

Furthermore, it can be demonstrated that before Forshall and Madden proclaimed in 1850 that Purvey edited the late version (LV), there is a Scots version of the New Testament that identifies John Purvey as editor of the LV.[235] The prologue to that old Scots Bible in the dialect of the Scots says:

"The prolouug follows closely Purveys 'prolog on the Dedis of Apostlis.'"[236]

The conclusion of this controversy appears to favor John Purvey as the translator and writer of the prologue of the LV. Perhaps John Trevisa and Purvey cooperated in its revision. Trevisa was doctrinally compatible with Wycliffe and Purvey. Most likely, both men were involved in the translation work. This is appropriate. Why try to separate them; why not give credit to both men for the brave effort during a frightful time? They should both be given credit for placing a translation containing the Words of God into the hands of the people in a perilous time!

Controversy #9

Are the EV and LV really separate translations or a translation in progress (i.e. retranslation, revision, improvement)?

[234] Westcott, p. 326, footnote (*Quarterly Review,* "The English Bible").
[235] Thomas Graves Law, LL.D., *The New Testament in Scots being Purvey's of the Wycliffe Version turned into Scots by Murdoch Nesbit c. 1520, Vol. III* (William Blackwood and Sons, Edinburgh and London, 1905 edited from the unique MS. In the possession of Lord Amherst of Hackney).
[236] Ibid. p. 1 (Law, *The New Testament in Scots).*

Previous quotes which could not be separate from other issues confirm that the Wycliffe Bibles are works of translation in progress. Dr. Daniell affirms this concept. He said:

> "...the effect of 'Forshall and Madden' has been to solidify the Wycliffe Bible into Block A (EV or Wycliffe edition) and Block B (Purvey edition). What they, obviously unwittingly, concealed, was that there could have been a more **continuous process of retranslation**, revision and improvement than their separation suggests. Their textual apparatus, remarkable as it is, does not allow a picture of manuscript succession, which could be labeled EV^1, EV^2, EV^3 and so on...Yet, probing manuscripts can reveal an interesting fluidity, with implications for the greater activities of Lollards, and the organic life of Lollardy.... **Going back to Bodley's MS 959, we find that, separate from the work of translation, the scribing, the writing-out, had been done by five different people**...What is clear however, is that this manuscript, Bodley MS 959, is a draft at an earlier stage than the four manuscripts which make up Forshall and Madden's left-hand column."[237]

Controversy #10

If Dr. Wycliffe was the most outstanding "scholastic" scholar at Oxford in the thirteen hundreds, would he be unfamiliar with Greek (or Hebrew), since most classics used for scholasticism were written in Greek?

In Dr. Wycliffe's treatise, *De veritae sacrae scripture* (*The Truth of Holy Scriptures*), he says:

---

237 Daniell, p. 80-81.

> "Jews were dispersed among the nations, taking with them their Hebrew manuscripts. Now this happened...that we might have recourse to their manuscripts as witnesses to the fact that there is no difference in the sense found in our Latin books and those Hebrew ones"[238]

Wycliffe also mentions manuscripts being corrected according to the Greek manuscripts.[239] Does this mean that contemorary translators of the Wycliffe Bibles used the Greek manuscripts or did earlier translators? However, the following information is included in another controversy below. It is significant enough to be included here, also.

Another author said:

> "...comparing all three versions (KJB, EV, & LV), side-by-side, it becomes clear the KJB translators rejected numerous revisions made in the "Later Version," and chose instead individual words and phraseology found in one variant or another of the "Early Version."..Why did they do this? ...**the "Early Version," both the poetry of the language and fidelity to the original Greek text** are superior to that found in the "Later Version."[240]

The quote above also suggests that the earlier version was translated from Greek manuscripts as opposed to the Latin Vulgate. This cannot be confirmed! Almost every researcher affirms the close

---

238 Ian Christopher Levy, translated Wycliffe's *"On the Truth of Holy Scripture* (1378), from Latin, (Medieval Institute Publications, Western Michigan University, Kalamazoo, MI, 2001) p. 160.
239 Ibid. pp. 143, 157 (Levy).
240 Terrance P. Noble, "Version Information." *Wycliffe New Testament."* Introduction, Endnotes, Conclusion." www.biblegateway.com/versions/index.php?action=getVersionInfo&vid=53; accessed 6/16/2008. Terrance Noble's version is a "modernized version" of the Old and New Testaments which can be downloaded from: http://www.ibiblio.org/tnoble/.

relationship of the EV and LV to the Latin Vulgate, but that the LV was an improvement in English phrasing. The EV is reported to be an ME gloss of the Latin Vulgate that often cannot be understood without reference to the Vulgate.

> The portion of the Old Testament printed in this volume a reprint from the *later* of the two Wycliffite versions of the same, as exhibited in 'The Holy Bible, containing the Old and New Testaments, with the Apocryphal Books, in the earliest English 'Versions **made from the Latin Vulgate** by John Wycliffe and his followers: edited by the Rev. Josiah Forshall, F.R.S., &c., and Sir Frederic ,Madden, K.H., F.R.S., &c.; Oxford, at the University Press, l850. The later Wycliffite version of the New Testament was reprinted in 1879, with·an Introduction which fully explains all that is most necessary to be known concerning these interesting Middle-English versions... The earlier version is rougher and more literal, and contains, on the whole a large number of unusual words rendering it somewhat more valuable for purely philological purposes, but less legible on other grounds. The earlier version is mainly the work of John de Wycliffe and Nicholas de Hereford, about 1380-1383, the later version revised by John Purvey about 1388...It is well remembered that *both* versions are, not infrequently, almost unintelligible in certain passages until the Latin version has been consulted."[241]

Controversy #11

Did KJB translators use earlier English phrases, Wycliffe's phraseology, or Tyndale's phraseology?

[241] *The Books of Job, Psalms, Proverbs, Ecclesiastes, and song of Solomon according to the Wycliffe Version made by Nicholas Hereford about 1381 and Revised by John Purvey about 1388* (Clarendon Press, Oxford, reprint of Rev. Josiah Forshall, late fellow of Exeter Hall, and Frederic Madden, keeper of the MSS in the British Museum, 1881) p. Introduction, v-vi.

Dr. Schaff said:

"While for a century and a half these volumes helped to keep alive the spirit of Wyclif in England, it is impossible to say how far Wyclif's version influenced the Protestant Reformers. In fact, it is unknown whether they used it at all. Some of its words, such as mote and beam and strait gate, which are found in the version of the 16th century, seem to indicate, to say the least, that these terms had become common property through the medium of Wyclif's version. The priceless heirloom which English speaking peoples possess in the English version and in an open Bible free to all who will read, learned and unlearned, lay and cleric, will continue to be associated with the Reformer of the 14th century."[242]

Daniell said:

"Writers on the English Bible have noticed that phrases from the later version are familiar, because they appear in KJV. At Matthew 25:21, KJV's admired words towards the end of the Parable of the Talents, 'enter thou into the joy of thy lord', have been traced in origin to Coverdale's 1535 revision of Tyndale's 1526 New Testament. That they appear at that point in the later Wyclif has been seized as evidence that Coverdale 'lifted this magnificent rendering straight from the Wycliffe bible'. Tyndale, in both his earlier, 1526, and later, 1534, translations has 'enter in into thy master's joy.' The Greek at that point has εἴσελθε εἰς τὴν χαρὰν τοῦ κυρίου σου (eisthe eis ten charan tou kuriou sou). The Vulgate has *Intra in gaudium domini tui.* Tyndale is more exact to both. Coverdale's is a fine phrase, and it is hard to think in to joy of the lord'. Part of the work on the Wyclif Bibles waiting to be done is a thorough analysis of such apparent borrowings. Whether or not the first translator from the Greek into English, William Tyndale,

242 Schaff, p. 258.

had a Wyclif LV beside him as he worked is an open question."[243]

And:

"We may for the moment postulate that one effect of solid preaching from Wyclif's Bibles, before the standardization that came with printed Bibles, was the creation of just such a common pool of English Bible phrases and passages in people's memories."[244]

Other authors said:

"...comparing all three versions (KJB, EV, & LV), side-by-side, it becomes clear the **KJB translators rejected numerous revisions made in the "Later Version**," and chose instead individual words and phraseology found in one variant or another of the "Early Version."..Why did they do this? ...the "Early Version," both the poetry of the language and fidelity to the original Greek text are superior to that found in the "Later Version."[245]

The quote above also suggests that the earlier version was translated from the Greek text as opposed to the Latin Vulgate. This cannot be confirmed. Almost every researcher affirms the close relationship of the EV and LV to the Latin Vulgate, but that the LV was an improvement in English phrasing. The EV is reported to be an ME gloss

---

[243] Daniell, 85.

[244] Daniell, 89.

[245] Terrance P. Noble, "Version Information." *Wycliffe New Testament."* Introduction, Endnotes, Conclusion." www.biblegateway.com/versions/index.php?action=getVersionInfo&vid=53; accessed 6/16/2008. Terrance Noble's version is a "modernized version" of the Old and New Testaments which can be downloaded from: http://www.ibiblio.org/tnoble/.

of the Latin Vulgate that often cannot be understood without reference to the Vulgate.

> The portion of the Old Testament printed in this volume is a reprint from the *later* of the two Wycliffite versions of the same, as exhibited in 'The Holy Bible, containing the Old and New Testaments, with the Apocryphal Books, in the earliest English 'Versions **made from the Latin Vulgate** by John Wycliffe and his followers: edited by the Rev. Josiah Forshall, F.R.S., &c., and Sir Frederic ,Madden, K.H., F.R.S., &c.; Oxford, at the University Press, I850. The later Wycliffite version of the New Testament was reprinted in 1879, with·an Introduction which fully explains all that is most necessary to be known concerning these interesting Middle-English versions...The earlier version is rougher and more literal, and contains, on the whole a large number of unusual words rendering it somewhat more valuable for purely philological purposes, but less legible on other grounds. The earlier version is mainly the work of John de Wycliffe and Nicholas de Hereford, about 1380-1383, the later version revised by John Purvey about 1388...It is well remembered that *both* versions are, not infrequently, almost unintelligible in certain passages until the Latin version has been consulted."[246]

Furthermore, it can be demonstrated that before Forshall and Madden proclaimed in 1850 that Purvey edited the late version (LV), there is a Scots version of the New Testament that identifies John Purvey as editor of the LV (q.v.).[247]

---

[246] *The Books of Job, Psalms, Proverbs, Ecclesiastes, and song of Solomon according to the Wycliffe Version made by Nicholas Hereford about 1381 and Revised by John Purvey about 1388* (Clarendon Press, Oxford, reprint of Rev. Josiah Forshall, late fellow of Exeter Hall, and Frederic Madden, keeper of the MSS in the British Museum, 1881) p. Introduction, v-vi.

[247] Thomas Graves Law, *The New Testament in Scots being Purvey's of the Wycliffe Version turned into Scots by Murdoch Nesbit c. 1520* (William

Controversy #12

Did the martyr John Huss study under Wycliffe at Oxford or did Queen Anne's attendants from Bohemia bring Wycliffe's writings to Huss after her death?

John Huss

Many works mention that Wycliffe's books or writings were brought back to Bohemia to John Huss (or Hus or John of Hassinetz) by Queen Anne's attendants, who were Bohemians, after her death. Queen Anne was the sister of the King of Bohemia. Also, James and Conrad of Canterbury, who studied under Wycliffe at Oxford and were probably some of his "poore preacher" missionaries, came to Bohemia.[248] The Reformation Society of South Africa said:

> "Scripture translations from the persecuted Waldensian refugees had begun entering Bohemia in the 13th Century. When Anne of Bohemia married King Richard II (1367-1400) she sent copies of Wycliffe's writings back to her homeland. Queen Anne's love for the Bible was shared by many of her countryman."[249] (HDW, my addition).

Blackwood and Sons, Edinburgh and London, 1905 edited from the unique MS. In the possession of Lord Amherst of Hackney).

[248] H. D. Williams, *The Lie That Changed the Modern World* (Bible For Today Press, Collingswood, NJ, 2004) p. 134-135.

[249] Reformation SA, "Truth Conquers, John Huss, Reformer of Prague" (Reformation Society of South Africa, Cape Town, South Africa, 2006 taken from *The Greatest Century of Reformation* By Peter Hammond) accessed 06/09/2008 at http://www.reformationsa.org/truth_conquers.htm.

Some books mention that John Huss studied at Oxford and became familiar with Wycliffe's writings, which influenced him greatly. James A. Wylie said:

> "We read in the Book of the Persecutions of the Bohemian Church: "In the year A.D. 1400, Jerome of Prague returned from England, bringing with him the writings of Wicliffe." "A Taborite chronicler of the fifteenth century, Nicholaus von Pelhrimow, testifies that the books of the evangelical doctor, Master John Wicliffe, opened the eyes of the blessed Master John Huss, as several reliable men know from his own lips, whilst he read and re-read them together with his followers."[250]

Some authors report that Jerome was in Prague obtaining a theological bachelor's degree and a master of arts diploma during the years Huss was said to be at Oxford. However, G. V. Lechler said:

> "John [Huss] studied at Prague, taking the degree of Bachelor of Theology in 1394, and Master of Arts 1396. In 1398 he delivered his first lectures, in 1401 was made dean of the philosophical faculty, and in 1403 rector of the university."[251] [HDW, my addition].

Therefore, Huss was in Bohemia studying when it is claimed he was in England. Similarly, other articles report that John Huss never studied at Oxford. Jeff Young said:

---

[250] James A. Wylie, *History of Protestanism, Vol. 1* (Cassell and Company, Lmt., London, New York, J. A. Wylie, 1808-1890) Section: 3rd Book, John Huss and Hussite Wars, Chapter 1.

[251] G.V. Lechler, "Hus, John" Philip Schaff, ed., *A Religious Encyclopaedia or Dictionary of Biblical, Historical, Doctrinal, and Practical Theology* (Funk & Wagnalls Company, Toronto, New York & London, 3rd edn, Vol. 2. 1894) pp. 1043-1045.

> "It could be said that the story of Hus actually began in Oxford, England. **Although Hus never studied there**, Oxford was the home of Hus' greatest human influence, Jon Wyclif. Wyclif died in 1384 but several Bohemians were students at Oxford in the late 1300s and, upon their return to Bohemia, they brought many of Wyclif's writings with them. These were soon translated into Czech. Hus himself translated some of Wyclif's work at the turn of the century."[252]

It is reported that Huss' supporter and colleague, Jerome of Prague, studied at Oxford at the behest of Huss.

> "At Hus's suggestion Jerome sailed to England and studied at Oxford, Wycliffe's old seat of learning. For the next several years, Jerome moved about a good deal, spreading reform doctrines in Paris, Jerusalem, Heidelberg, Vienna, Russia, Lithuania, Hungary and Cologne. In his native Bohemia he sided with nationalistic students. He denounced a bull proclaiming an indulgence for a crusade against Naples."[253]

It seems obvious that John Huss was in Bohemia obtaining his doctorate during the time he is reported to be in England by some authors.

---

[252] Jeff Young, John Huss, The Prereformer (Biblical Insights, Dec. 2005) accessed 06/09/2008. www.lavistachurchofchrist.org/LVarticles/JohnHus ThePreReformer.
[253] Christian History Institute, "Into the Fires Goes Jerome of Prague" (Christianity Today International, History Institute, 2007, accessed 06/09/2008 at http://chi.gospelcom.net/DAILYF/2001/05/daily-05-30-2001.shtml

Controversy #13

How significant was the "transubstantiation" controversy of Wycliffe's time?

Dr. Schaff said:

> "It was in 1381, the year before Courtenay said his memorable words, that Walden reports that Wyclif "began to determine matters upon the sacrament of the altar." To attempt an innovation at this crucial point required courage of the highest order. In 12 theses he declared the Church's doctrine unscriptural and misleading. For the first time since the promulgation of the dogma of transubstantiation by the Fourth Lateran (1213 A.D.) was it seriously called in question by a theological expert. It was a case of Athanasius standing alone. The mendicants waxed violent. Oxford authorities, at the instance of the archbishop and bishops, instituted a trial, the court consisting of Chancellor Berton and 12 doctors. Without mentioning Wyclif by name, the judges condemned as pestiferous the assertions that the bread and wine remain after consecration, and that Christ's body is present only figuratively or tropically in the eucharist."[254] (HDW, my addition).

The controversy was so significant that it resulted in John of Gaunt, Duke of Lancaster, asking his long term friend, Wycliffe, to not speak on this subject:

> "But in the king's council, to which he made appeal, **the duke of Lancaster** took sides against him and forbade him to speak any more on the subject at Oxford. This prohibition Wyclif met with a still more positive avowal of his views in his Confession, which

---

[254] Schaff, p. 241.

> closes with the noble words, "**I believe that in the end the truth will conquer.**"[255] (HDW, my emphasis).

Wycliffe eventually lost the support of the King Richard II and parliament in 1381 because of his stand against transubstantiation.

> "Courtenay followed up the synod's decisions by summoning Rygge, then chancellor of Oxford, to suppress the heretical teachings and teachers (particularly Wycliffe)... Courtenay would permit no trifling and, summoning Rygge and the proctors to Lambeth, made them promise on their knees to take the action indicated. Parliament supported the primate. The new preaching was suppressed, but Wyclif stood undaunted. He sent a Complaint of 4 articles to the king and parliament, in which he pleaded for the supremacy of English law in matters of ecclesiastical property, for the liberty for the friars to abandon the rules of their orders and follow the rule of Christ, and **for the view that on the Lord's table the real bread and wine are present, and not merely the accidents**."[256] (HDW, my emphasis).

Perhaps John of Gaunt was simply trying to restore order as a leader of the nation. Later after Wycliffe's death, John of Gaunt defended the translation of the Scriptures into English, which his old friend was so intimately involved. However, Wycliffe's stand against transubstantiation augmented Rome's rejection of the quote, unquote "pestilent wretch's" translation.

> "The work speedily received reprobation at the hands of the Church authorities. A bill presented in the English parliament, 1891, to condemn English versions, was rejected through the influence of the duke of Lancaster (John of Gaunt), but an Oxford synod, of

---

[255] Ibid. p. 241 (Schaff).

[256] Schaff, p. 240

> 1408, passed the ominous act, that upon pain of greater excommunication, no man, by his own authority, should translate into English or any other tongue, until such translation were approved by the bishop, or, if necessary, by the provincial council. It distinctly mentions the translation "set forth in the time of John Wyclif." Writing to John XXIII., 1412, Archbishop Arundel took occasion to denounce "that pestilent wretch of damnable memory, yea, the forerunner and disciple of anti-christ who, as the complement of his wickedness, invented a new translation of the Scriptures into his mother-tongue." The same year, 1381, the "Peasants' Revolt" broke out causing irreparable harm to Wyciffe's cause, even though he had nothing to do with it."[257] (HDW, my addition)

It was an excuse to persecute the leader. Even 150 years later the apostates and heretics continued to blame Wycliffe.

> "One hundred and fifty years after this time, Tyndale said, "They said it in Wyclif's day, and the hypocrites say now, that God's Word arouseth insurrection."[258]

Controversy #14

Wycliffe is called the "Father of the English Bible"[259], but was he? (see Controversy #6.)

G. A. Riplinger said:

> "Wycliffe, in the 1300s, states in his Bible's preface that Bede had translated the Bible into Saxon.

[257] Schaff, p. 257.
[258] Schaff, p. 242.
[259] http://www.wayoflife.org/fbns/john-wycliffe.html

> 'Bede translatide the bible…in Saxon,
> that was English, either comoun lagage
> of th lond, in hi tyme'
>
> Bede's Saxon Bible is attested to by Dore who brings this fact to his readers in the 1800s affirming, "he translated the Bible into the vulgar tongue of his day…'"…The 1611 KJV translators of the scriptures, note that Bede 'turned a great part of them in Saxon…'"[260]

Furthermore:

> "The Lord Chancellor of England in the early 1500s 'says he could show English Bibles earlier than Wycliffe's.'"[261]

Encyclopedia Britannica reports that Wycliffe admits to gathering many old English Bibles for his translation.[262] Even so, he is called the "Father of the English Bible" just like William Tyndale, because "Bible" in that age often referred to portions of the Bible. Wycliffe was responsible for a translation of the 'whole bible' (which was called a pandect) from the Latin Vulgate into English. Therefore, it is appropriate to speak of him as the Father of the English Bible because of his influence on those to follow as translators and proponents of placing the 'entire' Bible into the hands of the laity.

However, it appears that portions of the Bible during this time were called "Bibles" and the question remains, were there complete OT and NT Bibles before Wycliffe? No complete Bible can be demonstrated as far as this author knows prior to Wycliffe; only those who claim there were. Therefore, the title of "Father of the English Bible" belongs to

---

[260] Riplinger, *In Awe of Thy Word* (A.V. Publications Corp., Ararat, VA., 2003) p. 693

[261] Ibid. p. 745 (Riplinger).

[262] Riplinger, 749.

Wycliffe, especially since previous translations seem to be in a vernacular closer to the Saxon dialect. Wycliffe's middle English translations are much closer to the lingua franca of current English and are of the entire OT and NT, but they also contained the Apocrypha.

Controversy #15

Did Wycliffe write the tracts commonly attributed to him until recent times?

Encyclopedia Britannia said:

> "From its early days the Lollard movement tended to discard the scholastic subtleties of Wycliffe, **who probably wrote few or none of the popular tracts in English formerly attributed to him**. The most complete statement of early Lollard teaching appeared in the *Twelve Conclusions*, drawn up to be presented to the Parliament of 1395."[263]

Dr. Daniell said:

> "It seems unlikely that Wyclif himself, pen in hand, translated any of 'his' Bible.... It is the same with the second most extensively preserved Wycliffe English text (again surviving in spite of systematic destruction of such material), the thirty-one fine manuscripts which contain a complete cycle of 294 anonymous sermons. These present a comprehensive view of Wyclif's views,

---

263 Lollard. (2008). In *Encyclopædia Britannica*. Retrieved May 29, 2008, from Encyclopædia Britannica Online: http://www.britannica.com/EBchecked/topic/346626/Lollards.

> theological, ecclesiastical, social and political **but are not by Wyclif.**"[264] (HDW my emphasis).

In 1869, Thomas Arnold said:

> "SPURIOUS AND DOUBT WRITINGS.—For some time after I had begun to read the works which the *Catalogue* ascribes to Wycif, I was strongly disposed to question the authenticity of a considerable number of them, for various reasons. With regard to some of these, farther inquiry has not removed my doubts, while in the case of others, that internal evidence on which I relied to establish for the high probability, if not certainty, of a date subsequent to the death of Wyclif, has been proved by fuller investigation to be far less cogent than I had at first supposed...'Early English Sermons', it is a collection of fifty-four sermons on the Sunday gospels, together with five others on great festivals. No one except Dr. Vaughn, has ever ascribed these sermons to Wyclif...and the partial examination which I was able to make of them at Cambridge last year, convinced me that they were the production of a traveler in the well-worn track of homiletics, who posed no spark of the erratic and daring spirit of our author [Wyclif]."[265]

There continues to be great controversy concerning this subject. It seems that too much emphasis has been placed upon "internal evidence" by some scholars, a tenet fraught with great danger to exclude Wycliffe's authorship. However, just as there are psuedoepigraphal books attributed to the Apostles, there are most likely tracts that are falsely claimed to have been written by Wycliffe.

---

264 Daniell, p. 73 (*The Bible in English*).

265 Thomas Arnold, M.A., *Select English Works of John Wyclif, Vol. I, Sermons on The Gospels For Sundays and Festivals* (Clarendon Press, Oxford, 1869, Edited from the originals by Thomas Arnold, M.A. of University College, Oxford) p. iii.

Controversy #16

Did Wycliffe write his own commentary on the Bible?

Dr. Schaff said:

> "Although Wyclif wrote **no commentaries** on books of Scripture, he gave expositions of the Lord's Prayer and the Decalogue and of many texts, which are thoroughly practical and popular. In his treatise on the *Truth of Scripture*, he seems at times to pronounce the discovery of the literal sense the only object of a sound exegesis."[266]

Others have said the opposite:

> "...already existing (English) version, with changes when necessary, were incorporated and made use of by the translators...[and the] text of the Gospels [a translation into English Wycliffe used at Oxford] was extracted from the **Commentary** upon them by Wycliffe "[267] (HDW, my addition).

Other authors have reported on this controversy in quotes throughout this work. Without a doubt, Wycliffe wrote commentaries; most likely on the whole Bible that he used for teaching purposes at Oxford, at Canterbury Hall, and at his last rectory, Lutterworth. His commentary depended upon his gloss of the Latin Vulgate, and vice versa.

---

[266] Schaff, p. 530.
[267] Riplinger, p. 775.

Other Considerations

There are several other considerations of references to controversies surrounding Wycliffe in the literature. For example, it is well known that the Wycliffe versions (the EV and LV) contained apocryphal books just like Jerome's Latin Vulgate or the LXX produced by Origen et al. A consideration of which aprocryphal books were included by Wycliffe and his associates has arisen such as the *Letter to the Laodiceans*. F. F. Bruce makes the following comment:

> "Although it (*Letter to the Laodiceans*) did not form part originally of either the earlier or the later Wycliffite Bibles, two independent Middle English versions of the work made their way into the manuscript tradition of the Wycliffite Bible, and were repeatedly reproduced from the first half of the fifteenth century onward."[268] (HDW, my addition)

Conclusion:

Some laud and some disparage the man. Encyclopedia Britannica said:

> "At Oxford in the 1370s, Wycliffe came to advocate increasingly radical religious views. He denied the doctrine of transubstantiation and stressed the importance of preaching and the primacy of Scripture as the source of Christian doctrine. Claiming that the office of the papacy lacked scriptural justification, he equated the pope with Antichrist and welcomed the 14th-century schism in the papacy as a prelude to its destruction. Wycliffe was charged with heresy and retired from Oxford in 1378. Nevertheless, he was never brought to

---

[268] F. F. Bruce, *The Canon of Scripture* (Intervarsity Press, Downers Grove, IL, 1988) pp. 239-240.

trial, and he continued to write and preach until his death in 1384."[269]

George Trevelyan said:

> "It is probable that few will ever study his writings. The interest and meaning of his Latin books are obscured to the modern reader by the jargon of the medieval schools. His English pamphlets, written in the simple and vigorous language of that day, well repay study. But even these have a certain want of attractiveness, owing to the predominance of hard intellectual and moral qualities over the emotions. But although his writings tell us little about himself, we can read in their every line the severity which appeared also in his actions, and was certainly the characteristic of the man."[270]

Whatever anyone concludes about these controversies surrounding Wycliffe and his associates, one thing is for certain: Wycliffe was a courageous leader of men who exalted Truth and proclaimed *"fides est summa thologia"* (faith the supreme theology).

Wycliffe mentioned the Lord Jesus Christ on almost every page of his writings. His views, though influenced by Ockham, Bardwardine or others, were not from them, but from the Scripture. He denied most doctrines of the Roman Catholic Church such as the infallibility of the pope, transubstantiation, indulgences, and many others. Undoubtedly, he was a man of faith who relied on Scripture. This author looks forward to sitting down and talking with him "in our home in heaven."

---

[269] Lollard. (2008). In *Encyclopædia Britannica*. Retrieved May 29, 2008, from Encyclopædia Britannica Online: http://www.britannica.com/EBchecked/topic/346626/Lollards.
[270] Trevelyan, p. 182 (England in the Age of Wycliffe).

CHAPTER 4

A Chart Comparison

[of 150 Verses in four versions: the KJB, Wycliffe EV (Hexapla), Wycliffe EV (Forshall and Madden), Wycliffe LV, and Catholic Douay Rheims]

(The one hundred and fifty verses are from:
Dr. D. A. Waite's *Defending the King James Bible*, pp. 137ff.)

Explanation of the Chart

I. Italics in the **KJB** verses quoted in this chart stand for words, phrases, or verses **missing** from modern Greek texts and versions. **Brackets** indicate words in the KJB added by the translators for clarity. Brackets were used to indicate the translators' italicized words in the 1611 KJB.

II. For the **theological implications of these 150 verses in the chart, which are VERY significant,** see Dr. Waite's classic work, *Defending the King James Bible,* which is available from www.biblefortoday.org.

III. Wycliffe's Late Version (1395) usded in this chart can be found at: www.studylight.org/desk/?l=en&query=Genesis+1§ion=0&translation=wyc&oq

IV. The Douay-Rheims (DR) Catholic version can be located online at: http://www.drbo.org/. The DR is a "half-way house" between the Critical

Text and the Textus Receptus. The Wycliffe versions (EV and LV) are the same textual basis as the DR.

> "The Douay-Rheims Bible, also known as the Rheims-Douai Bible or Douai Bible and abbreviated as D-R, is a translation of the Bible from the Latin Vulgate into English. The New Testament was published in one volume with extensive commentary and notes in 1582. The Old Testament followed in 1609–10 in two volumes, also extensively annotated. The notes took up the bulk of the volumes and had a strong polemical and patristic character. They also offered insights on issues of translation, and on the Hebrew and Greek source texts of the Vulgate. The purpose of the version, both the text and notes, was to uphold Catholic tradition in the face of the Protestant Reformation which was heavily influencing England. As such it was an impressive effort by English Catholics to support the Counter-Reformation.
>
> "Although the New Jerusalem Bible and New American Bible are most commonly used in English-speaking Catholic Churches, the Challoner revision of the Douay-Rheims is still often the Bible of choice of Traditional Roman Catholics today."[271]

V. The **EV** in this chart is from *"The English Hexapla"* by Samuel Bagster in 1851.

VI. The **EV*** in this chart is from Forshall and Madden's 1850 parallel publication of the Wycliffe Bible in two columns.

VII. A few verses from the **Gothic and Anglo-Saxon versions** were placed in the chart to demonstrate the linguistic changes. They are from Joseph Bosworth and George Waring's *The Gothic and Anglo-Saxon*

[271] From Wikipedia, the free encyclopedia

Gospels in Parallel Columns with the Versions of Wycliffe and Tyndale, second edition, printed by Russel Smith in London in 1874. On page xxxvi of their work is a transliteration chart that may be useful to some researchers. Some parts (verses) were missing in the manuscripts.

VIII. The abbreviations in the following chart in this work are:

1. KJB = King James Bible, 1769;
2. EV = Wycliffe 1380 Early Version (EV) from *The English Hexapla* by Samuel Bagster (1380, New Testament Bible)[272];
3. EV* = "The Holy Bible, containing the Old and New Testaments, with the apocryphal books*, in the earliest English versions made from the Latin Vulgate by John Wycliffe and his followers" from Forshall & Madden's work published in 1850. It is an edited "Early Version" of **1388**[273].

---

[272] Samuel Bagster, *The English Hexapla* (Samuel Bagster and Sons, Paternoster Kow, 1851, by Still Waters Revival Books, Edmonton, AB, Canada, ISBN 0-921148-66-6) Compares Wiclif M.CCC.LXXX.; Genevan M.D.LXX.; Tyndale M.D.XXXIV; Cranmer M.D.XXXIX.; Anglo-Rhemish, M.D.XXXII.; Authorized. M.DC.XI. However, in an article by Brooke Foss Westcott, The Quarterly Review, 1870, p. 305, he says: "The Preface to Wycliffe's Bible is, upon this department, far too brief, and, in some respects, vague; the notices in the historical account prefixed to Bagster·s' Hexapla 'are confused, and not always trustworthy;" but this opinion by B. F. Westcott does not seem accurate by the testimony of many authors who quote Bagster.

[273] "The Wycliffe Bible, by John Wycliffe, The first complete English translation of the Bible. Old and New Testaments, 1388; Retains original spellings (see below). Taken from an 1850 reprint which states: "The Holy Bible, containing the Old and New Testaments, with the apocryphal books*, in the earliest English versions made from the Latin Vulgate by John Wycliffe and his followers." Edited by The Rev. Josiah Forshall, F.R.S. etc. Late Fellow of Exeter College, and Sir Frederic Madden, K.H. F.R.S. etc. Keeper of the MSS. in the British Museum. Oxford, Oxford University Press, 1850." (From SwordSearcher, Ver. 5.2.1.1, 2007, Broken Arrow, OK) It is important to note the "Retains original spellings" in this statement simply means some old English spellings, and not the original spellings in or by Wycliffe's EV.

4. LV = Wycliffe Late Version, LV, 1395 alleged Purvey version from www.studylight.org/desk/?l=en&query=Genesis+1§ion=0&translation=wyc&oq.
5. DR = Douay-Rheims Catholic Version from SwordSearcher, Ver. 5.2.1.1.
6. { } = the word(s) were italicized in the 1611 KJB.
7. ***Italicized* words in this chart** = those words missing in many new versions and the Greek text underlying them.
8. NIV = New International Version
9. NASV = New American Standard Version
10. NB = New Berkley Version
11. Aleph = Sinaiticus MS (which is corrupted)
12. B = Vaticanus MS (which is corrupted)
13. Note the "picking and choosing" by the translators of the 'new' or modern versions, which is called eclecticism (e.g. generally, if the word(s) are missing in the MSS Aleph/B, they are missing in the 'new' versions. But, occasionally even though words are missing in the MSS Aleph/B, they are in the 'new' version, example 2 Jn. 1:9, 1 Cor. 15:54, 1 Tim. 1:1, J:n. 9:38).

VERSE	VERSION	QUOTE
1 Jn. 5:7-9	KJB	7. For there are three that bear record *in heaven, the Father, the Word, and the Holy Ghost: and these three are one.* 8. *And there are three that bear witness in earth,* the Spirit, and the water, and the blood: and these three agree in one. 9. If we receive the witness of men, the witness of God is greater: for this is the witness of God which he hath testified of his Son. (missing in modern Gr. tx. and versions, B/Aleph, NIV, NASV, NKJV-FN, NB)
	EV	for thre ben that yeuen witnessynge in heuene, the fadir the sone the holi goost: and thes thre ben oon. 8. & thre ben that yeuen witnesaynge in erthe, the spirit water & blood: and thes thre ben oon. 9. If we reaceyuen the witnessnge of men, the witnessing of god, that is more: for he witnesaid of his sone,
	EV*	7. For thre ben, that yyuen witnessing in heuene, the Fadir, the Sone, and the Hooli Goost; and these thre ben oon. 8 `And thre ben, that yyuen witnessing in erthe, the spirit, water, and blood; and these thre ben oon. 9 If we resseyuen the witnessing of men, the witnessing of God is more; for this is the witnessing of God, that is more, for he witnesside of his sone.
	LV	:7 For thre ben, that yyuen witnessing in heuene, the Fadir, the Sone, and the Hooli Goost; and these thre ben oon. 5:8 `And thre ben, that yyuen witnessing in erthe, the spirit, water, and blood; and these thre ben oon. 5:9 If we resseyuen the witnessing of men, the witnessing of God is more; for this is the witnessing of God, that is more, for he witnesside of his sone.
	DR	7 And there are three who give testimony in heaven, the Father, the Word, and the Holy Ghost. And these three are one. **8** And there are three that give testimony on earth: *the spirit, and the water, and the blood*: and these three are one. **9** If we receive the testimony of men, the testimony of God is greater. For this is the testimony of God, which is greater,

		because he hath testified of his Son.
Rev. 2:15	KJB	"So hast thou also them that hold the doctrine of the Nicolaitans, *which thing I hate.*" (missing in modern Gr. tx. and versions, Aleph, B is missing Rev., NIV, NASV, NKJV-FN, NB .
	EV	so also thou hast men holdynge the techinge of Nycholaitis, also do thou penannce
	EV*	15 so also thou hast men holdinge the teching of Nycholaitis. 16 Also do thou penaunce;
	LV	so also thou hast men holdinge the teching of Nycholaitis. 16 Also do thou penaunce
	DR	**15** So hast thou also them that hold the doctrine of the Nicolaites. **16** In like manner do penance:
Lk. 22:43	KJB	*43. And there appeared an angel unto him from heaven, strengthening him.* 44. And being in an agony he prayed more earnestly: and his sweat was as it were great drops of blood falling down to the ground. (missing in Gr. tx. & Eng. Versions; B/Aleph; NKJV-FN)
	EV	43. and an aungel apperid to hym fro heuene, and coumfortid hym, and he was made in agony, and preied the lenger 44. and his swoot was made as dropis of blood rennynge doun in to the erthe.
	EV*	43. And an aungel apperide to hym fro heuene, and coumfortide hym. And he was maad in agonye, and preyede the lenger; 44. and his swot was maad as dropis of blood rennynge doun in to the erthe.
	LV	And an aungel apperide to hym fro heuene, and coumfortide hym. And he was maad in agonye, and preyede the lenger;
	Gothic	missing
	Anglo-Saxon	43 Da set-ywde him Godes engel of heofene, and hine gestrangode. 44 And he was on gewinne, and hine lange gebaed; and his swat waes swylee

		blodes dropan on eorqan yrnnende.
	DR	43 And there appeared to him an angel from heaven, strengthening him. And being in an agony, he prayed the longer. 44 And his sweat became as drops of blood, trickling down upon the ground.
Lk. 22:43	KJB	And there appeared an angel unto him from heaven, strengthening him. (missing in modern Gr. text and versions; B/Aleph; NKJV-FN)
	EV	and an aungel apperide to hym fro heuene, and coumfortide hym, and he was made in agony and preied the lenger
	EV*	And an aungel apperide to hym fro heuene, and coumfortide hym. And he was maad in agonye, and preyede the lenger;
	LV	And an aungel apperide to hym fro heuene, and coumfortide hym. And he was maad in agonye, and preyede the lenger;
	Gothic	absent in MSS
	Anglo-Saxon	43 Da set-ywde him Godes engel of heofene, and hine gestrangode.
	DR	And there appeared to him an angel from heaven, strengthening him. And being in an agony, he prayed the longer.
Lk. 4:8	KJB	8. And Jesus answered and *said unto him, Get thee behind me, Satan*: for it is written, Thou shalt worship the Lord thy God, and him only shalt thou serve. (missing in modern Gr. text and versions; B/Aleph; NIV, NASV, NKJV-FN, NB)
	EV	8. and ihesus answered: and seide to hym, it is writun, thou shcalt worschip thi lord god; and to hym alone thou schalt serue
	EV*	8 And Jhesus answeride, and seide to hym, It is writun, Thou schalt worschipe thi Lord God, and to hym aloone thou schalt serue.
	LV	And Jhesus answeride, and seide to hym, It is writun, Thou schalt worschipe thi Lord God, and to hym aloone thou schalt serue.

	Gothic	8 Yah andhafyands imma lesus Gamelid ist, Frauyan Gur teinana inweitais, yah imma ainamma fullafahyals.
	Anglo-Saxon	8. Da andswarode him se Haclend, • Hit is awriten, Drihten dinne God du ge-eadmetst, and him anum qeowast.
	DR	8 And Jesus answering said to him: It is written: Thou shalt adore the Lord thy God, and him only shalt thou serve.
Mk. 16:9-20	KJB	present. Denial of text in modern Gr. and versions; (missing in modern Gr. text and versions; B/Aleph; [NIV], [NASV], NKJV-FN; bracketed in the NIV, NASV casting doubt)
	EV	present
	EV*	present
	LV	present
	Gothic	Mk. 16:17-20 missing
	Anglo-Saxon	present
	DR	present
Jn. 7:53-8:11	KJB	present ; Denial of text in modern Gr. and versions. (missing in modern Gr. text and versions; B/Aleph; [NIV], [NASV], NKJV-FN, bracketed in the NIV, NASV casting doubt). Verse 9 changed significantly in other versions: 9. "And they which heard *it*, being convicted by *their own* conscience, went out one by one, beginning at the eldest, *even* unto the last: and Jesus was left alone, and the woman standing in the midst." 10. When Jesus had lifted up himself, and saw none but the woman, he said unto her, Woman, where are those thine accusers? hath no man condemned thee?
	EV	(present but changed in v. 9 particularly) 9. and thei herynge these thingis wenten awei; oon aftir anothir, and thei bigunne fro the eldir; and ihesus dwelte aloone; and the woman stondynge in the myddil, 10. and ihesus reisid hym silf, and seide to hir,

		woman, where ben thei that accuseden thee? No man hath dampned thee,
	EV*	(present but changed in v. 9 particularly) 9 And thei herynge these thingis, wenten awei oon aftir anothir, and thei bigunnen fro the eldre men; and Jhesus dwelte aloone, and the womman stondynge in the myddil. 10 And Jhesus reiside hym silf, and seide to hir, Womman, where ben thei that accusiden thee? no man hath dampned thee.
	LV	(present but changed in v. 9 particularly) And thei herynge these thingis, wenten awei oon aftir anothir, and thei bigunnen fro the eldre men; and Jhesus dwelte aloone, and the womman stondynge in the myddil.
	Gothic	John 8:1-2
	Anglo-Saxon	all verses present
	DR	Verse 8:9 changed significantly: (present but changed in v. 9 particularly) 9. But they hearing this, went out one by one, beginning at the eldest. And Jesus alone remained, and the woman standing in the midst. **10** Then Jesus lifting up himself, said to her: Woman, where are they that accused thee? Hath no man condemned thee?
Mk. 13:14	KJB	13. But when ye shall see the abomination of desolation, *spoken of by Daniel the prophet*, standing where it ought not, (let him that readeth understand,) then let them that be in Judaea flee to the mountains: (missing in Gr. texts and modern versions; B/Aleph; NIV, NASV, NKJV-FN, NB).
	EV	13. but whanne ȝe schulen se the abhomynacioun of discounforte stondynge where it owith not; he that redith, vndirstonde, thane thei that ben in iudee, fle in to hellis,
	EV*	14 But whanne ye schulen se the abhomynacioun of discoumfort, stondynge where it owith not; he that redith, vndurstonde; thanne thei that be in Judee, fle `in to hillis.
	LV	But whanne ye schulen se the abhomynacioun

		of discoumfort, stondynge where it owith not; he that redith, vndurstonde; thanne thei that be in Judee, fle `in to hillis.
	Gothic	missing
	Anglo-Saxon	14. Donne ge gcseow daere toworpennysse asceonunge, • • • • . . •• • • • • • • • standan dar heo ne sceal; donne ongyte se de raet; fleon donne on muntas, da de synd on ludea.
	DR	**14** And when you shall see the abomination of desolation, standing where it ought not: he that readeth let him understand: then let them that are in Judea, flee unto the mountains:
2 Pe. 3:2	KJB	That ye may be mindful of the words which were spoken before by the holy prophets, and of the commandment of *us* the apostles of the Lord and Saviour: (missing in modern Gr. text and versions, denies Peter's apostleship)
	EV	2. that je be myndeful of tho wordis, that I biforseide of the holi profetis; and of the manundementis of the holi apostlis of the lord and sauyour,
	EV*	2 that ye be myndeful of tho wordis, that Y biforseide of the hooli prophetis, and of the maundementis of the hooli apostlis of the Lord and sauyour.
	LV	that ye be myndeful of tho wordis, that Y biforseide of the hooli prophetis, and of the maundementis of the hooli apostlis of the Lord and sauyour.
	DR	**2** That you may be mindful of those words which I told you before from the holy prophets, and of your apostles, of the precepts of the Lord and Saviour.
Lk. 4:4	KJB	And Jesus answered him, saying, It is written, That man shall not live by bread alone, *but by every word of God.* (missing in Gr. texts and modern versions; B/Aleph; NIV, NASV, NKJV-FN).
	EV	4. and ihesus answeride to hym, it is writun, that a man lyueth not in breed aloone; but in eueri word of god.,
	EV	4 And Jhesus answeride to hym, It is writun, That a man lyueth not in breed aloone, but in euery word of God.

	LV	And Jhesus answeride to hym, It is writun, That a man lyueth not in breed aloone, but in euery word of God.
	DR	4 And Jesus answered him: It is written, that Man liveth not by bread alone, but by every word of God.
Jn. 17:17	KJB	Sanctify them through *thy* truth: thy word is truth. (missing in Gr. texts and modern versions; B; NIV, NASV, NB)
	EV	17. halowe thou hem in truthe, thi word is truthe.
	EV*	17 Halewe thou hem in treuth; thi word is treuthe.
	LV	Halewe thou hem in treuth; thi word is treuthe.
	Gothic	17 Weihai ins in sunyai; waurd peinata sunya ist.
	Anglo-Saxon	17 Gehalga him sofaestnysse; din spraec ys sofaestnysse;
	DR	17 Sanctify them in truth. Thy word is truth.
Mat. 27:34 (cf. Psa. 69:21)	KJB	They gave him *vinegar* to drink mingled with gall: and when he had tasted {thereof,} he would not drink. (missing in Gr. texts and modern versions; B/Aleph; NIV, NASV, NKJV-FN, NB).
	EV	34 And thei yauen hym to drynke wyne meynd with galle; and whanne he hadde tastid, he wolde not drynke.
	EV*	34. And thei yauen hym to drynke wyne meynd with galle; and whanne he hadde tastid, he wolde not drynke.
	LV	And thei yauen hym to drynke wyne meynd with galle; and whanne he hadde tastid, he wolde not drynke.
	DR	34 And they gave him wine to drink mingled with gall. And when he had tasted, he would not drink
Mat. 27:35 (cf. Psa.	KJB	And they crucified him, and parted his garments, casting lots: *that it might be fulfilled which was spoken by the prophet, They parted my garments among them, and upon my vesture did they cast lots.* (missing in Gr. texts and modern versions; B/Aleph; NIV, [NASV], NKJV-FN, NB)
	EV	35 And aftir that thei hadden crucified hym, thei departiden his clothis, and kesten lotte, to fulfille

22:18)		that is seid bi the prophete, seiynge, Thei partiden
	EV*	And aftir that thei hadden crucified hym, thei departiden his clothis, and kesten lotte, to fulfille that is seid bi the prophete, seiynge, Thei partiden to hem my clothis, and on my clooth thei kesten lott.
	LV	And aftir that thei hadden crucified hym, thei departiden his clothis, and kesten lotte, to fulfille that is seid bi the prophete, seiynge, Thei partiden to hem my clothis, and on my clooth thei kesten lott.
	DR	**35** And after they had crucified him, they divided his garments, casting lots; that it might be fulfilled which was spoken by the prophet, saying: They divided my garments among them; and upon my vesture they cast lots.
Mk. 1:2 (cf. Mal. 3:1; v. Mk. 1:3 is from Isa. but not verse 1:2)	KJB	As it is written *in the prophets,* Behold, I send my messenger before thy face, which shall prepare thy way before thee. (missing in Gr. texts and modern versions; B/Aleph; NIV, NASV, NKJV-FN)
	EV	2 As it is writun in Ysaie, the prophete, Lo! Y sende myn aungel bifor thi face, that schal make thi weie redi bifor thee.
	EV*	As it is writun in Ysaie, the prophete, Lo! Y sende myn aungel bifor thi face, that schal make thi weie redi bifor thee.
	LV	As it is writun in Ysaie, the prophete, Lo! Y sende myn aungel bifor thi face, that schal make thi weie redi bifor thee.
	DR	**2** As it is written in Isaias the prophet: Behold I send my angel before thy face, who shall prepare the way before thee.
Mk. 15:28 (cf. Isa. 53:12)	KJB	*And the scripture was fulfilled, which saith, And he was numbered with the transgressors.* (missing in Gr. texts and modern versions; B/Aleph; NIV, [NASV], NKJV-FN)
	EV	28 And the scripture was fulfillid that seith, And he is ordeyned with wickid men.
	EV*	And the scripture was fulfillid that seith, And he is ordeyned with wickid men.

	LV	28 And the scripture was fulfillid that seith, And he is ordeyned with wickid men
	DR	**28** And the scripture was fulfilled, which saith: And with the wicked he was reputed.
Mat. 25:13	KJB	Watch therefore, for ye know neither the day nor the hour *wherein the Son of man cometh.* (missing in Gr. texts and modern versions; B/Aleph; NIV, NASV, NKJV-FN)
	EV	13 Therfor wake ye, for ye witen not the dai ne the our.
	EV*	Therfor wake ye, for ye witen not the dai ne the our.
	LV	Therfor wake ye, for ye witen not the dai ne the our.
	DR	**13** Watch ye therefore, because you know not the day nor the hour.
Mk. 12:23	KJB	In the resurrection *therefore, when they shall rise,* whose wife shall she be of them? for the seven had her to wife. (missing in Gr. texts and modern versions; B/Aleph; NIV, NASV)
	EV	23 Thanne in the resurreccioun, whanne thei schulen rise ayen, whos wijf of these schal sche be? for seuene hadden hir to wijf.
	EV*	Thanne in the resurreccioun, whanne thei schulen rise ayen, whos wijf of these schal sche be? for seuene hadden hir to wijf.
	LV	Thanne in the resurreccioun, whanne thei schulen rise ayen, whos wijf of these schal sche be? for seuene hadden hir to wijf.
	DR	**23** In the resurrection therefore, when they shall rise again, whose wife shall she be of them? for the seven had her to wife.
Mk. 6:11	KJB	And whosoever shall not receive you, nor hear you, when ye depart thence, shake off the dust under your feet for a testimony against them. *Verily I say unto you, It shall be more tolerable for Sodom and Gomorrha in the day of judgment, than for that city.* (missing in Gr. texts and modern versions; B/Aleph; NIV, NASV, NKJV-FN)

	EV	11 And who euer resseyueth you not, ne herith you, go ye out fro thennus, and schake awei the powdir fro youre feet, in to witnessyng to hem.
	EV*	And who euer resseyueth you not, ne herith you, go ye out fro thennus, and schake awei the powdir fro youre feet, in to witnessyng to hem.
	LV	And who euer resseyueth you not, ne herith you, go ye out fro thennus, and schake awei the powdir fro youre feet, in to witnessyng to hem.
	DR	**11** And whosoever shall not receive you, nor hear you; going forth from thence, shake off the dust from your feet for a testimony to them.
Col. 3:6	KJB	For which things' sake the wrath of God cometh *on the children of disobedience*: (missing in Gr. texts and modern versions; B; NIV, NASV)
	EV	for whiche thingis; the wraththe of god cam on the sones of vnbileue
	EV*	for whiche thingis the wraththe of God cam on the sones of vnbileue;
	LV	for whiche thingis the wraththe of God cam on the sones of vnbileue;
	DR	For which things the wrath of God cometh upon the children of unbelief,
2 Pe. 3:10	KJB	But the day of the Lord will come as a thief in the night; in the which the heavens shall pass away with a great noise, and the elements shall melt with fervent heat, the earth also and the works that are therein shall be *burned up*. (missing in Gr. texts and modern versions; B/ALEPH; NIV, NKJV-FN)
	EV	For the day of the lord schal come as a theef, in whiche heuenes with greet bire schulen passé, and elementis schuln be dissolued be heete, and the erthe, and alle the werkis that ben in it, schulen be brente.
	EV*	For the dai of the Lord schal come as a theef, in which heuenes with greet bire schulen passe, and elementis schulen be dissoluyd bi heete, and the erthe, and alle the werkis that ben in it, schulen be brent.

	LV	For the dai of the Lord schal come as a theef, in which heuenes with greet bire schulen passe, and elementis schulen be dissoluyd bi heete, and the erthe, and alle the werkis that ben in it, schulen be brent.
	DR	But the day of the Lord shall come as a thief, in which the heavens shall pass away with great violence, and the elements shall be melted with heat, and the earth and the works which are in it, shall be burnt up.
Rom. 14:10	KJB	But why dost thou judge thy brother? or why dost thou set at nought thy brother? for we shall all stand before the judgment seat *of Christ.* (missing in Gr. texts and modern versions; B/ALEPH; NIV, NASV, NKJV-FN, NB)
	EV	But what demest thou thi brother? Or whi dispisist thou thi brother, for alle we shculen stoned bifor the trone of crist,
	EV*	But what demest thou thi brothir? or whi dispisist thou thi brothir? for alle we schulen stonde bifore the trone of Crist.
	LV	But what demest thou thi brothir? or whi dispisist thou thi brothir? for alle we schulen stonde bifore the trone of Crist.
	DR	But thou, why judgest thou thy brother? or thou, why dost thou despise thy brother? For we shall all stand before the judgment seat of Christ.
Jn. 3:15	KJB	That whosoever believeth in him *should not perish,* but have eternal life. (missing in Gr. texts and modern versions; B/ALEPH; NIV, NASV, NKJV-FN, NB)
	EV	that eche man that beleueth in hym, perisch not, but haue euerlastynge liif,
	EV*	that ech man that bileueth in hym, perische not, but haue euerlastynge lijf.
	LV	that ech man that bileueth in hym, perische not, but haue euerlastynge lijf.
	DR	That whosoever believeth in him, may not perish; but may have life everlasting.

Mk. 9:44, 46	KJB	44. *Where their worm dieth not, and the fire is not quenched.* 46. *Where their worm dieth not, and the fire is not quenched.* (missing in Gr. texts and modern versions; B/ALEPH; NIV, NASV, NKJV-FN, NB)
	EV	44. where the worme of hem dieth not, and the fier is not quenched, 46. where the worme of hem dieth not, and the fier is not quenched,
	EV*	44. (43) where the worm of hem dieth not, and the fier is not quenchid. 46. (45) where the worme of hem dieth not, and the fier is not quenchid.
	LV	44. where the worm of hem dieth not, and the fier is not quenchid. 46. where the worme of hem dieth not, and the fier is not quenchid.
	DR	44. (43)Where there worm dieth not, and the fire is not extinguished. 46. (47) Where there worm dieth not, and the fire is not extinguished.
Mk. 3:29	KJB	But he that shall blaspheme against the Holy Ghost hath never forgiveness, but is in danger of eternal *damnation*: (missing in Gr. texts and modern versions; B/ALEPH; NIV, NASV, NB)
	EV	But he that blasfemeth ayens the holi goost, hath not remyssioun in to with outen ende, but he schal be gulti of ouerlastynge trespass.
	EV*	But he that blasfemeth ayens the Hooli Goost, hath not remissioun in to with outen ende, but he schal be gilty of euerlastynge trespas.
	LV	But he that blasfemeth ayens the Hooli Goost, hath not remissioun in to with outen ende, but he schal be gilty of euerlastynge trespas.
	DR	But he that shall blaspheme against the Holy Ghost, shall never have forgiveness, but shall be guilty of an everlasting sin.
2 Pe. 2:17	KJB	These are wells without water, clouds that are carried with a tempest; to whom the mist of darkness is reserved *for ever*. (missing in Gr. texts and

		modern versions; B/ALEPH; NIV, NASV, NKJV-FN, NB)
	EV	These ben wellis with out water, and myistis dryuen with whirlynge wyndis, to whiche the thick myst of derknesse is reserued
	EV*	These ben wellis with out watir, and mystis dryuun with `whirlinge wyndys, to whiche the thicke mijst of derknessis is reseruyd.
	LV	These ben wellis with out watir, and mystis dryuun with `whirlinge wyndys, to whiche the thicke mijst of derknessis is reseruyd.
	DR	These are fountains without water, and clouds tossed with whirlwinds, to whom the mist of darkness is reserved
Lk. 11:2	KJB	And he said unto them, When ye pray, say, Our Father *which art in heaven,* Hallowed be thy name. *Thy kingdom come. Thy will be done, as in heaven,* so in earth. (missing in Gr. texts and modern versions; Luke 11:2 B/ALEPH; NIV, NASV, NKJV-FN, NB)
	EV	And he seide to hem, whanne je preien, seie je, fadir, halowid be thi name. thi kingdom come to
	EV*	And he seide to hem, Whanne ye preien, seie ye, Fadir, halewid be thi name. Thi kyngdom come to.
	LV	And he seide to hem, Whanne ye preien, seie ye, Fadir, halewid be thi name. Thi kyngdom come to.
	DR	**2** And he said to them: When you pray, say: Father, hallowed be thy name. Thy kingdom come.
Lk. 22:43-44	KJB	43. And there appeared an angel unto him from heaven, strengthening him. 44. And being in an agony he prayed more earnestly: and his sweat was as it were great drops of blood falling down to the ground. Luke 22:43-44 (missing in Gr. texts and modern versions; Luke 11:2 B/ALEPH; [NIV], [NKJV-FN])
	EV	43. And an aungel apperid to hym fro heuene, and coumfortide hym, and he was made in agony, and preied the lenger 44. and his swoot was made as deopis of blood

		rennynge doun in to the erthe.
	EV*	43. And an aungel apperide to hym fro heuene, and coumfortide hym. And he was maad in agonye, and preyede the lenger; 44. and his swot was maad as dropis of blood rennynge doun in to the erthe.
	LV	43. And an aungel apperide to hym fro heuene, and coumfortide hym. And he was maad in agonye, and preyede the lenger; 44. and his swot was maad as dropis of blood rennynge doun in to the erthe.
	DR	**43** And there appeared to him an angel from heaven, strengthening him. And being in an agony, he prayed the longer. **44** And his sweat became as drops of blood, trickling down upon the ground.
Heb. 10:34	KJB	For ye had compassion of me in my bonds, and took joyfully the spoiling of your goods, knowing in yourselves that ye have *in heaven* a better and an enduring substance. Hebrews 10:34 (missing in Gr. texts and modern versions; B/ALEPH; NIV, NASV, NKJV-FN, NB)
	EV	For also to bounden men je hadden compassioun, and ye resceyueden with ioye the robbyng of joure goodis, knowynge that je han a betere and a dwellynge substaunce.
	EV*	For also to boundun men ye hadden compassioun, and ye resseyueden with ioye the robbyng of youre goodis, knowinge that ye han a betere and a dwellinge substaunce.
	LV	For also to boundun men ye hadden compassioun, and ye resseyueden with ioye the robbyng of youre goodis, knowinge that ye han a betere and a dwellinge substaunce.
	DR	**34** For you both had compassion on them that were in bands, and took with joy the being stripped of

		your own goods, knowing that you have a better and a lasting substance.
1 Jn. 5:7-8	KJB	7. For there are three that bear record *in heaven, the Father, the Word, and the Holy Ghost: and these three are one.* 8. *And there are three that bear witness in earth*, the Spirit, and the water, and the blood: and these three agree in one. 1 John 5:7-8 (missing in Gr. texts and modern versions; B/ALEPH; NIV, NASV, NKJV-FN, NB)
	EV	For thre ben, that jeuen witnessynge in heuene, the fadir, the sone, the holi goost; and thes thre be noon 8. and thre ben, that jeuen witnessynge in erthe, the spirit, water, and blood; and thes thre be noon.
	EV*	7. For thre ben, that yyuen witnessing in heuene, the Fadir, the Sone, and the Hooli Goost; and these thre ben oon[b] 8. And thre ben, that yyuen witnessing in erthe, the spirit, water, and blood; and these thre ben oon.
	LV	7. For thre ben, that yyuen witnessing in heuene, the Fadir, the Sone, and the Hooli Goost; and these thre ben oon. 8. And thre ben, that yyuen witnessing in erthe, the spirit, water, and blood; and these thre ben oon.
	DR	***There is no verse 7 or 9 in the DR*** ***8*** "The spirit, and the water, and the blood.".. As the Father, the Word, and the Holy Ghost, all bear witness to Christ's divinity; so the spirit, which he yielded up, crying out with a loud voice upon the cross; and the water and blood that issued from his side, bear witness to his humanity, and are one; that is, all agree in one testimony
Rev. 16:17	KJB	And the seventh angel poured out his vial into the air; and there came a great voice out of the temple *of heaven*, from the throne, saying, It is done. Revelation 16:17 ALEPH, (no B in Rev.); NIV, NASV, NB)
	EV	and the seuenthe aungel schedde out his viol in to the eir, and a greet vois went out of heuene fro the

		trone, and seide, It is doon.
	EV*	And the seuenthe aungel schedde out his viol in to the eyr, and a greet vois wente out of heuene fro the trone, and seide, It is don.
	LV	And the seuenthe aungel schedde out his viol in to the eyr, and a greet vois wente out of heuene fro the trone, and seide, It is don.
	DR	**17** And the seventh angel poured out his vial upon the air, and there came a great voice out of the temple from the throne, saying: It is done.
Rev. 21:24	KJB	And the nations *of them which are saved* shall walk in the light of it: and the kings of the earth do bring their glory and honour into it. Revelation 21:24 (missing in Gr. texts and modern versions; ALEPH; (no B in Rev.) NIV, NASV, NKJV-FN, NB)
	EV	and folkis schulen walke in lijt of it; and the kingis of the erthe shculen bringe her glorie and honour in to it.
	EV*	And folkis schulen walke in liyt of it; and the kyngis of the erthe schulen brynge her glorie and onour in to it.
	LV	And folkis schulen walke in liyt of it; and the kyngis of the erthe schulen brynge her glorie and onour in to it.
	DR	**24** And the nations shall walk in the light of it: and the kings of the earth shall bring their glory and honour into it.
1 Pe. 2:2	KJB	As newborn babes, desire the sincere milk of the word, that ye may *grow thereby*: 1 Peter 2:2 (missing in Gr. texts and modern versions; B/ALEPH; NIV, NASV, NKJV-FN, NB)
	EV	as now borun jung children, resonale, with out gile, coueite je mylke, that in it je wexe in to helthe, if netheles je han tasstid that the lord is swete.
	EV*	as now borun yonge children, resonable, with out gile, coueite ye mylk, that in it ye wexe in to helthe; if netheles ye han tastid,

	LV	as now borun yonge children, resonable, with out gile, coueite ye mylk, that in it ye wexe in to helthe; if netheles ye han tastid,
	DR	**2** As newborn babes, desire the rational milk without guile, that thereby you may grow unto salvation:
James 5:16	KJB	Confess *{your} faults* one to another, and pray one for another, that ye may be healed. The effectual fervent prayer of a righteous man availeth much. James 5:16 (missing in Gr. texts and modern versions; B/ALEPH; NIV, NASV, NKJV-FN, NB)
	EV	therfor knowleche je to eche other joure synnes, and preie je eche for other, that je be saued. For the contynuel preier of a iust man, is myche worth.
	EV*	Therfor knouleche ye ech to othere youre synnes, and preye ye ech for othere, that ye be sauyd. For the contynuel preyer of a iust man is myche worth.
	LV	Therfor knouleche ye ech to othere youre synnes, and preye ye ech for othere, that ye be sauyd. For the contynuel preyer of a iust man is myche worth.
	DR	**(Not my emphasis, HDW)16** *Confess therefore your sins one to another*: and pray one for another, that you may be saved. For the continual prayer of a just man availeth much.
1 Tim. 6:19	KJB	Laying up in store for themselves a good foundation against the time to come, that they may lay hold on *eternal life*. 1 Timothy 6:19 (missing in Gr. texts and modern versions; ALEPH (no B here); NIV, NASV, NKJV-FN, NB)
	EV	to comoun, to trsoure to hem silf a good foundement in to tyme to comynge, that thei cacche euerlastynge liif.
	EV*	to comyne, to tresoure to hem silf a good foundement in to tyme to comynge, that thei catche euerlastinge lijf.
	LV	to comyne, to tresoure to hem silf a good foundement in to tyme to comynge, that

		thei catche euerlastinge lijf.
	DR	**19** To lay up in store for themselves a good foundation against the time to come, that they may lay hold on the true life.
Rom. 5:1	KJB	Therefore being justified by faith, *we have* peace with God through our Lord Jesus Christ: Romans 5:1 (missing in Gr. texts and modern versions; B/ALEPH; NKJV-FN, NB)
	EV	THERFOR we, iustified of faith, haue we pees at god bi oure lord ihesus crist.
	EV*	Therfor we, iustified of feith, haue we pees at God bi oure Lord Jhesu Crist.
	LV	Therfor we, iustified of feith, haue we pees at God bi oure Lord Jhesu Crist.
	DR	**1** Being justified therefore by faith, let us have peace with God, through our Lord Jesus Christ:
Lk. 23:45	KJB	And the sun *was darkened*, and the veil of the temple was rent in the midst. Luke 23:45 (missing in Gr. texts and modern versions; B/ALEPH; NIV, NASV, NKJV-FN, NB)
	EV	and the sunne was made derk, and the veil of the temple was torent atwo
	EV*	And the sun was maad derk, and the veile of the temple was to-rent atwo.
	LV	And the sun was maad derk, and the veile of the temple was to-rent atwo.
	DR	**45** And the sun was darkened, and the veil of the temple was rent in the midst.
1 Cor. 5:7	KJB	Purge out therefore the old leaven, that ye may be a new lump, as ye are unleavened. For even Christ our passover is sacrificed *for us*: 1 Corinthians 5:7 (missing in Gr. texts and modern versions; B/ALEPH; NIV, NASV, NKJV-FN, NB)
	EV	Clense ye out the oold sourdouw that ye be newe springinge togidre as ye ben therf, for crist offrid: is oure pask
	EV*	Clense ye out the old sourdow[c] that ye be new sprengyng togidere, as ye ben therf. For Crist offrid is oure pask.

	LV	Clense ye out the old sourdow, that ye be new sprengyng togidere, as ye ben therf. For Crist offrid is oure pask.
	DR	**7** Purge out the old leaven, that you may be a new paste, as you are unleavened. For Christ our pasch is sacrificed.
1 Pe. 4:1	KJB	Forasmuch then as Christ hath suffered *for us* in the flesh, arm yourselves likewise with the same mind: for he that hath suffered in the flesh hath ceased from sin; 1 Peter 4:1 (missing in Gr. texts and modern versions; B; NIV, NASV, NKJV-FN, NB)
	EV	THERFOR for crist suffrid in fleisch, be ye also armed bi the same thenkynge, for he that suffrid in fleisch ceesid fro synnes
	EV*	Therfor for Crist suffride in fleisch[a] be ye also armed bi the same thenkynge; for he that suffride in fleisch ceesside fro synnes,
	LV	Therfor for Crist suffride in fleisch, be ye also armed bi the same thenkynge; for he that suffride in fleisch ceesside fro synnes,
	DR	**1** Christ therefore having suffered in the flesh, be you also armed with the same thought: for he that hath suffered in the flesh, hath ceased from sins:
Acts 20:28	KJB	Take heed therefore unto yourselves, and to all the flock, over the which the Holy Ghost hath made you overseers, to feed the church *of God*, which he hath purchased with his own blood. Acts 20:28 (missing in many Gr. texts and modern versions; (B/Aleph follow TR); NKJV-FN)
	EV	take ye tente to you, and to alle the flocke in whiche the hooli gost hath sette you bischopis to rule the chirche of god whiche he purchased with his blood
	EV*	Take ye tente to you, and to al the flocke, in which the Hooli Goost hath set you bischops, to reule the chirche of God, which he purchaside with his blood.
	LV	Take ye tente to you, and to al the flocke, in which the Hooli Goost hath set you

		bischops, to reule the chirche of God, which he purchaside with his blood.
	DR	**28** Take heed to yourselves, and to the whole flock, wherein the Holy Ghost hath placed you bishops, to rule the church of God, which he hath purchased with his own blood.
Col. 1:14	KJB	In whom we have redemption *through his blood*, {*even*} the forgiveness of sins: Colossians 1:14 (missing in Gr. texts and modern versions; B; NIV, NASV, NKJV-FN, NB)
	EV	in whom we han ayenbiynge and remyssionn of synnes
	EV*	in whom we han ayenbiyng and remyssioun of synnes.
	LV	in whom we han ayenbiyng and remyssioun of synnes.
	DR	**14** In whom we have redemption through his blood, the remission of sins;
1 Jn. 1:7	KJB	But if we walk in the light, as he is in the light, we have fellowship one with another, and the blood of Jesus *Christ* his Son cleanseth us from all sin. 1 John 1:7 (missing in Gr. texts and modern versions; B/Aleph; NIV, NASV, NB)
	EV	but if we walken in liyt, as also he is in liyt; we han felowschip togidere, and the blood of Ihesus crist, his sone; clensith us fro al synne
	EV*	But if we walken in liyt, as also he is in liyt, we han felawschip togidere; and the blood of Jhesu Crist, his sone, clensith vs fro al synne.
	LV	But if we walken in liyt, as also he is in liyt, we han felawschip togidere; and the blood of Jhesu Crist, his sone, clensith vs fro al synne.
	DR	**7** But if we walk in the light, as he also is in the light, we have fellowship one with another, and the blood of Jesus Christ his Son cleanseth us from all sin.
	KJB	And whosoever shall offend one of *these* little ones that believe *in me*, it is better for him that a millstone

Mk. 9:42		were hanged about his neck, and he were cast into the sea. Mark 9:42 (missing in Gr. texts and modern versions; Aleph; NASV)
	EV	and who euer schal sclaundre oon of these litil that bileuen in me; it were bettir to hym, that a mylne stone of assis, were don aboute his necke, and he were cast in to the see.
	EV*	(9:41) And who euer schal sclaundre oon of these litle that bileuen in me, it were betere to hym that a mylne stoon `of assis were don aboute his necke, and he were cast in to the see.
	LV	And who euer schal sclaundre oon of these litle that bileuen in me, it were betere to hym that a mylne stoon `of assis were don aboute his necke, and he were cast in to the see.
	DR	**41** And whosoever shall scandalize one of these little ones that believe in me; it were better for him that a millstone were hanged around his neck, and he were cast into the sea.
Jn. 6:47	KJB	Verily, verily, I say unto you, He that believeth *on me* hath everlasting life. John 6:47 (missing in Gr. texts and modern versions; B/Aleph; NIV, NASV, NKJV-FN, NB)
	EV	sothli sothli I seie to you, he that bileueth in me; hath euerlastinge liif
	EV*	Sotheli, sotheli, Y seie to you, he that bileueth in me, hath euerlastynge lijf.
	LV	Sotheli, sotheli, Y seie to you, he that bileueth in me, hath euerlastynge lijf.
	DR	**47** Amen, amen I say unto you: He that believeth in me, hath everlasting life.
Rom. 1:16	KJB	For I am not ashamed of the gospel *of Christ*: for it is the power of God unto salvation to every one that believeth; to the Jew first, and also to the Greek. Romans 1:16 (missing in Gr. texts and modern versions; B/Aleph; NIV, NASV, NKJV-FN, NB)
	EV	for I schame not the gospel, for it is the uertu of god in to heelthe to eche man that bileued; to the Iewe

		first, and to the greek
	EV*	For Y schame not the gospel, for it is the vertu of God in to heelthe to ech man that bileueth, to the Jew first, and to the Greke.
	LV	For Y schame not the gospel, for it is the vertu of God in to heelthe to ech man that bileueth, to the Jew first, and to the Greke.
	DR	**16** For I am not ashamed of the gospel. For it is the power of God unto salvation to every one that believeth, to the Jew first, and to the Greek.
Gal. 3:17	KJB	And this I say, {*that*} the covenant, that was confirmed before of God *in Christ*, the law, which was four hundred and thirty years after, cannot disannul, that it should make the promise of none effect. Galatians 3:17 (missing in Gr. texts and modern versions; B/Aleph; NIV, NASV, NKJV-FN, NB)
	EV	but I seie this testament is confermed of god, the lawe that was made aftir foure hundred and thritti yere, makith not the testament veyn, to avoide awey the biheest
	EV*	But Y seie, this testament is confermed of God; the lawe that was maad after foure hundrid and thritti yeer, makith not the testament veyn to auoide awei the biheest.
	LV	But Y seie, this testament is confermed of God; the lawe that was maad after foure hundrid and thritti yeer, makith not the testament veyn to auoide awei the biheest.
	DR	**17** Now this I say, that the testament which was confirmed by God, the law which was made after four hundred and thirty years, doth not disannul, to make the promise of no effect.
Gal.	KJB	Wherefore thou art no more a servant, but a son; and if a son, then an heir of God *through Christ.* Galatians 4:7 (missing in Gr. texts and modern versions;

4:7		B/Aleph; NIV, NASV, NKJV-FN, NB)
	EV	and so there is not now a seruaunt but a sone, and if he is a sone; he is an eire bi god,
	EV*	And so ther is not now a seruaunt, but a sone; and if he is a sone, he is an eir bi God.
	LV	And so ther is not now a seruaunt, but a sone; and if he is a sone, he is an eir bi God.
	DR	**7** Therefore now he is not a servant, but a son. And if a son, an heir also through God.
Gal. 6:15	KJB	For *in Christ* Jesus neither circumcision availeth any thing, nor uncircumcision, but a new creature. Galatians 6:15 (missing in Gr. texts and modern versions; B; NIV, NASV, NB)
	EV	for in ihesus crist nether circumcisioun is ony thing worthe, ne prepucie, but a newe creature,
	EV*	For in Jhesu Crist nether circumcisioun is ony thing worth, ne prepucie, but a newe creature.
	LV	For in Jhesu Crist nether circumcisioun is ony thing worth, ne prepucie, but a newe creature.
	DR	**15** For in Christ Jesus neither circumcision availeth any thing, nor uncircumcision, but a new creature.
Heb. 1:3	KJB	Who being the brightness of *his* glory, and the express image of his person, and upholding all things by the word of his power, when he had *by himself* purged our sins, sat down on the right hand of the Majesty on high; Hebrews 1:3 (missing in Gr. texts and modern versions; B/Aleph; NIV, NASV, NKJV-FN, NB)
	EV	which whanne also he is the britnes of glorie, and figure of his substaunce and berith alle thingis bi word of his vertu, he makith purgacioun of synnes, and sittith on the riythalf of the maieste in heuenes
	EV*	Which whanne also he is the briytnesse of glorie, and figure of his substaunce, and berith alle thingis bi word of his vertu, he makith purgacioun of synnes, and syttith on the riythalf of the maieste in heuenes;

	LV	Which whanne also he is the briytnesse of glorie, and figure of his substaunce, and berith alle thingis bi word of his vertu, he makith purgacioun of synnes, and syttith on the riythalf of the maieste in heuenes;
	DR	**(Not my emphasis) 3** Who being the brightness of his glory, and *the figure* of his substance, and upholding all things by the word of his power, *making purgation* of sins, sitteth on the right hand of the majesty on high.
1 Pe. 2:24	KJB	Who his own self bare our sins in his own body on the tree, that we, being dead to sins, should live unto righteousness: by *whose* stripes ye were healed. 1 Peter 2:24 (missing in Gr. texts and modern versions; B/Aleph; NIV, NASV, NKJV-FN, NB)
	EV	and he hym silf bare oure synnes in his bodi on a tre, that we be deed to synnes, and lyue to riytwisnesse, bi whos wane wounde ye ben heelid.
	EV*	And he hym silf bar oure synnes in his bodi on a tre, that we be deed to synnes, and lyue to riytwisnesse, bi whos wan wounde ye ben heelid.
	LV	And he hym silf bar oure synnes in his bodi on a tre, that we be deed to synnes, and lyue to riytwisnesse, bi whos wan wounde ye ben heelid.
	DR	**24** Who his own self bore our sins in his body upon the tree: that we, being dead to sins, should live to justice: by whose stripes you were healed
Jn. 3:13	KJB	And no man hath ascended up to heaven, but he that came down from heaven, *even* the Son of man *which is in heaven.* John 3:13 (missing in Gr. texts and modern versions; B/Aleph; NIV, NASV, NKJV-FN, NB)
	EV	and no man stieth in to heuene, but he that cam doun from heuene; mannes sone that is in heuene
	EV*	And no man stieth in to heuene, but he that cam doun fro heuene, mannys sone that is in heuene.
	LV	And no man stieth in to heuene, but he

		that cam doun fro heuene, mannys sone that is in heuene.
	DR	**13** And no man hath ascended into heaven, but he that descended from heaven, the Son of man who is in heaven.
1 Cor. 11:24	KJB	And when he had given thanks, he brake *{it}*, and said, *Take, eat*: this is my body, which is *broken* for you: this do in remembrance of me. 1 Corinthians 11:24 (missing in Gr. texts and modern versions; B/Aleph; NIV, NASV, NKJV-FN)
	EV	and dide thankyngis and brak and seide, take ye and ete ye; this is my bodi, whiche schal be bitraied for you, do ye this thing in to my mynde
	EV*	took breed, and dide thankyngis, and brak, and seide, Take ye, and ete ye; this is my bodi, which schal be bitraied for you; do ye this thing in to my mynde.
	LV	took breed, and dide thankyngis, and brak, and seide, Take ye, and ete ye; this is my bodi, which schal be bitraied for you; do ye this thing in to my mynde.
	DR	**24** And giving thanks, broke, and said: Take ye, and eat: this is my body, which shall be delivered for you: this do for the commemoration of me.
1 Cor. 11:29	KJB	For he that eateth and drinketh *unworthily*, eateth and drinketh damnation to himself, not discerning the Lord's body. 1 Corinthians 11:29 (missing in Gr. texts and modern versions; B/Aleph; NIV, NASV, NKJV-FN)
	EV	for the that etith and drynkith vnworthili etith and drinkith dome to hym, not wisely demynge the bodi of the lord
	EV*	For he that etith and drinkith vnworthili, etith and drinkith doom to hym, not wiseli demyng the bodi of the Lord.
	LV	For he that etith and drinkith vnworthili, etith and drinkith doom to hym, not wiseli demyng the bodi of the Lord.
	DR	**29** For he that eateth and drinketh unworthily, eateth and drinketh judgment to himself, not discerning the

		body of the Lord.
1 Tim. 3:16	KJB	And without controversy great is the mystery of godliness: *God* was manifest in the flesh, justified in the Spirit, seen of angels, preached unto the Gentiles, believed on in the world, received up into glory. 1 Timothy 3:16 (missing in Gr. texts and modern versions; B/Aleph; NIV, NASV, NKJV-FN, NB)
	EV	and opunli it is a greet sacrament of pitee, that thing that was schewid in fleisch it is iustified in spirit, it apperid to aungels, it is prechid to hethen men, it is bileued in the world, it is takun up in glorie
	EV*	And opynli it is a greet sacrament of pitee, that thing that was schewid in fleisch, it is iustified in spirit, it apperid to aungels, it is prechid to hethene men, it is bileuyd in the world, it is takun vp in glorie.
	LV	And opynli it is a greet sacrament of pitee, that thing that was schewid in fleisch, it is iustified in spirit, it apperid to aungels, it is prechid to hethene men, it is bileuyd in the world, it is takun vp in glorie.
	DR	**16** And evidently great is the mystery of godliness, which was manifested in the flesh, was justified in the spirit, appeared unto angels, hath been preached unto the Gentiles, is believed in the world, is taken up in glory.
1 Jn. 4:3	KJB	And every spirit that confesseth not that Jesus *Christ is come in the flesh* is not of God: and this is that *spirit* of antichrist, whereof ye have heard that it should come; and even now already is it in the world. 1 John 4:3 (missing in Gr. texts and modern versions; B (No Aleph here); NASV, NKJV-FN,)
	EV	and eche spieit that fordoith ihesu; is not of god, and this antichrist, of whom y herden that he cometh, and riyt now he is in the world
	EV*	and ech spirit that fordoith Jhesu, is not of God. And this is antecrist, of whom ye herden, that he cometh; and riyt now he is in the world.
	LV	and ech spirit that fordoith Jhesu, is not of God. And this is antecrist, of whom ye

		herden, that he cometh; and riyt now he is in the world.
	DR	**(Not my emphasis, HDW) 3** And every spirit *that dissolveth Jesus*, is not of God: and this is Antichrist, of whom you have heard that he cometh, and *he is now already in the world*.
Jn. 7:8	KJB	Go ye up unto this feast: I go not up *yet* unto this feast; for my time is not yet full come. John 7:8 (Aleph; NASV, NKJV-FN)
	EV	go ye up to this feest dai; but I schal not go up to this feeste dai, for my tyme is not yit fulfillid
	EV*	Go ye vp to this feeste dai, but Y schal not go vp to this feeste dai, for my tyme is not yit fulfillid
	LV	Go ye vp to this feeste dai, but Y schal not go vp to this feeste dai, for my tyme is not yit fulfillid.
	DR	**8** Go you up to this festival day, but I go not up to this festival day: because my time is not accomplished.
Lk. 2:22	KJB	And when the days of *her* purification according to the law of Moses were accomplished, they brought him to Jerusalem, to present {him} to the Lord; Luke 2:22 (missing in Gr. texts and modern versions; B/Aleph; NIV, NASV, NB)
	EV	and aftir that the daies of purcacioun of marie weren fulfilled aftir moyses lawe; thei token hym in to ierusalem to offer hem to the lord,
	EV*	And aftir that the daies of the purgacioun of Marie weren fulfillid, aftir Moyses lawe, thei token hym into Jerusalem, to offre hym to the Lord, as it is writun in the lawe of the Lord,
	LV	And aftir that the daies of the purgacioun of Marie weren fulfillid, aftir Moyses lawe, thei token hym into Jerusalem, to offre hym to the Lord, as it is writun in the lawe of the Lord,
	DR	**22** And after the days of her purification, according to the law of Moses, were accomplished, they carried

		him to Jerusalem, to present him to the Lord:
2 Jn. 1:9	KJB	Whosoever transgresseth, and abideth not in the doctrine *of Christ*, hath not God. He that abideth in the doctrine of Christ, he hath both the Father and the Son. 2 John 1:9 (missing in Gr. texts and modern versions; B/Aleph; NIV)
	EV	witing that ech man that goith bifor, and dwellith not in the techiynge of crist; hath not god, he that dwellith in the techinge, hath bothe the sone and the fadir
	EV*	witynge that ech man that goith bifore, and dwellith not in the teching of Crist, hath not God. He that dwellith in the teching, hath bothe the sone and the fadir.
	LV	witynge that ech man that goith bifore, and dwellith not in the teching of Crist, hath not God. He that dwellith in the teching, hath bothe the sone and the fadir.
	DR	**9** Whosoever revolteth, and continueth not in the doctrine of Christ, hath not God.
Lk. 24:51	KJB	And it came to pass, while he blessed them, he was parted from them, and *carried up into heaven.* Luke 24:51 (missing in Gr. texts and modern versions; Aleph; NASV)
	EV	and it was don the while he blessed hem, he departed fro hem, and was borun in to heuene
	EV*	And it was don, the while he blesside hem, he departide fro hem, and was borun in to heuene.
	LV	And it was don, the while he blesside hem, he departide fro hem, and was borun in to heuene.
	DR	**51** And it came to pass, whilst he blessed them, he departed from them, and was carried up to heaven.
Lk. 23:34	KJB	*Then said Jesus, Father, forgive them; for they know not what they do.* And they parted his raiment, and cast lots. Luke 23:34 (missing in Gr. texts and modern versions; B/Aleph;NIV-FN, NKJV-FN)
	EV	but ihesus seid, fadir, foryyue hem; for thei witen not what thei don, and thei departiden hiss clothis and kesten lottis

	EV*	34. But Jhesus seide, Fadir, foryyue hem, for thei witen not what thei doon. 35. And thei departiden his clothis, and kesten lottis.
	LV	But Jhesus seide, Fadir, foryyue hem, for thei witen not what thei doon.
	DR	**34** And Jesus said: Father, forgive them, for they know not what they do. But they, dividing his garments, cast lots.
Mat. 18:11	KJB	*For the Son of man is come to save that which was lost.* Matthew 18:11 (missing in Gr. texts and modern versions; B/Aleph; NIV, [NASV], NKJV-FN)
	EV	for mannes sone cam to saue that thing that perischid
	EV*	For mannus sone cam to saue that thing that perischide.
	LV	For mannus sone cam to saue that thing that perischide.
	DR	**11** For the Son of man is come to save that which was lost.
Lk. 9:56	KJB	*For the Son of man is not come to destroy men's lives, but to save{them}.* And they went to another village. Luke 9:56 (missing in Gr. texts and modern versions; B/Aleph; NIV, NASV, NKJV-FN)
	EV	for mannes sone cam not to lese mennes soulis; but to saue, and thei wenten in to another castil
	EV*	for mannus sone cam not to leese mennus soulis, but to saue. And thei wenten in to another castel.
	LV	for mannus sone cam not to leese mennus soulis, but to saue. And thei wenten in to another castel.
	DR	**56** The Son of man came not to destroy souls, but to save. And they went into another town.
Mat. 1:25	KJB	And knew her not till she had brought forth her *firstborn* son: and he called his name JESUS. Matthew 1:25 (missing in Gr. texts and modern versions; B/Aleph; NIV, NASV, NKJV-FN)
	EV	and he knewe hir not til she hadde borun hir first bigetun sone, and clepide his name Ihesus

	EV*	and he knew her not, til she hadde borun her firste bigete sone, and clepide his name Jhesus.
	LV	and he knew her not, til she hadde borun her firste bigete sone, and clepide his name Jhesus.
	DR	**(Not my emphasis, HDW) 25** And he knew her not *till she brought forth her firstborn son*: and he called his name JESUS.
Lk. 2:33	KJB	And *Joseph* and his mother marvelled at those things which were spoken of him. Luke 2:33 (missing in Gr. texts and modern versions; B/Aleph; NIV, NASV, NKJV-FN, NB)
	EV	and his fadir and his modir weren wondrynge on these thinges that weren seid of hym
	EV*	And his fadir and his modir weren wondrynge on these thingis, that weren seid of hym.
	LV	And his fadir and his modir weren wondrynge on these thingis, that weren seid of hym.
	DR	**33** And his father and mother were wondering at those things which were spoken concerning him.
Lk. 24:6	KJB	*He is not here, but is risen*: remember how he spake unto you when he was yet in Galilee, Luke 24:6 (missing in Gr. texts and modern versions; D; NASV-FN)
	EV	he is not here; but is risun, haue ye mynde hou he spake to you, whanne he was yit in galile
	EV*	He is not here, but is risun. Haue ye mynde, hou he spak to you, whanne he was yit in Galile,
	LV	He is not here, but is risun. Haue ye mynde, hou he spak to you, whanne he was yit in Galile,
	DR	**6** He is not here, but is risen. Remember how he spoke unto you, when he was in Galilee,
	KJB	*Then arose Peter, and ran unto the sepulchre; and stooping down, he beheld the linen clothes laid by*

Lk. 24:12		*themselves, and departed, wondering in himself at that which was come to pass.* Luke 24:12 (missing in Gr. texts and modern versions; D; NASV-FN)
	EV	but petir roos vp, and rane to the graue, and he bowid doun and saiy the lynnen clothis liynge aloone, and he wente bi hym silf, wondringe on that that was don
	EV*	But Petir roos vp, and ran to the graue; and he bowide doun, and say the lynen clothis liynge aloone. And he wente bi him silf, wondrynge on that that was don.
	LV	But Petir roos vp, and ran to the graue; and he bowide doun, and say the lynen clothis liynge aloone. And he wente bi him silf, wondrynge on that that was don.
	DR	**12** But Peter rising up, ran to the sepulchre, and stooping down, he saw the linen cloths laid by themselves; and went away wondering in himself at that which was come to pass.
Lk. 24:40	KJB	*And when he had thus spoken, he shewed them {his} hands and {his} feet.* Luke 24:40 (missing in Gr. texts and modern versions; D; NASV-FN, NKJV-FN)
	EV	and whanne he hadde seid this thing he shcewid hondis and feet to hem
	EV*	And whanne he hadde seid this thing, he schewide hoondis and feet to hem.
	LV	And whanne he hadde seid this thing, he schewide hoondis and feet to hem.
	DR	**40** And when he had said this, he showed them his hands and feet.
Acts 2:30	KJB	Therefore being a prophet, and knowing that God had sworn with an oath to him, that of the fruit of his loins, a*ccording to the flesh, he would raise up* Christ to sit on his throne; Acts 2:30 (missing in Gr. texts and modern versions; B/Aleph; NIV, NASV, NKJV-FN)
	EV	therefore whanne he was a profete, and wiste, that with a greet ooth god hadde swoor to hym that of the fruyt of his leende, schulde oon sitte on his seet

	EV*	Therfore whanne he was a prophete, and wiste, that with a greet ooth God hadde sworn to hym, that of the fruyt of his leende schulde oon sitte on his seete,
	LV	Therfore whanne he was a prophete, and wiste, that with a greet ooth God hadde sworn to hym, that of the fruyt of his leende schulde oon sitte on his seete,
	DR	**30** Whereas therefore he was a prophet, and knew that God hath sworn to him with an oath, that of the fruit of his loins one should sit upon his throne.
1 Cor. 15:54	KJB	So when *this corruptible shall have put on incorruption*, and this mortal shall have put on immortality, then shall be brought to pass the saying that is written, Death is swallowed up in victory. 1 Corinthians 15:54 (missing in the Greek text Aleph, but not missing in the new versions = eclecticism)
	EV	53. for it bihoueth this corruptible thing to clothe vncorrupcioun; and this deedli thing to putte aweye vndeedlynesse, 54. but whanne this deedli thing schal clothe vndeedlynesse; thane schal the word be don that is writun, deeth is sipun up in victorie
	EV*	53. For it byhoueth this corruptible thing to clothe vncorrupcioun, and this deedli thing to putte awei vndeedlinesse. 54. But whanne this deedli thing schal clothe vndeedlynesse, thanne schal the word be doon, that is writun, Deth is sopun vp in victorie.
	LV	53. For it byhoueth this corruptible thing to clothe vncorrupcioun, and this deedli thing to putte awei vndeedlinesse. 54. But whanne this deedli thing schal clothe vndeedlynesse, thanne schal the word be doon, that is writun, Deth is sopun vp in victorie.
	DR	**54** And when this mortal hath put on immortality, then shall come to pass the saying that is written: Death is swallowed up in victory.

Jn. 1:18	KJB	No man hath seen God at any time; the only begotten *Son*, which is in the bosom of the Father, he hath declared {him}. John 1:18 (missing in Gr. texts and modern versions; B/Aleph; NIV, NASV, NKJV-FN)
	EV	no man saie euer god; no but the oon bigetun sone, that is in the bosum of the fadir, he hath teld out
	EV*	No man sai euer God, no but the `oon bigetun sone, that is in the bosum of the fadir, he hath teld out.
	LV	No man sai euer God, no but the `oon bigetun sone, that is in the bosum of the fadir, he hath teld out.
	DR	**18** No man hath seen God at any time: the only begotten Son who is in the bosom of the Father, he hath declared him.
Jn. 5:30	KJB	I can of mine own self do nothing: as I hear, I judge: and my judgment is just; because I seek not mine own will, but the will of the *Father* which hath sent me. John 5:30 (missing in Gr. texts and modern versions; B/Aleph; NIV, NASV, NB)
	EV	I mai no thing of my silf; but as I haere I deme, and my doom is iust, for I seke not my wille, but the wille of the fadir that sente me
	EV*	Y may no thing do of my silf, but as Y here, Y deme, and my doom is iust, for Y seke not my wille, but the wille of the fadir that sente me.
	LV	Y may no thing do of my silf, but as Y here, Y deme, and my doom is iust, for Y seke not my wille, but the wille of the fadir that sente me.
	DR	**30** I cannot of myself do any thing. As I hear, so I judge: and my judgment is just; because I seek not my own will, but the will of him that sent me.
Rev. 1:8	KJB	I am Alpha and Omega, *the beginning and the ending*, saith the Lord, which is, and which was, and which is to come, the Almighty. Revelation 1:8 (missing in Gr. texts and modern versions; Aleph (No B in Rev); NIV, NASV, NKJV-FN, NB)

	EV	I am Alpha and O the bigynnynge and the ende seith the lord god; that is, and that was and that is to comynge almyyti
	EV*	Yhe, Amen! Y am alpha and oo, the bigynnyng and the ende, seith the Lord God, that is, and that was, and that is to comynge, almyyti.
	LV	Yhe, Amen! Y am alpha and oo, the bigynnyng and the ende, seith the Lord God, that is, and that was, and that is to comynge, almyyti.
	DR	**(Not my emphasis, HDW) 8** *I am Alpha and Omega*, the beginning and the end, saith the Lord God, who is, and who was, and who is to come, the Almighty.
Rev. 1:11	KJB	Saying, *I am Alpha and Omega, the first and the last*: and, What thou seest, write in a book, and send *it* unto the seven churches which are in Asia; unto Ephesus, and unto Smyrna, and unto Pergamos, and unto Thyatira, and unto Sardis, and unto Philadelphia, and unto Laodicea. Revelation 1:11 (missing in Gr. texts and modern versions; Aleph (No B in Rev); NIV, NASV, NKJV-FN, NB)
	EV	seiynge to me, write thou in a book that thing that thou seest; and sende to the seuene chirchis that ben in asie, to effesus, to smyrma, and to pergamus, and to tiatira, and to sardis, and to philadelfia, and to laodicia
	EV*	seiynge to me, Write thou in a book that thing that thou seest, and sende to the seuene chirchis that ben in Asie; to Ephesus, to Smyrma, and to Pergamus, and to Tiatira, and to Sardis, and to Filadelfia, and to Loadicia.
	LV	seiynge to me, Write thou in a book that thing that thou seest, and sende to the seuene chirchis that ben in Asie; to Ephesus, to Smyrma, and to Pergamus, and to Tiatira, and to Sardis, and to Filadelfia, and to Loadicia.

	DR	**11** Saying: What thou seest, write in a book, and send to the seven churches which are in Asia, to Ephesus, and to Smyrna, and to Pergamus, and to Thyatira, and to Sardis, and to Philadelphia, and to Laodicea. **11** Saying: What thou seest, write in a book, and send to the seven churches which are in Asia, to Ephesus, and to Smyrna, and to Pergamus, and to Thyatira, and to Sardis, and to Philadelphia, and to Laodicea.
Rev. 5:14	KJB	And the four beasts said, Amen. And the four {and} twenty elders fell down and worshipped *him that liveth for ever and ever.* Revelation 5:14 (missing in Gr. texts and modern versions; Aleph (No B in Rev); NIV, NASV, NKJV-FN, NB)
	EV	and the foure beestis seiden amen, and the foure and twenty elder men filden doun on her facis; and worschipiden him that lyueth in to worldis of worldis.
	EV*	And the foure beestis seiden, Amen. And the foure and twenti eldre men fellen doun on her faces, and worschipiden hym that lyueth in to worldis of worldis.
	LV	And the foure beestis seiden, Amen. And the foure and twenti eldre men fellen doun on her faces, and worschipiden hym that lyueth in to worldis of worldis.
	DR	**14** And the four living creatures said: Amen. And the four and twenty ancients fell down on their faces, and adored him that liveth for ever and ever.
Rev. 11:17	KJB	Saying, We give thee thanks, O Lord God Almighty, which art, and wast, *and art to come*; because thou hast taken to thee thy great power, and hast reigned. Revelation 11:17 (missing in Gr. texts and modern versions; Aleph (No B in Rev); NIV, NASV, NKJV-FN, NB)
	EV	and seiden, we don thankyngis to thee, lord god almyyti, which art and which were and which art to comynge; which hast takun thi greet vertu and hast regned
	EV*	and seiden, We don thankyngis to thee, Lord God almyyti, which art, and which

		were, and which art to comynge; which hast takun thi greet vertu, and hast regned.
	LV	and seiden, We don thankyngis to thee, Lord God almyyti, which art, and which were, and which art to comynge; which hast takun thi greet vertu, and hast regned.
	DR	**17** We give thee thanks, O Lord God Almighty, who art, and who wast, and who art to come: because thou hast taken to thee thy great power, and thou hast reigned.
Rev. 16:5	KJB	And I heard the angel of the waters say, Thou art righteous, O Lord, which art, and wast, *and shalt be*, because thou hast judged thus. Revelation 16:5 (missing in Gr. texts and modern versions; Aleph (No B in Rev); NIV, NASV, NB)
	EV	4. And the thridde aungel schedde out his viol on the flodis and on the wellis of watris and seide, 5. iust art thou lord; that art and that were hooli; that demest these thingis
	EV*	4. And the thridde aungel schedde out his viol on the floodis, and on the wellis of watris, and seide, 5. Just art thou, Lord, that art, and that were hooli, that demest these thingis;
	LV	4. And the thridde aungel schedde out his viol on the floodis, and on the wellis of watris, and seide, 5. Just art thou, Lord, that art, and that were hooli, that demest these thingis;
	DR	**5** And I heard the angel of the waters saying: Thou art just, O Lord, who art, and who wast, the Holy One, because thou hast judged these things:
Mat. 21:44	KJB	*And whosoever shall fall on this stone shall be broken: but on whomsoever it shall fall, it will grind him to powder.* Matthew 21:44 (missing in Gr. texts and modern versions; D, NIV-FN)
	EV	and he that schal falle on this stoon, schal be brokun, but on whom it schal falle it schal al to brise him

	EV*	And he that schal falle on this stoon, schal be brokun; but on whom it schal falle, it schal al tobrise hym.
	LV	And he that schal falle on this stoon, schal be brokun; but on whom it schal falle, it schal al to brise hym.
	DR	**44** And whosoever shall fall on this stone, shall be broken: but on whomsoever it shall fall, it shall grind him to powder.
Jn. 8:59	KJB	Then took they up stones to cast at him: but Jesus hid himself, and went out of the temple, *going through the midst of them, and so passed by.* John 8:59 (missing in Gr. texts and modern versions; B/Aleph; NIV, NASV, NKJV-FN, NB)
	EV	therfor thei token stonis to caste to hym, but ihesus hidde hym; and wente out of the temple.
	EV*	Therfor thei token stonys, to caste to hym; but Jhesus hidde hym, and wente out of the temple.
	LV	Therfor thei token stonys, to caste to hym; but Jhesus hidde hym, and wente out of the temple.
	DR	
Phil. 4:13	KJB	I can do all things through *Christ* which strengtheneth me. Philippians 4:13 (missing in Gr. texts and modern versions; B/Aleph; NIV, NASV, NKJV-FN, NB)
	EV	I may alle thingis in hym that coumfortith me.
	EV*	Y may alle thingis in hym that coumfortith me.
	LV	Y may alle thingis in hym that coumfortith me.
	DR	**13** I can do all these things in him who strengtheneth me.
2 Cor. 4:14	KJB	Knowing that he which raised up the Lord Jesus shall raise up us also *by* Jesus, and shall present {us} with you. 2 Corinthians 4:14 (missing in Gr. texts and modern versions; B/Aleph; NIV, NASV, NKJV-FN, NB)

	EV	witinge that he that reisid ihesus schal reise also us with ihesus, and schal ordeyne with you
	EV*	witynge that he that reiside Jhesu, schal reise also vs with Jhesu, and schal ordeyne with you.
	LV	witynge that he that reiside Jhesu, schal reise also vs with Jhesu, and schal ordeyne with you.
	DR	**14** Knowing that he who raised up Jesus, will raise us up also with Jesus, and place us with you.
Eph. 3:9	KJB	And to make all {men} see what {is} the fellowship of the mystery, which from the beginning of the world hath been hid in God, who created all things *by Jesus Christ*: Ephesians 3:9 (missing in Gr. texts and modern versions; B/Aleph; NIV, NASV, NKJV-FN, NB)
	EV	8. to me leest of alle seyntis, this grace is youun to preche among hethen men, the vnserchable richessis of crist, and to liytne alle men 9. whiche si the dispensacioun of sacramente hide fro worldis in god; that made alle thingis of nouyt
	EV*	8. To me, leeste of alle seyntis, this grace is youun to preche among hethene men the vnserchable richessis of Crist, and to liytne alle men, 9. which is the dispensacioun of sacrament hid fro worldis in God, that made alle thingis of nouyt;
	LV	8. To me, leeste of alle seyntis, this grace is youun to preche among hethene men the vnserchable richessis of Crist, and to liytne alle men, 9. which is the dispensacioun of sacrament hid fro worldis in God, that made alle thingis of nouyt;
	DR	**9** And to enlighten all men, that they may see what is the dispensation of the mystery which hath been hidden from eternity in God, who created all things:
	KJB	Jesus saith unto them, Have ye understood all these things? They say unto him, Yea, *Lord*. Matthew 13:51

Mat. 13:51		(missing in Gr. texts and modern versions; B/Aleph; NIV, NASV, NKJV-FN, NB)
	EV	han ye vndirstonden alle these thingis? Thei seyn to hym, yhe
	EV*	Han ye vndirstonde alle these thingis? Thei seien to hym, Yhe.
	LV	Han ye vndirstonde alle these thingis? Thei seien to hym, Yhe.
	DR	**51** Have ye understood all these things? They say to him: Yes.
Mk. 9:24	KJB	And straightway the father of the child cried out, and said with tears, *Lord*, I believe; help thou mine unbelief. Mark 9:24 (missing in Gr. texts and modern versions; B/Aleph; NIV, NASV, NB)
	EV	24. and anoon the fadir of the child criede with teeris and seide, lord I beleue; lord help thou myn vnbileue
	EV*	(9:23) And anoon the fadir of the child cried with teeris, and seide, Lord, Y bileue; Lord, helpe thou myn vnbileue.
	LV	And anoon the fadir of the child criede with teeris, and seide, Lord, Y bileue; Lord, helpe thou myn vnbileue.
	DR	**23** And immediately the father of the boy crying out, with tears said: I do believe, Lord: help my unbelief.
Lk. 9:57	KJB	And it came to pass, that, as they went in the way, a certain {man} said unto him, *Lord*, I will follow thee whithersoever thou goest. Luke 9:57 (missing in Gr. texts and modern versions; B/Aleph; NIV, NASV, NB)
	EV	and it was don whanne thei walkiden in the weie; a man seide to hym, I schal sue thee; whidir euer thou go
	EV*	And it was don, whanne thei walkeden in the weie, a man seide to hym, Y schal sue thee, whidur euer thou go.
	LV	And it was don, whanne thei walkeden in the weie, a man seide to hym, Y schal sue thee, whidur euer thou go.

	DR	**57** And it came to pass, as they walked in the way, that a certain man said to him: I will follow thee withersoever thou goest.
Lk. 22:31	KJB	*And the Lord said,* Simon, Simon, behold, Satan hath desired {to have} you, that he may sift {you} as wheat: Luke 22:31 (missing in Gr. texts and modern versions; B; NIV, NASV, NKJV-FN, NB)
	EV	and the lord seide to symount, symount lo sathanas hath axed you; that he schulde reddile as whete; but I haue preied for thee.
	EV*	And the Lord seide to Symount, Symount, lo, Satanas hath axid you, that he schulde ridile as whete; but Y haue preyede for thee,
	LV	And the Lord seide to Symount, Symount, lo, Satanas hath axid you, that he schulde ridile as whete; but Y haue preyede for thee,
	DR	**31** And the Lord said: Simon, Simon, behold Satan hath desired to have you, that he may sift you as wheat:
Lk. 23:42	KJB	And he said unto Jesus, *Lord,* remember me when thou comest into thy kingdom. Luke 23:42 (missing in Gr. texts and modern versions; B/Aleph; NIV, NASV, NB)
	EV	and he seide to ihesus, lord haue mynde on me; whanne thou comest in lto thi hyngdom
	EV*	And he seide to Jhesu, Lord, haue mynde of me, whanne thou comest \`in to thi kyngdom.
	LV	And he seide to Jhesu, Lord, haue mynde of me, whanne thou comest \`in to thi kyngdom.
	DR	**42** And he said to Jesus: Lord, remember me when thou shalt come into thy kingdom.
Rom. 6:11	KJB	Likewise reckon ye also yourselves to be dead indeed unto sin, but alive unto God through Jesus Christ *our Lord.* Romans 6:11 (missing in Gr. texts and modern versions; B; NIV, NASV, NB)
	EV	so ye deme you silf to be deed to synne; but lyuynge

		to god in ihesus crist oure lord
	EV*	So ye deme you silf to be deed to synne, but lyuynge to God in `Jhesu Crist oure Lord.
	LV	So ye deme you silf to be deed to synne, but lyuynge to God in `Jhesu Crist oure Lord.
	DR	**11** So do you also reckon, that you are dead to sin, but alive unto God, in Christ Jesus our Lord.
1 Cor. 15:47	KJB	The first man {is} of the earth, earthy: the second man {is} *the Lord* from heaven. 1 Corinthians 15:47 (missing in Gr. texts and modern versions; B/Aleph; NIV, NASV, NKJV-FN, NB)
	EV	the first man of erthe is erthli, the secunde man of heuene is heuynli
	EV*	The firste man of erthe is ertheli; the secounde man of heuene is heuenelich.
	LV	and that thing that thou sowist, `thou sowist not the bodi that is to come, but a nakid corn, as of whete, or of summe othere seedis;
	DR	**47** The first man was of the earth, earthly: the second man, from heaven, heavenly.
2 Cor. 4:10	KJB	Always bearing about in the body the dying of *the Lord* Jesus, that the life also of Jesus might be made manifest in our body. 2 Corinthians 4:10 (missing in Gr. texts and modern versions; B/Aleph; NIV, NASV, NB)
	EV	and euer more we beren aboute the sleyng of ihesus in oure bodi; that also the liif of ihesus be schewid in oure bodies
	EV*	And euere more we beren aboute the sleyng of Jhesu in oure bodi, that also the lijf of Jhesu be schewid in oure bodies.
	LV	And euere more we beren aboute the sleyng of Jhesu in oure bodi, that also the lijf of Jhesu be schewid in oure bodies.
	DR	**10** Always bearing about in our body the mortification of Jesus, that the life also of Jesus may

		be made manifest in our bodies.
Gal. 6:17	KJB	From henceforth let no man trouble me: for I bear in my body the marks of *the Lord* Jesus. Galatians 6:17 (missing in Gr. texts and modern versions; B (no Aleph here); NIV, NASV, NB)
	EV	and heraftir no man be heuy to me, for I bere in my bodi the tokens of oure lord ihesus crist
	EV*	And heraftir no man be heuy to me; for Y bere in my bodi the tokenes of oure Lord Jhesu Crist.
	LV	And heraftir no man be heuy to me; for Y bere in my bodi the tokenes of oure Lord Jhesu Crist.
	DR	**17** From henceforth let no man be troublesome to me; for I bear the marks of the Lord Jesus in my body.
1 Tim. 1:1	KJB	Paul, an apostle of Jesus Christ by the commandment of God our Saviour, and *Lord* Jesus Christ, {which is} our hope; 1 Timothy 1:1 (missing in Gr. texts and modern versions; D (no B here); NIV, NASV, NB)
	EV	Poul apostil of ihesus crist bi the comaundement of god oure sauyour and of ihesus crist oure hope
	EV*	Poul, apostle `of Jhesu Crist, bi the comaundement of God oure sauyour, and of Jhesu Crist oure hope,
	LV	Poul, apostle `of Jhesu Crist, bi the comaundement of God oure sauyour, and of Jhesu Crist oure hope,
	DR	**1** Paul, an apostle of Jesus Christ, according to the commandment of God our Saviour, and of Christ Jesus our hope:
1 Tim. 5:21	KJB	I charge {thee} before God, and the *Lord* Jesus Christ, and the elect angels, that thou observe these things without preferring one before another, doing nothing by partiality. 1 Timothy 5:21 (missing in Gr. texts and modern versions; Aleph (no B here); NIV, NASV, NB)
	EV	I preie bifor god and ihesus crist and hise chosun aungels, that thou kepe these thingis with out preiudice, and do not thing in bowynge in to the

		other side
	EV*	Y preie bifor God, and Jhesu Crist, and hise chosun aungelis, that thou kepe these thingis with oute preiudice, and do no thing in bowynge `in to the othere side.
	LV	Y preie bifor God, and Jhesu Crist, and hise chosun aungelis, that thou kepe these thingis with oute preiudice, and do no thing in bowynge `in to the othere side.
	DR	**21** I charge thee before God, and Christ Jesus, and the elect angels, that thou observe these things without prejudice, doing nothing by declining to either side.
2 Tim. 4:1	KJB	I charge {thee} therefore before God, and *the Lord* Jesus Christ, who shall judge the quick and the dead at his appearing and his kingdom; 2 Timothy 4:1 (missing in Gr. texts and modern versions; Aleph (no B here); NIV, NASV, NB)
	EV	I WITNESSE bifor god and crist ihesus that schal deme the quike and the deede, and bi the comynge of hym, and the kingdom of him
	EV*	I witnesse bifore God and Crist Jhesu, that schal deme the quike and the deed, and bi the comyng of hym, and the kyngdom of hym,
	LV	I witnesse bifore God and Crist Jhesu, that schal deme the quike and the deed, and bi the comyng of hym, and the kyngdom of hym,
	DR	**1** I charge thee, before God and Jesus Christ, who shall judge the living and the dead, by his coming, and his kingdom:
Tit. 1:4	KJB	To Titus, {mine} own son after the common faith: Grace, mercy, {and} peace, from God the Father and the *Lord* Jesus Christ our Saviour. Titus 1:4 (missing in Gr. texts and modern versions; Aleph (no B here); NIV, NASV, NKJV-FN, NB)
	EV	to tite moost dereworthe sone, bi the comyn faith;

		grace and pees of god the fadir, and of crist ihesus oure sauyoure
	EV*	to Tite, most dereworthe sone bi the comyn feith, grace and pees of God the fadir, and of Crist Jhesu, oure sauyour.
	LV	to Tite, most dereworthe sone bi the comyn feith, grace and pees of God the fadir, and of Crist Jhesu, oure sauyour.
	DR	**4** To Titus my beloved son, according to the common faith, grace and peace from God the Father, and from Christ Jesus our Saviour.
2 Jn. 1:3	KJB	Grace be with you, mercy, {and} peace, from God the Father, and from *the Lord* Jesus Christ, the Son of the Father, in truth and love. 2 John 1:3 (missing in Gr. texts and modern versions; B; NIV, NASV, NB)
	EV	grace be with you merci and pees of god the fadir; and of ihesus crist the sone of the fadir in truthe and charite
	EV*	Grace be with you, merci, and pees of God the fadir, and of Jhesu Crist, the sone of the fadir, in treuthe and charite.
	LV	Grace be with you, merci, and pees of God the fadir, and of Jhesu Crist, the sone of the fadir, in treuthe and charite.
	DR	**3** Grace be with you, mercy, and peace from God the Father, and from Christ Jesus the Son of the Father; in truth and charity.
Lk. 24:52	KJB	And they *worshipped* him, and returned to Jerusalem with great joy: Luke 24:52 (missing in Gr. texts and modern versions; D; NASV)
	EV	and thei worschipiden, and wenten ayen in to ierusalem with greet ioie
	EV*	And thei worschipiden, and wenten ayen in to Jerusalem with greet ioye,
	LV	And thei worschipiden, and wenten ayen in to Jerusalem with greet ioye,
	DR	**52** And they adoring went back into Jerusalem with great joy.

Jn. 9:38	KJB	*And he said, Lord, I believe. And he worshipped him.* John 9:38 (missing in Gr. texts and modern versions; Aleph not missing in 'new' versions
	EV	and he seide, lord, I bileue, and he fel doun and worschipid hym
	EV*	And he seide, Lord, Y byleue. And he felle doun, and worschipide hym.
	LV	And he seide, Lord, Y byleue. And he felle doun, and worschipide hym.
	DR	**38** And he said: I believe, Lord. And falling down, he adored him.
Mk. 1:1	KJB	The beginning of the gospel of Jesus Christ, *the Son of God*; Mark 1:1 (missing in Gr. texts and modern versions; Aleph, [NASV-FN]
	EV	THE bigynnynge of the gospel of ihesus crist the sone of god
	EV*	The bigynnyng of the gospel of Jhesu Crist, the sone of God.
	LV	The bigynnyng of the gospel of Jhesu Crist, the sone of God.
	DR	**1** The beginning of the gospel of Jesus Christ, the Son of God.
Jn. 6:69	KJB	And we believe and are sure that thou art that *Christ, the Son of the living God.* John 6:69 (missing in Gr. texts and modern versions; B/Aleph; NIV, NASV, NKJV-FN, NB)
	EV	and we bileuen and han knowen; that thou art crist the sone of god
	EV*	(6:70) and we bileuen, and han knowun, that thou art Crist, the sone of God.
	LV	and we bileuen, and han knowun, that thou art Crist, the sone of God.
	DR	**70** And we have believed and have known, that thou art the Christ, the Son of God.
Jn. 9:35	KJB	Jesus heard that they had cast him out; and when he had found him, he said unto him, Dost thou believe on the Son of *God*? John 9:35 (missing in Gr. texts and modern versions; B/Aleph; NIV, NASV, NKJV-FN, NB)

	EV	ihesus herde that thei hadden putte hym out; and whanne he hadde founden hym, he seide to hym, bileuest thou in the sone of god?
	EV*	Jhesus herd, that thei hadden putte hym out; and whanne he hadde founde hym, he seide to hym, Bileuest thou in the sone of God?
	LV	Jhesus herd, that thei hadden putte hym out; and whanne he hadde founde hym, he seide to hym, Bileuest thou in the sone of God?
	DR	**35** Jesus heard that they had cast him out: and when he had found him, he said to him: Dost thou believe in the Son of God?
Acts 8:37	KJB	*And Philip said, If thou believest with all thine heart, thou mayest. And he answered and said, I believe that Jesus Christ is the Son of God.* Acts 8:37 (missing in Gr. texts and modern versions; B/Aleph; NIV, NASV, NKJV-FN)
	EV	and fillip seide, if thou bileuest of alle the herte, it is leeful, and he answeride and seide, I bileue that ihesus crist is the sone of god
	EV*	And Filip seide, If thou bileuest of al the herte, it is leueful. And he answeride, and seide, Y bileue that Jhesu Crist is the sone of God.
	LV	And Filip seide, If thou bileuest of al the herte, it is leueful. And he answeride, and seide, Y bileue that Jhesu Crist is the sone of God.
	DR	**(Not my emphasis, HDW) 37** And Philip said: <u>If thou believest with all thy heart</u>, thou mayest. And he answering, said: I believe that Jesus Christ is the Son of God.
Jn. 8:28	KJB	Then said Jesus unto them, When ye have lifted up the Son of man, then shall ye know that I am {he}, and {that} I do nothing of myself; but as *my* Father hath taught me, I speak these things. John 8:28 (missing in Gr. texts and modern versions; B/Aleph; NIV, NASV, NB)

	EV	therfor ihesus seith to hem, whanne ye han areisid mannes sone; thanne ye schuln knowe, that I am, and of my silf I do no thing, but as my fadir tauyte me; I speke these thingis,
	EV*	Therfor Jhesus seith to hem, Whanne ye han areisid mannus sone, thanne ye schulen knowe, that Y am, and of my silf Y do no thing; but as my fadir tauyte me, Y speke these thingis.
	LV	Therfor Jhesus seith to hem, Whanne ye han areisid mannus sone, thanne ye schulen knowe, that Y am, and of my silf Y do no thing; but as my fadir tauyte me, Y speke these thingis.
	DR	**28** Jesus therefore said to them: When you shall have lifted up the Son of man, then shall you know, that I am he, and that I do nothing of myself, but as the Father hath taught me, these things I speak:
Jn. 10:32	KJB	Jesus answered them, Many good works have I shewed you from *my* Father; for which of those works do ye stone me? John 10:32 (missing in Gr. texts and modern versions; B/Aleph; NIV, NASV, NB)
	EV	ihesus answered to hem, I haue schewid to you many good werkis of my fadir, for whiche werke of hem stonen ye me?
	EV*	Jhesus answerde to hem, Y haue schewide to you many good werkis of my fadir, for which werk of hem stonen ye me?
	LV	Jhesus answerde to hem, Y haue schewide to you many good werkis of my fadir, for which werk of hem stonen ye me?
	DR	**32** Jesus answered them: Many good works I have showed you from my Father; for which of these works do you stone me?
	KJB	Ye have heard how I said unto you, I go away, and come {again} unto you. If ye loved me, ye would

Jn. 14:28		rejoice, because I said, I go unto the Father: for *my* Father is greater than I. John 14:28 (missing in Gr. texts and modern versions; B/Aleph; NIV, NASV, NB)
	EV	ye han herde that I seide to you; I go and I come to you, if ye loueden me; forsothe ye schulden haue ioie, for I go to the fadir for the fadir is greetter thane I
	EV*	Ye han herd, that Y seide to you, Y go, and come to you. If ye loueden me, forsothe ye schulden haue ioye, for Y go to the fadir, for the fadir is grettere than Y.
	LV	Ye han herd, that Y seide to you, Y go, and come to you. If ye loueden me, forsothe ye schulden haue ioye, for Y go to the fadir, for the fadir is grettere than Y.
	DR	**(Not my emphsis, HDW) 28** You have heard that I said to you: I go away, and I come unto you. If you loved me, you would indeed be glad, because I go to the Father: *for the Father is greater than I.*
Jn. 16:10	KJB	Of righteousness, because I go to *my* Father, and ye see me no more; John 16:10 (missing in Gr. texts and modern versions; B/Aleph; NIV, NASV, NB)
	EV	and of riytwisnesse; for I go to the fadir, and now ye schulen not se me,
	EV*	and of riytwisnesse, for Y go to the fadir, and now ye schulen not se me;
	LV	and of riytwisnesse, for Y go to the fadir, and now ye schulen not se me;
	DR	**10** And of justice: because I go to the Father; and you shall see me no longer.
Eph. 3:14	KJB	For this cause I bow my knees unto the Father *of our Lord Jesus Christ*, Ephesians 3:14 (missing in Gr. texts and modern versions; B/Aleph; NIV, NASV, NKJV-FN, NB)
	EV	for grace of this thing I bowe my knees to the fadir of oure lord ihesus crist,

	EV*	For grace of this thing Y bowe my knees to the fadir of oure Lord Jhesu Crist,
	LV	For grace of this thing Y bowe my knees to the fadir of oure Lord Jhesu Crist,
	DR	**14** For this cause I bow my knees to the Father of our Lord Jesus Christ,
Col. 1:2	KJB	To the saints and faithful brethren in Christ which are at Colosse: Grace *be* unto you, and peace, from God our Father *and the Lord Jesus Christ.* Colossians 1:2 (missing in Gr. texts and modern versions; B; NIV, NASV, NKJV-FN)
	EV	2. hem that een at colise, holi and faithful britheren in crist ihesus; grace and pees to you of god oure fadir and of the lord ihesus crist, 3. we don thankyngis to god, and to the fadir of oure lord ihesus crist, euermore preiynge for you, 4. herynge you faith in crist ihesus,…
	EV*	2. and Tymothe, brother, to hem that ben at Colose, hooli and feithful britheren in Crist Jhesu, 3. grace and pees to you of God oure fadir and of the Lord Jhesu Crist. We don thankyngis to God, and to the fader of oure Lord Jhesu Crist, euermore preiynge for you, herynge youre feith in Crist Jhesu,
	LV	2. and Tymothe, brother, to hem that ben at Colose, hooli and feithful britheren in Crist Jhesu, 3. grace and pees to you of God oure fadir and of the Lord Jhesu Crist. We don thankyngis to God, and to the fader of oure Lord Jhesu Crist, euermore preiynge for you, herynge youre feith in Crist Jhesu,
	DR	**2** To the saints and faithful brethren in Christ Jesus, who are at Colossa. **3** Grace be to you and peace from God our Father, and from the Lord Jesus Christ. We give thanks to God, and the Father of our Lord Jesus Christ,

		praying always for you.
Acts 9:29	KJB	And he spake boldly in the name of the Lord *Jesus*, and disputed against the Grecians: but they went about to slay him. Acts 9:29 (missing in Gr. texts and modern versions; B/Aleph; NIV, NASV, NB)
	EV	and did tristli in the name of ihesus, and he spake with hethen men; and disputed with grekis, and thei souyten to sle hym
	EV*	And he spak with hethene men, and disputide with Grekis[f] And thei souyten to sle hym.
	LV	And he spak with hethene men, and disputide with Grekis. And thei souyten to sle hym.
	DR	**29** He spoke also to the Gentiles, and disputed with the Greeks; but they sought to kill him
1 Cor. 5:5	KJB	To deliver such an one unto Satan for the destruction of the flesh, that the spirit may be saved in the day of the Lord *Jesus*. 1 Corinthians 5:5 (missing in Gr. texts and modern versions; B; NIV, NASV, NKJV-FN)
	EV	to take suche a man to sathanas in to the perischynge of fleisch, that the spirit be saaf in the dai of oure lord ihesus crist.
	EV*	to take siche a man to Sathanas, in to the perischyng of fleisch[a] that the spirit be saaf in the dai of oure Lord Jhesu Crist.
	LV	to take siche a man to Sathanas, in to the perischyng of fleisch, that the spirit be saaf in the dai of oure Lord Jhesu Crist.
	DR	**5** To deliver such a one to Satan for the destruction of the flesh, that the spirit may be saved in the day of our Lord Jesus Christ.
1 Cor. 16:22	KJB	If any man love not the Lord *Jesus Christ*, let him be Anathema Maranatha. 1 Corinthians 16:22 (missing in Gr. texts and modern versions; B; NIV, NASV, NB)
	EV	if ony man loueth not oure lord ihesus crist; be he cursed, maranatha
	EV*	If ony man loueth not oure Lord Jhesu

		Crist, be he cursid, Mara natha.
	LV	If ony man loueth not oure Lord Jhesu Crist, be he cursid, Maranatha.
	DR	**(Not my emphasis, HDW) 22** If any man love not our Lord Jesus Christ, <u>*let him be anathema, maranatha*</u>.
Acts 3:26	KJB	Unto you first God, having raised up his Son *Jesus*, sent him to bless you, in turning away every one of you from his iniquities. Acts 3:26 (missing in Gr. texts and modern versions; B; NIV, NASV, NB)
	EV	god reisid his sone first to you, and sente hym blessed you; that ech man conuertid hym ; from his wickidnesse.
	EV*	God reiside his sone first to you, and sente hym blessynge you, that ech man conuerte hym from his wickidnesse.
	LV	God reiside his sone first to you, and sente hym blessynge you, that ech man conuerte hym from his wickidnesse.
	DR	**26** To you first God, raising up his Son, hath sent him to bless you; that every one may convert himself from his wickedness.
Mat. 8:29	KJB	And, behold, they cried out, saying, What have we to do with thee, *Jesus*, thou Son of God? art thou come hither to torment us before the time? Matthew 8:29 (missing in Gr. texts and modern versions; B; NIV, NASV, NB)
	EV	and lo thei crieden and seiden, what to us and to thee thou ihesus the sone of god? art thou comen hider bifor the tyme to turmente us?
	EV*	And lo! thei crieden, and seiden, What to vs and to thee, Jhesu, the sone of God? \`art thou comun hidir bifore the tyme to turmente vs?
	LV	And lo! thei crieden, and seiden, What to vs and to thee, Jhesu, the sone of God? \`art thou comun hidir bifore the tyme to turmente vs?
	DR	**29** And behold they cried out, saying: What have we to do with thee, Jesus Son of God? art thou come

		hither to torment us before the time?
Rom. 15:8	KJB	Now I say that *Jesus* Christ was a minister of the circumcision for the truth of God, to confirm the promises *made* unto the fathers: Romans 15:8 (missing in Gr. texts and modern versions; B/Aleph; NIV, NASV, NB)
	EV	for I seie, that ihesus crist was a mynystre of circumcisioun for the truthe of god; to conferme the biheestis of fadris
	EV*	For Y seie, that Jhesu Crist was a mynystre of circumcisioun for the treuthe of God, to conferme the biheestis of fadris.
	LV	For Y seie, that Jhesu Crist was a mynystre of circumcisioun for the treuthe of God, to conferme the biheestis of fadris.
	DR	**(Not my emphasis, HDW) 8** For I say that Christ Jesus was *minister of the circumcision* for the truth of God, to confirm the promises made unto the fathers.
1 Cor. 9:1	KJB	Am I not an apostle? am I not free? have I not seen Jesus *Christ* our Lord? are not ye my work in the Lord? 1 Corinthians 9:1 (missing in Gr. texts and modern versions; B/Aleph; NIV, NASV, NB)
	EV	WHERE I am not free, am I not apostle? Where I sai not crist ihesus oure lord? Where ye ben not my werke in the lord,
	EV*	Whether Y am not fre? Am Y not apostle? Whether Y saiy not `Crist Jhesu, `oure Lord? Whether ye ben not my werk in the Lord?
	LV	Whether Y am not fre? Am Y not apostle? Whether Y saiy not `Crist Jhesu, `oure Lord? Whether ye ben not my werk in the Lord?
	DR	**1** Am not I free? Am not I an apostle? Have not I seen Christ Jesus our Lord? Are not you my work in the Lord?
	KJB	And all things *are* of God, who hath reconciled us to

2 Cor. 5:18		himself by *Jesus* Christ, and hath given to us the ministry of reconciliation; 2 Corinthians 5:18 (missing in Gr. texts and modern versions; B/Aleph; NIV, NASV, NB)
	EV	17…and lo alle thingis ben of god, 18. whiche recounceilid us to hym bi crist and yaf to us the seruyce of recounceilynge,
	EV*	And lo! alle thingis ben of God, which recounselide vs to hym bi Crist, and yaf to vs the seruyce of recounselyng.
	LV	And lo! alle thingis ben of God, which recounselide vs to hym bi Crist, and yaf to vs the seruyce of recounselyng.
	DR	**18** But all things are of God, who hath reconciled us to himself by Christ; and hath given to us the ministry of reconciliation.
Col. 1:28	KJB	Whom we preach, warning every man, and teaching every man in all wisdom; that we may present every man perfect in Christ *Jesus*: Colossians 1:28 (missing in Gr. texts and modern versions; B/Aleph; NIV, NASV, NB)
	EV	whom we schewen, repreuynge eche man, and techynge eche man in al wisdom, that we offer eche man perfiyt in crist ihesus,
	EV*	Whom we schewen, repreuynge ech man, and techinge `ech man in al wisdom, that we offre ech man perfit in Crist Jhesu.
	LV	Whom we schewen, repreuynge ech man, and techinge `ech man in al wisdom, that we offre ech man perfit in Crist Jhesu.
	DR	**28** Whom we preach, admonishing every man, and teaching every man in all wisdom, that we may present every man perfect in Christ Jesus.
Heb. 3:1	KJB	Wherefore, holy brethren, partakers of the heavenly calling, consider the Apostle and High Priest of our profession, *Christ* Jesus; Hebrews 3:1 (missing in Gr. texts and modern versions; B/Aleph; NIV, NASV, NB)
	EV	THERFOR hooli britheren, and parteneris of heuenli clepynge, biholde ye the apostle, and the bischop of

		oure confessioun ihesus,
	EV*	Therfor, hooli britheren, and parceneris of heuenli cleping, biholde ye the apostle and the bischop of oure confessioun, Jhesu,
	LV	Therfor, hooli britheren, and parceneris of heuenli cleping, biholde ye the apostle and the bischop of oure confessioun, Jhesu,
	DR	**1** Wherefore, holy brethren, partakers of the heavenly vocation, consider the apostle and high priest of our confession, Jesus:
1 Pe. 5:10	KJB	But the God of all grace, who hath called us unto his eternal glory by Christ *Jesus*, after that ye have suffered a while, make you perfect, stablish, strengthen, settle {you}. 1 Peter 5:10 (missing in Gr. texts and modern versions; B/Aleph; NIV, NASV, NB)
	EV	and god of al grace that clepid you in to his euerlastynge glorie you suffrynge a litil he schal perfourme and schal conferme, and schal make sad.
	EV*	And God of al grace, that clepide you in to his euerlastinge glorie, you suffrynge a litil, he schal performe, and schal conferme, and schal make sad.
	LV	And God of al grace, that clepide you in to his euerlastinge glorie, you suffrynge a litil, he schal performe, and schal conferme, and schal make sad.
	DR	**10** But the God of all grace, who hath called us into his eternal glory in Christ Jesus, after you have suffered a little, will himself perfect you, and confirm you, and establish you.
1 Pe. 5:14	KJB	Greet ye one another with a kiss of charity. Peace *be* with you all that are in Christ *Jesus*. Amen. 1 Peter 5:14 (missing in Gr. texts and modern versions; B/Aleph; NIV, NASV, NB)
	EV	grete ye wel togidre in holi coose, grace be to you alle that ben in crist amen.
	EV*	Grete ye wel togidere in hooli cos. Grace

		be to you alle that ben in Crist. Amen.
	LV	Grete ye wel togidere in hooli cos. Grace be to you alle that ben in Crist. Amen.
	DR	**14** Salute one another with a holy kiss. Grace be to all you, who are in Christ Jesus. Amen
Rev. 1:9	KJB	I John, who also am your brother, and companion in tribulation, and in the kingdom and patience of Jesus *Christ*, was in the isle that is called Patmos, for the word of God, and for the testimony of Jesus Christ. Revelation 1:9 (missing in Gr. texts and modern versions; Aleph (No B in Rev); NIV, NASV, NKJV-FN, NB)
	EV	I ioon youre brother and partener in tribulacioun and kingdom and pacience in crist ihesus; was in an ile that is clepid pathmos, for the word of god and for the witnessinge of ihesus,
	EV*	I, Joon, youre brothir, and partener in tribulacioun, and kingdom, and pacience in Crist Jhesu, was in an ile, that is clepid Pathmos, for the word of God, and for the witnessyng of Jhesu.
	LV	I, Joon, youre brothir, and partener in tribulacioun, and kingdom, and pacience in Crist Jhesu, was in an ile, that is clepid Pathmos, for the word of God, and for the witnessyng of Jhesu.
	DR	**9** I John, your brother and your partner in tribulation, and in the kingdom, and patience in Christ Jesus, was in the island, which is called Patmos, for the word of God, and for the testimony of Jesus.
Rev. 12:17	KJB	And the dragon was wroth with the woman, and went to make war with the remnant of her seed, which keep the commandments of God, and have the testimony of Jesus *Christ*. Revelation 12:17 (missing in Gr. texts and modern versions; Aleph (No B in Rev.); NIV, NASV, NKJV-FN, NB)
	EV	and the dragoun was wroth ayens the woman; and he wente to make bateil with other of hir seed, that kepen the maundementis of god, and han the witnessynge of ihesus crist; and he stood on the

		graueil of the see.
	EV*	And the dragoun was wrooth ayens the womman, and he wente to make batel with othere of hir seed, that kepen the maundementis of God, and han the witnessing of Jhesu Crist.
	LV	And the dragoun was wrooth ayens the womman, and he wente to make batel with othere of hir seed, that kepen the maundementis of God, and han the witnessing of Jhesu Crist.
	DR	**17** And the dragon was angry against the woman: and went to make war with the rest of her seed, who keep the commandments of God, and have the testimony of Jesus Christ.
Lk. 4:41	KJB	And devils also came out of many, crying out, and saying, Thou art *Christ* the Son of God. And he rebuking {them} suffered them not to speak: for they knew that he was Christ. Luke 4:41 (missing in Gr. texts and modern versions; B/Aleph; NIV, NASV, NKJV-FN, NB)
	EV	and feendis wenten out fro many; and crieden and seiden, for thou art the sone of god, and he blamed and suffrid hem not to speke; for thei wisten hym, that he was crist
	EV*	And feendis wenten out fro manye, and crieden, and seiden, For thou art the sone of God. And he blamede, and suffride hem not to speke, for thei wisten hym, that he was Crist.
	LV	And feendis wenten out fro manye, and crieden, and seiden, For thou art the sone of God. And he blamede, and suffride hem not to speke, for thei wisten hym, that he was Crist.
	DR	**41** And devils went out from many, crying out and saying: Thou art the Son of God. And rebuking them he suffered them not to speak, for they knew that he was Christ.
	KJB	And said unto the woman, Now we believe, not

Jn. 4:42		because of thy saying: for we have heard *him* ourselves, and know that this is indeed *the Christ*, the Saviour of the world. John 4:42 (missing in Gr. texts and modern versions; B/Aleph; NIV, NASV, NKJV-FN, NB)
	EV	and seiden to the woman, that now not for thi speche, we bileuen, for we han herde, and we witen, that this is verrili the sauyour of the world.
	EV*	and seiden to the womman, That now not for thi speche we bileuen; for we han herd, and we witen, that this is verili the sauyour of the world.
	LV	and seiden to the womman, That now not for thi speche we bileuen; for we han herd, and we witen, that this is verili the sauyour of the world.
	DR	**42** And they said to the woman: We now believe, not for thy saying: for we ourselves have heard him, and know that this is indeed the Saviour of the world.
Acts 15:11	KJB	But we believe that through the grace of the Lord Jesus *Christ* we shall be saved, even as they. Acts 15:11 (missing in Gr. texts and modern versions; B/Aleph; NIV, NASV, NKJV-FN, NB)
	EV	but bi the grace of oure lord ihesus crist, we bileuen to be saued; as also thei,
	EV*	But bi the grace of oure Lord Jhesu Crist we bileuen to be saued, as also thei.
	LV	But bi the grace of oure Lord Jhesu Crist we bileuen to be saued, as also thei.
	DR	**11** But by the grace of the Lord Jesus Christ, we believe to be saved, in like manner as they also.
Acts 16:31	KJB	And they said, Believe on the Lord Jesus *Christ*, and thou shalt be saved, and thy house. Acts 16:31 (missing in Gr. texts and modern versions; B/Aleph; NIV, NASV, NB)
	EV	and thei seiden, bileue thou in the lord ihesus, and thou schalt be saaf and thin hous,
	EV*	And thei seiden, Bileue thou in the Lord Jhesu, and thou schalt be saaf, and thin

		hous.
	LV	And thei seiden, Bileue thou in the Lord Jhesu, and thou schalt be saaf, and thin hous.
	DR	**31** But they said: Believe in the Lord Jesus, and thou shalt be saved, and thy house.
Acts 20:21	KJB	Testifying both to the Jews, and also to the Greeks, repentance toward God, and faith toward our Lord Jesus *Christ*. Acts 20:21 (missing in Gr. texts and modern versions; B; NIV, NB)
	EV	and I witnessed to iewis and to hethen men penaunce in to god; and faith in to oure lord ihesus crist,
	EV*	and Y witnesside to Jewis and to hethene men penaunce in to God, and feith in to oure Lord Jhesu Crist.
	LV	and Y witnesside to Jewis and to hethene men penaunce in to God, and feith in to oure Lord Jhesu Crist.
	DR	**21** Testifying both to Jews and Gentiles penance towards God, and faith in our Lord Jesus Christ.
1 Cor. 5:4	KJB	In the name of our Lord Jesus *Christ*, when ye are gathered together, and my spirit, with the power of our Lord Jesus Christ, 1 Corinthians 5:4 (missing in Gr. texts and modern versions; B/Aleph; NIV, NASV, NB)
	EV	whanne ye ben gaderid to gidre in the name of oure lord ihesus crist, and my spirit with the vertu of the lord ihesus
	EV*	ye ben gaderid togidere in the name of oure Lord Jhesu Crist, and my spirit, with the vertu of the Lord Jhesu,
	LV	ye ben gaderid togidere in the name of oure Lord Jhesu Crist, and my spirit, with the vertu of the Lord Jhesu,
	DR	**4** In the name of our Lord Jesus Christ, you being gathered together, and my spirit, with the power of our Lord Jesus;
	KJB	The grace of our Lord Jesus *Christ* {be} with you. 1 Corinthians 16:23 (missing in Gr. texts and modern

1 Cor. 16:23		versions; B/Aleph; NIV, NASV, NB)
	EV	the grace of oure lord ihesus crist; be with you,
	EV*	The grace of oure Lord Jhesu Crist be with you.
	LV	The grace of oure Lord Jhesu Crist be with you.
	DR	
2 Cor. 11:31	KJB	The God and Father of our Lord Jesus *Christ*, which is blessed for evermore, knoweth that I lie not. 2 Corinthians 11:31 (missing in Gr. texts and modern versions; B/Aleph; NIV, NASV, NB)
	EV	god and the fadir of oure lord ihesus crist, that is blessed in to worldis; woot that I lie not,
	EV*	God and the fadir of oure Lord Jhesu Crist, that is blessid in to worldis, woot that Y lie not.
	LV	God and the fadir of oure Lord Jhesu Crist, that is blessid in to worldis, woot that Y lie not.
	DR	**31** The God and Father of our Lord Jesus Christ, who is blessed for ever, knoweth that I lie not.
1 Thess. 3:11	KJB	Now God himself and our Father, and our Lord Jesus *Christ*, direct our way unto you. 1 Thessalonians 3:11 (missing in Gr. texts and modern versions; B/Aleph; NIV, NASV, NB)
	EV	but god hym silf and oure fadir, and the lord ihesus crist; dresse oure weie to you,
	EV*	But God hym silf and oure fadir, and the Lord Jhesu Crist, dresse oure weye to you.
	LV	But God hym silf and oure fadir, and the Lord Jhesu Crist, dresse oure weye to you.
	DR	**11** Now God himself and our Father, and our Lord Jesus Christ, direct our way unto you.
1 Thess. 3:13	KJB	To the end he may stablish your hearts unblameable in holiness before God, even our Father, at the coming of our Lord Jesus *Christ* with all his saints. 1 Thessalonians 3:13 (missing in Gr. texts and modern

		versions; B/Aleph; NIV, NASV, NB)
	EV	that youre hertis ben confermed with outen playnte in holynesse bifor god and oure fadir, in the comynge of oure lord ihesus crist with al his seyntis Amen
	EV*	that youre hertis ben confermyd with outen pleynt in holynesse, bifor God and oure fadir, in the comyng of oure Lord Jhesu Crist with alle hise seyntis. Amen.
	LV	that youre hertis ben confermyd with outen pleynt in holynesse, bifor God and oure fadir, in the comyng of oure Lord Jhesu Crist with alle hise seyntis. Amen.
	DR	**13** To confirm your hearts without blame, in holiness, before God and our Father, at the coming of our Lord Jesus Christ, with all his saints. Amen.
2 Thess. 1:8	KJB	In flaming fire taking vengeance on them that know not God, and that obey not the gospel of our Lord Jesus *Christ*: 2 Thessalonians 1:8 (missing in Gr. texts and modern versions; B; NIV, NASV, NB)
	EV	in the flawme of fire that schal yue veniaunce to hem that knowen not god; and that obeien not to the euangeli of oure lord ihesus crist,
	EV*	in the flawme of fier, that schal yyue veniaunce to hem that knowen not God, and that obeien not to the euangelie of oure Lord Jhesu Crist.
	LV	in the flawme of fier, that schal yyue veniaunce to hem that knowen not God, and that obeien not to the euangelie of oure Lord Jhesu Crist.
	DR	**8** In a flame of fire, giving vengeance to them who know not God, and who obey not the gospel of our Lord Jesus Christ.
2 Thess. 1:12	KJB	That the name of our Lord Jesus *Christ* may be glorified in you, and ye in him, according to the grace of our God and the Lord Jesus Christ. 2 Thessalonians 1:12 (missing in Gr. texts and modern versions; B/Aleph; NIV, NASV, NB)
	EV	that the name of oure lord ihesus crist be clarified in

		you and ye in hym; bi the grace of oure lord ihesus crist.
	EV*	that the name of oure Lord Jhesu Crist be clarified in you, and ye in hym, bi the grace of oure Lord Jhesu Crist.
	LV	that the name of oure Lord Jhesu Crist be clarified in you, and ye in hym, bi the grace of oure Lord Jhesu Crist.
	DR	**12** That the name of our Lord Jesus may be glorified in you, and you in him, according to the grace of our God, and of the Lord Jesus Christ.
Rev. 22:21	KJB	The grace of our Lord Jesus *Christ be* with you all. Amen. Revelation 22:21 (missing in Gr. texts and modern versions; Aleph (No B in Rev.); NIV, NASV)
	EV	the grace of oure lord ihesus crist be with you alle amen.
	EV*	The grace of oure Lord Jhesu Crist be with you alle. Amen.
	LV	The grace of oure Lord Jhesu Crist be with you alle. Amen.
	DR	**21** The grace of our Lord Jesus Christ be with you all. Amen.

CHAPTER 5

CONCLUSION

Wycliffe's Translation

By examination of the 150 verses in chapter four, there is little doubt that Wycliffe's NT was translated from the Latin Vulgate NT. Little difference is seen in the EV and LV Wycliffe NT Bible except for spelling. Also, there is no evidence that the LV was edited back to the Latin Vulgate after Wycliffe's death. The editions were a translation according to the syntax of Middle English; a language that was undergoing significant rapid changes. The EV verses examined demonstrate no evidence that the EV was translated from Old Latin MSS rather than the Latin Vulgate. Hopefully, the OT will be examined by a similar technique in the future. A few OT verses are compared by other authors below.

John Purvey indicated in his preface to the Wycliffe Bible revision of 1388-1395 that the Hebrew text was compared to Jerome's translation and comments were made in the margin, but apparently changes in the English translation of the OT Latin Vulgate were not made, except for English phrasing (q.v.). Many scholars have pointed out that English phraseology was improved in the LV as compared with the EV. The EV OT was primarily more of a gloss of the Latin Vulgate, than the EV NT. The process of translating was interrupted by the death of Wycliffe in 1384, but Wycliffe's curate John Purvey, John Trevisa, and other associates of Wycliffe continued to work on the translation between the years 1384 and

1395. John Trevisa was protected by a benefactor, like John of Gaunt protected Wycliffe, and that allowed him to continue to help.

> "John Trevisa or John of Trevisa (1342 - 1402), translator, was a Cornishman, educated at Oxford, who became Vicar of Berkeley, Gloucestershire, chaplain to the 4th Lord Berkeley, and Canon of Westbury on Trym. He translated for his patron the *Polychronicon* of Ranulf Higden... A fellow of Queen's College, Oxford from 1372-76 at the same time as John Wycliff and Nicholas of Hereford,..."[274]

However, Nicholas de Hereford, Wycliffe's supporter, was imprisoned, severly persecuted, and recanted, becoming a Carthusian monk; so, he probably did not help with later editions. In the end, most scholars agree that the Latin Vulgate was the text used by Wycliffe and his associates for translating the OT and NT for the EV and the LV. In this author's opinion, the circumstantial evidence supports John Purvey as the writer of the LV preface (q.v.).

Although there is no proof that Dr. Wycliffe and the other translators used "Old Latin Texts," there is factual support that they noted the corruption in the Latin Vulgate. They also had access to the earlier portions of Scripture (particularly the Psalter and the Gospels) translated from Old Latin MSS into Anglo-Saxon before the Latin Vulgate arrived in England. Surely they noted the difference in those (translated) texts compared with the common Latin Vulgate used in Wycliffe's age. The question that arises however, is if they thought the translations in Anglo-Saxon were inaccurate or whether they suspected problems with the underlying text.

---

[274] Wikipedia, The Free Encyclopedia, John Trevisa.

It is significant that Wycliffe greatly respected Aristotle, Augustine, and Jerome.[275] Recall, he was a scholastically trained scholar and Roman Catholic Priest. He believed Jerome's translation should be:

> "approved as much by the sanctity of his life, which Augustine recounts in his letter *On the Holiness of Jerome*, as by his expertise in the Hebrew language and the complete agreement of his translation with the Hebrew and Greek manuscripts."[276]

He also believed that:

> "many apocryphal books are Holy Scripture, since they are inscribed in the book of Life."[277]

Notice he said "holy" (set aside to) and did not use the word inspired. And he said:

> "Concerning the manuscripts, one must comprehend them as they have been corrected by the sense and authority of the Church. And with respect to the meaning, one must receive it from the head; for that is faith as well as Holy Scripture."[278]

Note however, that Wycliffe said that only Christ is the "head" of the church (q.v.) saying: "it is blasphemy to call any head of the church, save Christ alone." (q.v.) And he also said:

---

[275] Levy, pp. 59, 142-149.
[276] Ibid. p. 157. Whether he meant he himself compared the Greek and Hebrew MSS with Jerome's translation is not clear in the text. However, his comments combined with Purvey's suggest they may have done some comparisons with the help of Jews of the dispersion (q.v.).
[277] Ibid. p. 163
[278] Ibid. p. 156

> "it still does not appear that we must believe in the aforementioned fifth level of Scripture and that which is apocryphal."[279]

Wycliffe believed as many of us today that the Scripture was preserved through the church.[280] But, he is speaking of the Roman Catholic Church that he called the "Mother Church" in spite of all its problems that he fought against.

In addition, it is clear that Wycliffe and Purvey knew some Hebrew and probably some Greek. The information in the writings by Wycliffe is ambiguous, but in light of other evidence, they were scholars who most likely learned everything they could about 'things' pertaining to the Scriptures. They were men of faith. This author read from cover to cover Wycliffe's book on *The Truth of the Holy Scriptures*. It is a difficult read, but it does seem to suggest some knowledge of original Biblical languages. The problem Wycliffe had was that attention to the Greek MSS of the Scriptures had not occurred in England secondary to the use of Latin by Rome and by the Roman Church's dominance. As a matter of fact, the Greek MSS did not arrive in Europe in abundance until the fall of Constantinople to the Turks in the fifteen century. Wycliffe was forced to utilize what he was most familiar with and what was available. Travel in many parts of the world in Wycliffe's age was dangerous and difficult, just as it is more and more in these last days. Also remember this important fact, Benedict Biscop (founder of Northumbria) brought many Latin texts to England in the seventh century from Rome **after** several translations into Anglo-Saxon had been made earlier in England from texts other than the Latin Vulgate.

---

[279] Ibid. p. 159.
[280] Ibid. p. 156.

Conservative authors, such as this author, will be tempted to disregard Wycliffe and his work in light of the information presented in this work. However, before we throw the baby out with the bath water, please note what Miles Coverdale said in the preface to the 1611 King James Bible about Jerome and Augustine and recall the KJB 1611 contained the apocrypha.

> "TRANSLATION OUT OF HEBREW AND GREEK INTO LATIN: There were also within a few hundred years after CHRIST, translations many into the Latin tongue: for this tongue also was very fit to convey the Law and the Gospel by, because in those times very many Countries of the West, yea of the South, East and North, spake or understood Latin, being made Provinces to the Romans. But now the Latin Translations were too many to be all good, for they were infinite (Latini Interprets nullo modo numerari possunt, saith S. Augustine.) [S. Augustin. de doctr. Christ. lib 2 cap II]. Again they were not out of the Hebrew fountain (we speak of the Latin Translations of the Old Testament) but out of the Greek stream, therefore the Greek being not altogether clear, the Latin derived from it must needs be muddy. This moved S. Jerome a most learned father, and the best linguist without controversy, of his age, or of any that went before him, to undertake the translating of the Old Testament, out of the very fountain with that evidence of great learning, judgment, industry, and faithfulness, that he had forever bound the Church unto him, in a debt of special remembrance and thankfulness."[281]

Furthermore, Wycliffe acknowledged that Aristotle, Jerome and Augustine were capable of error. He said:

---

[281] Preface, King James Bible, Section: Translation out of Hebrew and Greek into Latin, modernized spelling as found at: www.ccel.org/bible/kjv/preface/pref10.htm

> "One need not believe that St. Jerome's translation is free from error, since many other interpreters disagree with him. Indeed, in his own time he was reproached by Augustine and his other rivals..."[282]

He also disdained those who would put logic above Scripture. He said:

> Therefore, just as the sophist is like a hypocrite more interested in gaining a reputation for knowledge in the eyes of men, than he is in his existence in the sight of God, so on the contrary, the evangelical logician, having put aside worldly fame, would rather be considered a fool in the eyes of the world for Christ's sake, in order that he might be counted wise before God."[283]

However, the final conclusion of the whole matter concerning any Bible translated from the Latin MSS, whether the Latin Vulgate or the Old Latin versions, the Itala and the North African Latin MSS, is summarized by this statement:

> "There can be no doubt nor denying of the massive influence of the Latin Scriptures in the Western World, where for over a thousand years it was 'The Bible'. But it was only ever a version; the Latin language has no standing over against the Hebrew and Greek, so that all translations made from it are doubly at fault. It is true that all Bible texts before the general use of the printing presses are subject to the problems of hand-copying, but the Latin texts more so by their very popularity. Textbooks talk of the Old Latin, the Itala, the Hieronymian (Jerome's 405) and the Vulgate as if there were only a single text of each, but none of these were

---

[282] Levy, p. 156.
[283] Ibid. p. 54.

in any way stable, always begging the question, 'Which particular one?'"[284]

Wycliffe and Trevisa

John Trevisa is pointed out as the translator of the Wycliffe Bible as opposed to Dr. Wycliffe. More circumstantial evidence points to Wycliffe as the author rather than John Trevisa. Trevisa's work may have been utilized as a tool and for comparison, but Wycliffe was the leader and was the translator of the whole Bible as noted by his enemies as well as by his friends.

Wycliffe and Purvey

The evidence is accumulating that John Purvey is truly the author of the LV preface and a major associate and translator of the Wycliffe Bible. Maureen Jurkowski's evidence found in preserved prison records (q.v.) and other information indicates Purvey was indeed a Lollard, an adherent to the doctrines of Scripture, a scholar who understood Hebrew, a close associate of Wycliffe (more so than Trevisa), an apologist for the Lollards and against Roman Catholic doctrine, a probable martyr, and one tried by the fires of persecution. He renounced his Lollard positions for about two years after severe persecution in prison. He accepted a rectory that was nearby the Archbishop's residence for obvious reasons; the prelate was carefully monitoring him. Shortly thereafter, he is discovered by prison records again in the fight against Rome's suppression of the Scriptures and violence toward their opposer's violence and against the authorities who were supporting Rome.

---

[284] Hallihan, p. 14 (Quarterly Review, Trinitarian Bible Society).

The translation of the entire Bible was actively pursued by Wycliffe. As indicated in this work above, Wycliffe stated that **he** had translated the Bible. Other scholars report that he wrote a commentary on the **whole** Bible for teaching purposes. Those who make the claim that Wycliffe did little if any of the translation work are sadly mistaken. Furthermore, the comment is repeatedly made in the literature that Nicholas of Hereford translated the OT up to Baruck 3:20.[285]

> "Bodleian Douce MS 369 ends at precisely the same word, though this time the break, in the second column on the page, is about a third of the way down. At this point in Douce 369 another hand, contemporary with the test, has added the words 'Explicit translacionem Nicholay de Hereford'. This is important in apparently giving rare information about a translator, someone in Wyclif's Oxford circle. A similar note in the Cambridge manuscript (University Library, MS Ee.1.10), in English, appears at the same place, though there is a break: 'Here endith the translacioun of N, and noe begynneth the translacioun of J and of othere men.'...we find that the work of translation, the scribing, the writing out, had been done by five different people."[286]

This does not mean that Wycliffe was not involved, was not making suggestions, or was not helping to translate. As a matter of fact, many authors report several scribes involved in the handwritten MSS and even the mixing of various editions of the Wycliffe Bibles at different stages of the translation work.[287] Any proper and good translator will utilize counsel from as many sound individuals as possible. Perhaps Nicholas was recording or scribing the translating as the work proceeded

---

[285] Brown, p. 118 (*The Incomparable Book*) Dr. Brown is quoting Margaret Deanesly, M.A., *The Lollard Bible and Other Medieval Biblical Versions* (Cambridge University Press, 1920, p. 253)

[286] Daniell, p. 80-81 (*The Bible in English).*

[287] Ibid. p. 81 (Daniel, *The Bible in English).*

and then was removed secondary to Rome's persecution, and other associates took over scribing and assisting with the translation. This is the pattern of good translation work through the ages; multiple counselors. They may have acted primarily as amanuenses.

Wycliffe's Sympathies

There is no doubt that John de Wycliffe was a Lollard. Being a Lollard did not mean that you joined an organization by signing on the dotted line. Lollardism was a loosely knit organization of people who believed the Scriptures above the pronouncements of man, particularly the pope, salvation through faith, local church organization and government, and denied the doctrine of transubstantiation, pedobaptism, sacramentalism, Mariolatry, and other similar teaching of the Catholic Church. The Lollards were Waldensians who were named in England after Walter Reynard, derogatorily called Walter Lollard, a Waldensian barb, who came to England with the "good news."

> "And how shall they preach, except they be sent? as it is written, How beautiful are the feet of them that preach the gospel of peace, and bring glad tidings of good things!" (Romans 10:15).

He was martyred in Cologne, France for his beliefs. His influence in England was centered in Herefordshire near Olchon and the steep valley traversing the area. His influence was also through men like Bradwardine who helped light the way for Wycliffe.

The Influence of Wycliffe's Translation

Wycliffe's Bibles had a great influence on many aspects of life. Their influence continues to reach into the present age. His Bibles influenced the English population to call into question or reject many aspects of the practice of religion by the Roman Catholic Church. Significantly, his translations helped establish the modern English language.

Writing in the 1911 Encyclopedia Britannica, Anna C. Paues said:

> "For it is a well-known fact that Wycliffe proclaimed the Bible, not the Church or Catholic tradition, as a man's supreme spiritual authority, and that he sought in consequence by every means in his power to spread the knowledge of it among the people. It is, therefore, in all likelihood to the zeal of Wycliffe and his followers that we owe the two noble 14th-century translations of the Bible which tradition has always associated with his name, and which are the earliest complete renderings that we possess of the Holy Scriptures into English."[288]

There is no doubt that Wycliffe's accomplishment to make the Scriptures available to the laity helped introduce certain phrases into the English language. Those phrases have undoubtedly found their way into all translations of the Bible from Wycliffe to the KJB. It is certain that John de Wycliffe would be adverse to claiming that he is responsible. Having said that, many authors attribute many phrases in the KJB to

---

[288] Anna C. Paues, 1911, "Bible, English" (Encyclopedia Britannia, 11th edition). Section: Middle English Versions Before Wycliffe.

Wycliffe as opposed to Tyndale.[289] However, many phrases retained in the KJB are found only in Tyndale's translation, also. [290]

Wycliffe's Theological Influence

There is no question that Dr. John de Wycliffe is a giant in the history of Bible translation, theology, and missionary endeavors. Although he probably did not travel much from the location of his duties at Oxford and Lutterworth, there is overwhelming evidence that he understood:

> "But ye shall receive power, after that the Holy Ghost is come upon you: and ye shall be witnesses unto me both in Jerusalem, and in all Judaea, and in Samaria, and unto the uttermost part of the earth." Acts 1:8

His "poore preachers" traveled the highways and byway of Britain spreading the Gospel.

He clearly supported preservation of the Scripture to the jot and title. He said:

> "Christ says, *Heaven and earth will pass away but my words will not pass away.* Those words, however, are the sayings which he spoke of in the following chapter. And these words are explained in Luke 16:17 when the Savior says, *It is easier for heaven and earth to pass way, than for one point of the law to be revoked,*

[289] Terrance P. Noble, "Version Information" (*Wycliffe New Testament,* Introduction, Endnotes, Conclusion) www.biblegateway.com/versions/ index.php?action=getVersionInfo&vid=53; accessed 6/16/2008.

[290] Many authors attribute up to 90% or more of the KJB to Tyndale's translation from the Hebrew and Greek.

> because in Matt. 5:18 the Truth speaks in the same way: *not one jot, not one point, will pass from the law until all these things come to be* And undoubtedly that law, those words, and those sayings are this very Scripture, of which John 10:35 says, *the Scripture cannot be destroyed.*"[291]

Wycliffe is noted for his insistence on interpreting and relying on the Scriptures literally. This was in opposition to the Roman Catholic "doctors" such as Augustine who relied on allegorical interpretation. He said:

> "For this reason the doctors often counsel that sense which is contrary to the intended sense of the author should be dismissed. What is to be gained by verbose disputes, when the truth of the Christian faith does not depend upon the strength of our own manner of speaking (virtute sermonis nostril)? Indeed, there is little or no strength (virtus) to be found in sophistical speech. This is why I am accustomed to say that each part of Holy Scriptures is true according to the divinely intended literal sense (de virtute sermonis divine)."[292]

He was opposed to charismatic dependence on the senses. He said:

> "Because, beyond sense experience, we posses a complete knowledge of those things necessary for salvation through the faith of Scripture, it suffices for the Christian to press beyond sense experience and trust in that knowledge, and in Holy Scripture…"[293]

[291] Levy, pp. 100-101.
[292] Levy, p. 93 (*On the Truth of the Holy Scriptures*).
[293] Ibid. p. 163 (Levy, *On the Truth of the Holy Scriptures*).

He believed that God had preserved His Words through the Church, the church which is the body of Christ. He said:

> "[H]e (God) would have to preserve his own law within the Church"[294] (HDW, my addition).

He spoke of the Hebrew Scriptures being in every nation secondary to the dispersion, helping to preserve and confirm the Words of God by Jews witnessing to their sense in the Latin text.

> "First, that we might have recourse to their manuscripts as witnesses to the fact that there is no difference in the sense found in our Latin books and those Hebrew ones.[295]

He seemed to affirm that the Hebrew and Greek text agreed with that of Jerome's Latin text. He said:

> "as by his (Jerome's) expertise in the Hebrew language and the complete agreement of his translation with the Hebrew and Greek manuscripts."[296]

He did not accept the apocryphal books cart blance as Scripture or as on the same "level of Scripture" as the sixty-six books; he denied that transubstantiation was true doctrine; he denied baptism saves; he exalted faith in God, the Scriptures, and the Lord Jesus Christ. How can we not honor this man, who was hampered by the times in which he lived? We do not agree with all that he wrote, but how many of us get all of it right?

---

[294] Ibid. p. 156. (Levy, *On the Truth of the Holy Scriptures*).
[295] Ibid. p. 157. (Levy, *On the Truth of the Holy Scriptures*).
[296] Ibid. p. 157 (Levy, *On the Truth of the Holy Scriptures*).

This author is certain that Dr. Wycliffe would humbly direct the praise to Almighty God for his accomplishments were he alive today. I can also hear him giving due credit to others and his many Lollard (Waldensian) friends by saying:

> *"The Lord gave the word: great was the company of those that published it." (Psalms 68:11). "Thus saith the LORD, Let not the wise man glory in his wisdom, neither let the mighty man glory in his might, let not the rich man glory in his riches: But let him that glorieth glory in this, that he understandeth and knoweth me, that I am the LORD which exercise lovingkindness, judgment, and righteousness, in the earth: for in these things I delight, saith the LORD." (Jeremiah 9:23-24).*

Amen

H. D. Williams, M.D., Ph.D.

APPENDICES

SPREAD OF LATIN MSS

TITLE	YEAR	LANGUAGE	SCRIBE	LOCATION	PART OF SCRIPTURE
North Africa	c. 200	Old Latin	unknown	Africa	fragments primarily Old Testament; probably from Origin's LXX
Council of Carthage	397 A.D. (estab-lished the order of the Canon)	Old Latin translated from the Septuagint, from Origin	unknown	Africa	New Testament, copies widely different
	Old Latin from 1st three centuri es	Same	unknown, many	European Latin MSS vary greatly from African MSS	fragments of OT and NT, Latin reaches Britain before Jerome's Vulgate/Tertulli an & Origin (p. 28-29/Daniell)
Jerome's Latin Vulgate from the Hebrew for the OT	382 (by order of Pope Damas us) Finish-ed OT in 405	Same, but OT translated from the Hebrew; gospels from Greek; remainder probably from Old Latin MSS	Jerome	Rome	Jerome's Psalter known as the "Roman Psalter" Jerome's translation rapidly becomes corrupted.
St. Patrick	c. 390-460				quotes parts of Old Latin MSS as opposed to Latin Vulgate of Jerome
Gospel Book	c. 650	Old Latin	Irish Scribe, name?	Durham Cathedral Library	few leaves of the Gospels in Old Latin
Book of Darrow	c. 675	Northumbria Latin Vulgate		Trinity College Dublin	?
Otho-Corpus Gospels	?	? from Lindisfarne in an uncial script of Northumbria		British Library London and Corpus Christi College,	

		from Rome		Cambridge	
Echternach	?	small running cursive script			
Codex Grandior of Cassidorus brought by Abbot Ceolfrith from Italy;	c. 700				Whole Bible, Old testament at least is in Old Latin
Codex Amiatinus Ceolfrith imitates Codex Grandior at Monkwear mouth	c. 716			Monastery of Monte Amiata in central Italy; now in Florence at the Biblioteca Medicea-Laurenziana	3 copies of Jerome's Latin Vulgate, one in Florence is complete
Benedict Biscop (founder of North-umbria)	Found-ed mona-steries at Monk-wear-mouth in 674 and Jarrow in 681	Brought many books from Rome in Latin			
Codex Aureus	c. 800's			Royal Library Stockholm	Whole Bible from Southumbria probable Kent

EXTANT ENGLISH SCRIPTURES

TITLE	YEAR	LANGUAG E	SCRIBE	LOCATION	PART OF SCRIPTURE
Lindisfarn e Gospels	698 A.D.	Latin (glossed into Old English 946-968 by Aldred) Old English: c 450-1200 A.D.	Eadfrith	produced on the Isle of Lindisfarne at the monastic school founded by the Irish monk, Aidan; now at John Ritblat Gallery, British Library	Gospels, complete

				at St. Pancras	
Vespasian Psalter	c. 598 A.D.	Latin, glossed between the lines in Mercian Dialect		British Library	First 50 Psalms
The Book of Cerne	818 – 830 A.D.	Old English Introduction	A Private Prayer Book		Gospel extracts, Psalms and other devotional matter
Lindisfarn e Gospel Gloss	946-968 A.D.	Old English (Northumbri an dialect: modern word order—subject, verb, object)	Aldred	British Library	Gospels, complete, Latin Vulgate/Danie ll p. 46-47
Bede	Historia n d. 735, reporte d on Caedm on poems	Anglo-Saxon			translated Gospel of John to 6:9 but it has not survived; Caedmon' account by Bede is in Latin.
Book of Armagh	c. 800	Irish?		Ireland	New Testament
Rolle's Psalter	c. early 14th century , translat ed into English 1370-1380		Richard Rolle (c.1300-c.1349)		Latin, Translated later into English. He wrote mainly in Latin
Wycliffe' s Early and Late Versions	1380-1395	Middle English: c. 1200-1450	Wycliffe and associates known as Lollards: John Purvey, ?John Trevisa	Many locations	Whole Bible; the first extant record, 40 at Bodleian Library in Oxford, British Library has 40.

IMPORTANT CHRONOLOGICAL EVENTS DURING WYCLIFFE'S AGE

By Dr. David L. Brown[297]

Year – A.D.	Event
1215	Magna Carta signed by King John
1252	Pope Innocent VI officially sanctions the use of torture to obtain confessions from heretics
1324	Most scholars believe John Wycliffe was born about this year
1340	John Wycliffe is believed to have enrolled in Balliol Hall at about this time
1343	Pope Clement VI officially sanctions indulgences
1347	The Black Death infects Europe
1348	The Black Death kills 2.5 million people in England
1351	The Plague stops after killing 25 million people in Europe
1353	John Wycliffe's father dies and he becomes lord of the manor or estate
1361	John Wycliffe is ordained to the ministry
1372	A Doctors of Divinity degree is awarded to Wycliffe
1374-1376	-John Wycliffe is chosen by the English Crown to go to Burnges to negotiate with the papists -From 1376 to 1378 Wycliffe is the clerical advisor of John of Gaunt, the Duke of Lancaster
1377	-Charges of heresy are brought against Wycliffe and he appears at St. Paul's in London to be tried. The trial is broken up when John of Gaunt and Lord Percy insist that Wycliffe be seated and the Bishop demands that he stand. A riot breaks out, Wycliffe slips out uncharged and unharmed. -Pope Gregory XI issues 5 papal bulls against Wycliffe.
1378	-The beginning of the "Great Papal Schism" which lasted for the next 40 years with a pope and college of cardinals in Avignon, France and another in Rome, Italy with each pope excommunicating and anathematizing the other. -Wycliffe called to Lambeth Palace to be tied on charges of heresy, but the Queen Mother, Joan of Kent, warns the Bishops not to pass judgment on Wycliffe
1381	Wycliffe falsely accused of being responsible for the

[297] David L. Brown, Ph.D., *The Incomparable Book – The Holy Bible, The History of the English Bible* (Available from Dr. Brown, 8044 S. Verdev Dr. Oak Creek, WI, 53154, © August 2000) p. 90.

	Peasants Revolt.
1382	-The Entire Bible is translated into English for the first time -An earthquake stops a synod called to condemn Wycliffe, his writings and his Bible translation
1384	Wycliffe dies peacefully on New Years Eve
1401	The first English statute passed legalizing the burning of heretics
1414	Reading the English Scriptures is outlawed upon the pain of forfeiture "of lan, cattle, life, and goods from teir heirs forever."
1415	Council of Constance condemns Wycliffe as an heretic and his student John Hus is burned at the stake
1428	The remains of Wycliffe are exhumed, burned to ashes and scattered in the stream near the Lutterworth perish

Events in Wycliffe's Life

CHRONOLOGY OF EVENTS/CONNECTED WITH WYCLIFF[298]

CONNECTED WITH WYCLIFF			
A.D.	**Facts of Wycliffe's Life**	**King of England**	**Archbishop of Canterbury**
		Edward I	Wischelsey.
		1307, Edward II	
			1313. Reynolds.
	1320. Born [at Wycliffe-on-Tees or Speswell (Hipswell) Son of Roger and Catherine Wycliffe		
		1327. Edward III	1327. Simon Meopham

[298] Lewis Sergeant, *John Wycliff, The Last of the Schoolmen and the First of the Reformers* (Knickerbocker Press, G. P. Putman's Sons, 24 Bedford Street, London, 1893) pp. 360-372.

1301 to 1353	Probably heard Ockham, Bradwardine, and Fitzralph; and read Marsiglio and Cesena. Wyclif specially owns his obligations to Augustine and Grosteste. According to James he was a Doctor of Divinity soon after 1355?? Beneficed in Oxford? (James).		1333. John Stratford 1348. John Ufford. 1349. Thomas Bradwardine. 1349. Simon Islip

Chronology of Events		
Popes of Rome	Kings of France	Contemporary Events

CONNECTED WITH WYCLIFF			
A.D.	Facts of Wycliffe's Life	Kings of England	Archbishops of Canterbury
1354 to 1366	1356. Fellow Merton? Fellow of Balliol (date unrecorded). Master of Balliol (date unrecorded). Lord of the Manor of Wycliffe (a knights's fee)?	Edward III	Simon Islip
1361 to 1365	1361. Maintains authority of University against the Friars? Rector of Fillingham (college living). 1363. In residence at Queen's. Presents W. Wycliffe to family loving of Wycliffe? 1365. King's Chaplin. Probably begins to preach in London. Lectures on Divinity at Oxford. Writes scholastic works—*De Esse, De Compositions Hominins*, etc.	Edward III	
	1366. Called upon by Parliament to show cause against paying tribute to Rome: *Determinatio quadam de*	Edward III	1366. S. Langham

1366 to 1370	*Dominic.* 1368. In Oxford again. 1369. Presents H. Hugate of Balliol to Wycliffe rectory? Exchanges Fillingham for the poorer living of Ludgarshall. 1370. Doctor of Divinity.		1368. W. Whittlesea
1371	Personal influence of Wycliffe at Court, over Princess of Wales, Lancaster, Lord Latimer, Alice Perrers, etc. Also over Sir John Oldcastle, Lord Berkeley and many others.	Edward III	

Popes of Rome	**Chronology of Events** **Kings of France**	**Contemporary Events**
1362. Urban.	1364. Charles V.	1362. Jubilee of Edward's life. English language adopted in the courts. 1363. Suits in Papal court forbidden again.
		1366. Parliament refuses tribute to Pope. Wykeham Bishop of Winchester. 1367. Wykeham Chancellor of England. 1369. Portsmouth burnt by the French. 1370. Sack of Limoges.
1371. Gregory XI.		1371. Removal of ecclesiastics from offices of state on petition of Commons. Heavier taxation of the Church. Reverses in French and Spanish Wars.

CONNECTED WITH WYCLIFF			
A.D.	**Facts of Wycliffe's Life**	**Kings of**	**Archbishops of**

		England	Canterbury
1372 to 1375	1374. Appointed by Crown to living of Lutterworth. Appointed on Commission to confer with Papal legates at Bruges. 1375. Resides at Bruges as Commissioner, fifty days. Refuses the prebend of Aust.	Edward III	W. Whittlesea. 1375. S. Sudbury.
1376 to 1377	1376. Complaints of Wycliffe made by the friars to the English bishops, and then to Rome 1377. Summoned to St. Paul's by Courtenay; attended by Lancaster and Percy. Citizens break up the meeting. In residence at Black Hall, Oxford. Five Papal bulls against Wyclif, who makes his defense at Oxford and in Parliament. Wyclif, consulted by Parliament as to payment of Peter's Pence, refutes the claim, but declines to advise non-payment.	1377. Richard II.	

Chronology of Events

Popes of Rome	Kings of France	Contemporary Events
Gregory XI		1372. English navy destroyed. 1373. Mission to Avignon abut provisions, etc. Courtenay in Convocation demands relief for the Church. Commission on alien incumbents. 1374. Peace with France: mediation of Pope. 1375. Conferences at Bruges, political and ecclesiastical. Compromises effected in both cases. Senility of the King. Great influence of Alice Perrers. Parliament not summoned this

		year. Courtenay Bishop of London
		1376. Good Parliament. Ecclesiastics recalled. Prince of Wales dies. Parliament overruled. Wykeham disgraced and Speaker imprisoned. Pope excommunicates the Florentines. Attacks on foreigners in England. 1377. Courtenay demands the restoration of Wykeham. Commons packed by John of Gaunt. Attempt to curtail the privileges of the City. Riots in London and Westminster. First poll-tax. Death of Edward III. War renewed with France.

CONNECTED WITH WYCLIFF			
A.D.	**Facts of Wycliffe's Life**	**Kings of England**	**Archbishops of Canterbury**
1378 to 1380	1378. Cited to Lambeth; re-asserts his conclusions. Princess of Wales protects him. Lononers again interrupt. He withdraws to Lutterworth or Oxford. 1379. Serious illness at Oxford. Friars call upon him for retraction. He defies them. Sends his defense and challenge to Rome. Great literary activity; writes *De Veritate Sanctae Scripturae.*	Richard II.	
1381 to 1382	1381. Begins to lecture at Oxford against transubstantiation, and carries many with him. Inquire by Chancellor Berton and a Council of twelve. Wyclif's doctrine condemned, and he is forbidden to lecture. Appeals to the King; John of Gaunt asks him to desist. Writes his *Confession* or *Apologia,* claiming the authority of the earlier Church. Many replies from monks and others. Proceedings against the Poor Priests. 1382. Accused of complicity in the	Richard II.	1381. W. Courtenay.

	Peasants' Revolt. Cited by Courtenay before a Synod at the priory of the Black Friars in London. He does not attend (through illness or otherwise), but twenty-four of his conclusions are condemned, for heresy or error. (The Earthquake Synod.) His chief supporters condemned at subsequent meeting. He re-asserts his conclusions at Oxford.		

Popes of Rome	Chronology of Events Kings of France	Contemporary Events
SCHISM 1378 R. Urban VI A. Clement VII.		1378. England acknowledges Pope Urban. Courtenay excommunicates Lancaster's friends. Parliament sits at Gloucester, John of Gaunt reconciled to the Church. 1379 Sudbury appointed Chancellor. 1380. New and more stringent poll-tax imposed. John of Gaunt Envoy to Scotland and Lieutenant of the Marches.
		1381. Ruthless exaction of second poll-tax. **Peasants' Revolt;** the march on London; terms granted. Cruel suppression, and repudiation of the terms by parliament; 7,000 executed. Serfdom virtually ended. Courtenay Archbishop and Chancellor. 1382. Richard II, marries Anne of Bohemia. Parliament calls on Courtenay to proceed against Wycliffe and others. He assembles a Synod, sends Stokys to Oxford, reduces Rygge and others to submission. Processional Litany in London, Whitsunday. Convocation of St.

		Frideswide's, Oxford.

CONNECTED WITH WYCLIFF			
A.D.	**Facts of Wycliffe's Life**	**Kings of England**	**Archbishops of Canterbury**
1382 to 1384	1382. (Continued) Greater literary activity. Collects his sermons; writes a number of English tracts, in which he denounces the Papal crusade, the conduct of the Friars, etc. Engaged on English translation of the Bible. First stroke of paralysis. 1383. Persecution of his friends. Some fall away. Continued literary activity. Writes the *Trialogus.* Cited to Rome. Excuses himself on the ground if inability to travel. 1384. Has a second stroke at Lutterworth, Dec. 28th, and dies Dec. 31st.	Richard II.	W. Courtenay.
1385 to 1401	1385. Buried in the church at Lutterworth. Second text of his Bible prepared by Purvey. (The Pleshy Bible, copied for Thomas Woodstock, Duke of Gloucester, murdered 1397, was valued amongst his effects at 40s. It is now in the British Museum.) 1397. Arundel presides over a Synod which condemns eighteen conclusions of Wycliffe. 1401. Jerome of Prague and others carry many works of Wycliffe to Bohemia	Richard II 1399. Henry IV.	1396. T. Arundel.

Popes of Rome	**Chronology of Events** **Kings of France**	**Contemporary Events**
	Charles VI	1382. (Continued) Bishop Despencer's expedition (papal crusade) to Flanders ordered by

		Urban. Bulls and plenary indulgence proclaimed in England. Active assistance of the Friars. 1383. Crusade from May to September; disastrous result. The Scotts raid Northumberland. Hon of Gaunt retaliates. Chaucer assisted by Lancaster, Inclines to Church reform and ecclesiastical poverty. Gower in his Latin and English poems attacks the peasants, Lollardism, and the plicyh of Richard II. (1381-97).
    1389. R. Boniface IX. 1394. A. Benedict XIII.		1385. Commons demand secularization of Church property. 1388. Courtenay (under parliamentary powers) proceeds against heretics and seizes books. Lays Leicester under interdict, 1389. 1391. Statute of Mortmain confirmed. 1393. Second and more stringent Statute of *Praemunire*, Peace between England and France. 1395. Parliament petitions against alien clerics. 1396. Archbishop Arundel opens severely against the Lollards. Accused of intrigues and banished, 1397. 1399. Duke of Lancaster dies, Richard II, deposed. 1401. Statue *De Haeretico Comburendo.* Sawtre burned.

CONNECTED WITH WYCLIFF

A.D.	Facts of Wycliffe's Life	Kings of England	Archbishops of Canterbury
1402 to 1455	1403. Huss protests against condemnation of Wycliffism.	Henry IV.	T. Arundel.
	1407. Arundel's Council at Oxford.		
	1409. Two hundred and sixty-seven errors gathered by an Oxford committee from Wycliffe's works. The books burned at Carfax.		
	1410 Papal bull against Wycliffism in Bohemia. Seventeen works condemned. Huss and others protest; two hundred copies publicly burned.		
	1411. Huss excommunicated.	1413. Henry V.	
	1413. Wycliffe's books burned by the order of the Council of Rome.		1414. H. Chicheley.
	1415. The Council of Constance confirms the condemnation of the Council of Rome, and orders Wycliffe's bones to be exhumed and cast forth.		
	1416. Chicheley's Inquisition.	1422. Henry VI.	
	1423. Condemnation of Wycliffe by the Council of Pavia.		1443. J. Stafford. 1452. J. Kemp. 1454. T. Bourchier.
	1428. Bishop Flemmyng exhumes and burns Wycliffe's bones at Lutterworth.		

Chronology of Events		
Popes of Rome	**Kings of France**	**Contemporary Events**
1404. R. Innocent VII. 1406. R. Gregory XII. 1409. Alexander V		1404 and 1410. The Commons renew their demand for secularization. The Lollards take sides against Henry IV. At Shrewabury and elsewhere.

		1409. Council Pisa. Gregory and Benedict deposed.
1410. John XXIII		
		1410. Badby of Evesham burned.
(Interregnum; May 29, 1415-Nov. 11, 1417.)		1411. Arundel asserts his right to visit Oxford.
		1413. Henry IV. D. Sir John Oldcastle (Lord Cobham) condemned as a heretic. Council at Rome.
		1414. Abp. Arundel d. One hundred alien priories dissolved in England.
1417. Martin V.		1414-18. Council of Constance. John XXIII. Deposed. **End of Schism.**
	1422. Charles VII.	1415. Huss burned at Constance.
		1417. Cobham burned in England; afterwards Claydon and Taillour.
		1418. Beaufort, son of John of Gaunt, made Cardinal; afterwards Kemp and Bourchier.
		1423. Council of Pavia.
		1431. Council of Basle.
		1450. Rising in Kent.
		1455. Civil war breaks out in England. Indications of Lollard or anti-ecclesiastical leaning on the Yorkist side.

A Summary of Wycliffe's Contributions

"In looking over the career and opinions of John Wyclif, it becomes evident that in almost every doctrinal particular did this man anticipate the Reformers. The more his utterances are studied, the stronger becomes this conviction. He exalted preaching; he insisted upon the circulation of the Scriptures among the laity; he demanded purity and fidelity of the clergy; he denied infallibility to the papal utterances, and went so far as to declare that the papacy is not essential to the being of the Church. He defined the Church as the congregation of the elect; he showed the unscriptural and unreasonable character of the doctrine of transubstantiation; he pronounced priestly absolution a declarative act. He dissented from the common notion about pilgrimages; he justified marriage on biblical grounds as honorable among all men; he appealed for liberty for the monk to renounce his vow, and to betake himself to some useful work. The doctrine of justification by faith Wyclif did not state. However, he constantly uses such expressions as, that to believe in Christ is life. The doctrine of merit is denied, and Christ's mediation is made all-sufficient. He approached close to the Reformers when he pronounced "faith the supreme theology,"—*fides est summa theologia*,—and that only by the study of the Scriptures is it possible to become a Christian. Behind all Wyclif's other teaching is his devotion to Christ and his appeal to men to follow Him and obey His law. It is scarcely an exaggeration to say that the name of Christ appears on every page of his writings. To him, Christ was the supreme philosopher, yea, the content of all philosophy. In reaching his views Wyclif was, so far as we know, as independent as any teacher can well be. There is no indication that he drew from any of the medieval sects, as has been charged, nor from

Marsiglius and Ockam. He distinctly states that his peculiar views were drawn not from Ockam but from the Scriptures."[299]

[299] Schaff, p. 259 (*History of the Christian Church*).

John Wycliffe

His contribution to the development of language. The following is from: *Concise Oxford Companion to the English Language*, Oxford University Press, Date: 1998 by author, Tom Macarthur)

"**WYCLIFFE, John, also Wyclif, Wiclif,** and others [*c*.1320–1384]. English reformer and Bible translator, born at Wycliffe in Yorkshire, and Master of Balliol College, Oxford (*c*.1356–*c*.1382). His role in the Lollard movement and the politics of the Reformation have tended to overshadow his significant contribution to the language. His translations (with collaborators) of the Vulgate BIBLE were the first complete Bible in English and existed in two forms, the Early Version (*c*.1380–2) and the Late Version (*c*.1382–8), the second being more idiomatic, less archaic, and freer from Latinisms and generally more highly regarded. Wycliffe was a friend of Geoffrey Chaucer, who may have used him as the model for the Poor Parson in The Canterbury Tales. He did for Middle English prose what Chaucer did for poetry, making English a competitor with French and Latin; his sermons were written when London usage was coming together with the East Midlands dialect, to form a standard language accessible to all, and he included scientific references, such as to chemistry and optics. His style influenced Reformation and later nonconformist writing, and John Milton was among his admirers. More than 300 of his discourses survive, with some 170 manuscript copies of his Bible, circulated from Lutterworth, where he was rector (1374–84). Its opening words are: 'In the firste made God of nought heuene and erthe. The erthe forsothe was veyn withynne and void, and derknessis weren upon the face of the see.' Wycliffe's own share in the translations bearing his name is uncertain, but was probably considerable."[300]

The paragraphs below are excerpted from the article "Bible, English" by Anna C. Paues in the 11th edition of the Ecyclopædia Britannica (1911).

---

[300] Tom Mcarthur, *Concise Oxford Companion to the English Language* (Oxford University Press, 1998) paragraph: John Wycliffe.

Middle English Versions Before Wycliffe

(Excerpts from the 1911, 11th edition of the Encyclopedia Britannia article "Bible, English" by Anna C. Paues)[301]

"When English finally emerged victorious, towards the middle and latter half of the 14th century, it was for all practical purposes a new language, largely intermixed with French, differing from the language of the older period in sound, flexion and structure. It is evident that any Old English versions which might have survived the ravages of time would now be unintelligible, it was equally natural that as soon as French came to be looked upon as an alien tongue, the French versions hitherto in use would fail to fulfill their purpose, and that attempts should again be made to render the Bible into the only language intelligible to the greater part of the nation--into English. It was also natural that these attempts should be made where the need was most pressing, where French had gained least footing, where parliament and court were remote, where intercourse with France was difficult. In fact in the Northern Midlands, and in the North even before the middle of the 14th century, the book of Psalms had been twice rendered into English, and before the end of the same century, probably before the great Wycliffite versions had spread over the country, the whole of the New Testament had been translated by different hands into one or other of the dialects of this part of the country.

At the same time we can record only a single rendering during the whole century which originated in the south of England, namely the text of James, Peter, I John and the Pauline Epistles (edited by A. C. Paues, Cambridge, 1904).

Of these pre-Wycliffite versions possibly the earliest is the *West Midland Psalter*, once erroneously ascribed to William of Shoreham. (1) It occurs in three MSS., the earliest of which, Brit. Mus. Add. 17376, was probably written between 1340 and 1350. It contains a complete version of the book of Psalms, followed by the usual eleven canticles and the Athanasian Creed. The Latin original is a glossed version of the Vulgate, and in the English translation the words of the gloss are often substituted for the strong and picturesque expressions of the Biblical text; in other respects the rendering is faithful and idiomatic. The following two verses of the first psalm may exemplify this:—

MS. British Mus. Add. 17376. (i. I.) *Beatus vir, qui non abijt in consilio impiorum, & in uia peccatorum non stetit, et in cathedra i iudicio pestilencie i falsitatis non sedit.* Blesced be þe man þat ȝede nouȝt in þe counseil of wicked, ne stode nouȝt in þe waie of sinȝeres, ne sat

---

[301] See http://www.bible-researcher.com/1911-wyclif.html

nou3t in fals iugement. (2) *Set in lege domini voluntas eius, & in lege eius meditabitur die ac nocte.* Ac hijs wylle was in þe wylle of oure Lord, and he schal þenche in hijs lawe boþe daye and ny3t.

Before the middle of the century Richard Rolle (q.v.), the hermit of Hampole (+ 1349), turned into English, with certain additions and omissions, the famous *Commentary on the Psalms* by Peter Lombard. The work was undertaken, as the metrical prologue of one of the copies tells us (MS. Laud. misc. 286), "At a worthy recluse prayer, cald dame Merget Kyrkby." The Commentary gained immediate and lasting popularity, and spread in numerous copies throughout the country, the peculiarities of the hermit's vigorous northern dialect being either modified or wholly removed in the more southerly transcripts. The translation, however, is stiff and literal to a fault, violating idiomatic usage and the proper order of words in its strict adherence to the Latin. The following brief extracts may exemplify the hermit's rendering and the change the text underwent in later copies. (2)

MS. Univ. Coll. 64.	MS. Reg. 18 B.21
(1) Blisful man þe whilk oway 3ed noght in þe counsaile of wicked, and in þe way of synful stode noght, & in þe chaiere of pestilens he noght sate. (2) Bot in laghe of lord þe will of him; and in his laghe he sall thynke day & nyght.	Blessed is þat man þat haþ not gone in þe counsell of wicked men, and in þe weye of sinfull men haþ not stonde, and in þe chaire of pestilence sat not. 2. But in þe lawe of our lorde is þe wille of him; and [in] his lawe we shall þinke dday and nyght.

Approximately to the same period as these early renderings of the Psalter belongs a version of the Apocalypse with a Commentary, the earliest MS. of which (Harleian 874) is written in the dialect of the North Midlands. This Commentary, for a long time attributed to Wycliffe, is really nothing but a verbal rendering of the popular and widely-spread Norman Commentary on the Apocalypse (Paul Meyer and L. Delisle, *L'Apocalypse en Francais au XIII siècle*, Paris, 1901), which dates back as far as the first half of the 13th century, and in its general tenor represents the height of orthodoxy. The English apocalypse, to judge from the number of MSS. remaining, must have enjoyed great and lasting popularity. Several revisions of the text exist, the later of which present such striking agreement with the later Wycliffite version that we shall not be far wrong if we assume that they were made use of to a considerable extent by the revisers of this version.

To the North Midlands or the North belongs further a complete version of the Pauline Epistles found in the unique MS. 32, Corpus Christi College, Cambridge, of the 15th century.

Commentaries on the Gospels of St Matthew, St Mark and St Luke, we are told by the heading in one of the MSS. (Univ. Libr. Camb. Ii. 2. 12), were also translated into English by "a man of þe north cuntre." The translation of these Gospels as well as of the Epistles referred to above is stiff and awkward, the translator being evidently afraid of any departure from the Latin text of his original. The accompanying commentary is based on the Fathers of the Church and entirely devoid of any original matter. The opening lines of the third chapter of Matthew are rendered in the following way:—

MS. Camb. Univ. Libr. Ii. 2. 12. (iii. I.) In þo dayes come Ihone baptist prechand in desert of þe Iewry, & seyand, (2) Do ye penaunce; forwhy þe kyngdome of heuyne sal come negh. (3) this is he of whome it was seide be Isay þe prophete, sayand. "þe voice of þe cryand in þe desert, redye ye þe way of God, right made ye þe lityl wayes of him." (4) & Ihone his kleþing of þe hoerys of camels, & a gyrdyl of a skyn about his lendys; & his mete was þe locust & hony of þe wode.

A version of the Acts and the Catholic Epistles completes the number of the New Testament books translated in the northern parts of England. It is found in several MSS. either separately or in conjunction with a fragmentary Southern Version of the Pauline Epistles, Peter, James and I John in a curiously compiled volume, evidently made, as the prologue tells us, by a brother superior for the use and edification of an ignorant "sister," or woman vowed to religion. (3) The translation of this, our only southern text, surpasses all previous efforts from the point of view of clearness of expression and idiomatic use of English, and, though less exact, it may be even said in these respects to rank equal with the later or revised Wycliffite version.

Apart from these more or less complete versions of separate books of the Bible, there existed also numerous renderings of the Lord's Prayer, the Ten Commandments, accounts of the Life, Passion and Resurrection of our Lord, translations of the epistles and gospels used in divine service, and other means of familiarizing the people with Holy Scripture. It was the custom of the medieval preachers and writers to give their own English version of any text which they quoted, not resorting as in later times to a commonly received translation. This explains the fact that in collections of medieval homilies that have come down to us, no two renderings of the Biblical text used are ever alike, not even Wycliffe himself making use of the text of the commonly accepted versions that went under his name.

It is noteworthy that these early versions from Anglo-Saxon times onwards were perfectly orthodox, executed by and for good and faithful sons of the church, and, generally speaking, with the object of assisting those whose knowledge of Latin proved too scanty for a proper interpretation and understanding of the holy text. Thus Richard Rolle's version of the Psalms was executed for a nun; so was in all likelihood the southern version of the epistles referred to above. Again the earliest MS. (Harl. 874) of the Commentary on the Apocalypse gives the owner's name in a coeval hand as "Richard Schepard, presbiter," and the Catholic Epistles of MS. Douce 250 (4) were probably glossed for the benefit of men in religious orders, if one may judge from a short Commentary to James ii. 2, "& þerfore if eny man come into youre siyt, þat is, into youre cumpenye þat beþ Godes religiouse men in what degre so ye be." Nor do any of the remaining works contain anything but what is strictly orthodox.

The Wycliffite Versions

It is first with the appearance of Wycliffe (q.v.) and his followers on the arena of religious controversy that the Bible in English came to be looked upon with suspicion by the orthodox party within the Church. For it is a well-known fact that Wycliffe proclaimed the Bible, not the Church or Catholic tradition, as a man's supreme spiritual authority, and that he sought in consequence by every means in his power to spread the knowledge of it among the people. It is, therefore, in all likelihood to the zeal of Wycliffe and his followers that we owe the two noble 14th-century translations of the Bible which tradition has always associated with his name, and which are the earliest complete renderings that we possess of the Holy Scriptures into English. (5)

The first of these, the so-called Early Version, was probably completed about 1382, at all events before 1384, the year of Wycliffe's death. The second, or Later Version, being a thorough revision of the first, is ascribed to the year 1388 by Sir Frederic Madden and the Rev. Joshua Forshall in their edition of these two versions. (6)

It is a matter of uncertainty what part, if any, Wycliffe himself took in the work. The editors of the Wycliffite versions say in the Preface, pp. xv. ff. — "The New Testament was naturally the first object. The text of the Gospels was extracted from the Commentary upon them by Wycliffe, and to these were added the Epistles, the Acts and the Apocalypse, all now translated anew. This translation might probably be the work of Wycliffe himself; at least the similarity of style between the Gospels and the other parts favours the supposition." The Wycliffite authorship of the Commentaries on the Gospels, on which the learned editors base their argument, is, however, unsupported by any evidence beyond the fact that the writer of the Prologue to Matthew urges in strong language "the propriety of translating Scripture for the use of the laity." The Biblical text found in these Commentaries is in fact so far removed from the original type of the Early Version as to be transitional to the Late, and, what is still more convincing, passages from the Early Version, from both the Old

Testament and the New Testament, are actually quoted in the Commentary. Under such circumstances it would be folly to look upon them as anything but late productions, at all events later than the Early Version, and equal folly to assign these bulky volumes to the last two years of Wycliffe's life merely because the text used in them happens to be that of the Early Version. It is therefore at present impossible to say what part of the Early Version of the New Testament was translated by Wycliffe. (7)

The Old Testament of the Early Version was, according to the editors (Preface, p. xvii.), taken in hand by one of Wycliffe's coadjutors, Nicholas de Herford. The translator's original copy and a coeval transcript of it are still extant in the Bodleian library (Bodl. 959, Douce 369). Both break off abruptly at Baruch iii. 19, the latter having at this place a note inserted to the following effect: *Explicit translacionem Nicholay de herford.* There is consequently but little doubt that Nicholas de Herford took part in the translation of the Old Testament, though it is uncertain to what extent. The translator's copy is written in not less than five hands, differing in orthography and dialect. The note may therefore be taken to refer either to the portion translated by the last or fifth hand, or to the whole of the Old Testament up to Baruch iii. 19. Judging from uniformity of style and mode of translation the editors of the Bible are inclined to take the latter view; they add that the remaining part of the Old Testament was completed by a different hand, the one which also translated the New Testament. This statement is, however, not supported by sufficient evidence. In view of the magnitude of the undertaking it is on the contrary highly probable that other translators besides Wycliffe and Nicholas de Herford took part in the work, and that already existing versions, with changes when necessary, were incorporated or made use of by the translators.

The Early Version, apart from its completeness, shows but little advance upon preceding efforts. It is true that the translation is more careful and correct than some of the renderings noticed above, but on the other hand it shares all their faults. The translation of the Old Testament as far as Baruch iii. 19 is stiff and awkward, sometimes unintelligible, even nonsensical, from a too close adherence to the Latin text (e.g. Judges xx. 25). In the remaining parts the translation is somewhat easier and more skilful, though even here Latinisms and un-English renderings abound.

It is small wonder, therefore, if a revision was soon found necessary and actually taken in hand within a few years of the completion of the Earlier Version. The principles of work adopted by the revisers are laid down in the general prologue to their edition, the so-called "Later Version."

For these resons and othere ... a symple creature hath translatid the bible out of Latyn into English. First, this symple creature hadde myche trauaile, with diuerse felawis and helperis, to gedere manie elde biblis, and othere doctouris, and comune glosis, and to make oo Latyn bible sumdel trewe; and thanne to studie it of the newe, the text with the glose, and othere doctouris, as he miyte gete, and speciali Lire on the elde testament, that helpide ful myche in this work; the thridde tyme to counseile with elde gramariens, and elde dyuynis, of harde wordis, and harde sentencis, hou tho miyten best be vndurstonden and translatid; the iiij tyme to translate as cleerli as he coude to the sentence, and to haue manie gode felawis and kunnynge at the correcting of the translacioun.

It is uncertain who the revisers were; John Purvey, the leader of the Lollard party after Wycliffe's death, is generally assumed to have taken a prominent part in the work, but the evidence of this is extremely slight (cf. Wycl. Bible, Preface, pp. xxv. f.). The exact date of the revision is also doubtful: the editors of the Wycliffe Bible, judging from the internal evidence of the Prologue, assume it to have been finished about 1388. This Revised or Later Version is in every way a readable, correct rendering of the Scriptures, it is far more idiomatic than the Earlier, having been freed from the greater number of its Latinisms; its vocabulary is less archaic. Its popularity admits of no doubt, for even now in spite of neglect and persecution, in spite of the ravages of fire and time, over 150 copies remain to testify to this fact. The following specimens of the Early and Late Versions will afford a comparison with preceding renderings:—

Early Version.	Late Version.
(Psalm i. 1.) Blisful the man, that that went not awei in the counseil of vnpitouse, and in the wei off sinful stod not; and in the chayer of pestilence sat not, (2) But in the lawe of the Lord his wil; and in the lawe of hym he shal sweteli thenke dai and nygt.	(i. I.) Blessid is the man, that gede not in the councel of wickid men; and stood not in the weie of synneris, and sat not in the chaier of pestilence. (2) But his wille is in the lawe of the Lord; and he schal bithenke in the lawe of hym dai and nygt.
(Matthew iii. I.) In thilke days came Ioon Baptist, prechynge in the desert of Iude, sayinge, (2) Do ye penaunce, for the kyngdom of heuens shal neig,	(iii. I.) In tho daies Ioon Baptist cam, and prechide in the desert of Iudee, and seide, (2) Do ye penaunce, for the kyngdom of

or cume nige. (3) Forsothe this is he of whome it is said by Ysaye the prophet, A voice of a cryinge in desert, Make ye redy the wayes of the Lord; make ye rigtful the pathes of hym. (4) Forsothe that ilk loon hadde cloth of the heeris of cameylis, and a girdil of skyn aboute his leendis; sothely his mete weren locustis, and hony of the wode.	heuenes shal neige. (3) For this is he, of whom it is seid bi Ysaie, the prophete, seyinge, A vois of a crier in desert, Make ye redi the weies of the Lord; make ye rigt the pathis of hym. (4) And this loon hadde clothing of camels heeris, and a girdil of skynne aboute his leendis; and his mete was honysoukis and hony of the wode.

The 15th century may well be described as the *via dolorosa* of the English Bible as well as of its chief advocates and supporters, the Lollards. After the death of Wycliffe violence and anarchy set in, and the Lollards came gradually to be looked upon as enemies of order and disturbers of society. Stern measures of suppression were directed not only against them but against "Goddis Lawe," the book for which they pleaded with such passionate earnestness. The bishops' registers bear sufficient testimony to this fact. (8) It would appear, however, as if at first at all events the persecution was directed not so much against the Biblical text itself as against the Lollard interpretations which accompanied it. In a convocation held at Oxford under Archbishop Arundel in 1408 it was enacted "that no man hereafter by his own authority translate any text of the Scripture into English or any other tongue, by way of a book, booklet, or tract; and that no man read any such book, booklet, or tract, now lately composed in the time of John Wycliffe or since, or hereafter to be set forth in part or in whole, publicly or privately, upon pain of greater excommunication, until the said translation be approved by the ordinary of the place, or, if the case so require, by the council provincial. He that shall do contrary to this shall likewise be punished as a favourer of heresy and error." (9)

It must be allowed that an enactment of this kind was not without justification. The Lollards, for instance, did not hesitate to introduce into certain copies of the pious and orthodox Commentary on the Psalms by the hermit of Hampole interpolations of their own of the most virulently controversial kind (MSS. Trin. Coll. Camb. B.V. 25, Brit. Mus. Reg. 18. C. 26, &c.), and although the text of their Biblical versions was faithful and true, the General Prologue of the Later Version was interlarded with controversial matter. It is small wonder if the prelates and priests sought to repress such trenchant criticism of their lives and doctrines as appeared more especially in the former work, and probably in many others which since have perished in "faggots and burning."

For all this, manuscripts of Purvey's Revision were copied and recopied during this century, the text itself being evidently approved by the ecclesiastical authorities, when in the hands of the right people and if unaccompanied by controversial matter.

Of the Lollard movement in Scotland but little is known, but a curious relic has come down to our times in the shape of a New Testament of Purvey's Revision in the Scottish dialect of the early 16th century. The transcriber was in all probability a certain Murdoch Nisbet, who also showed his reforming tendencies by adding to it a rendering of Luther's Prologue to the New Testament. (10)

---

1. K. D. Bülbring, *The Earliest Complete English Prose Psalter* (E.E.T.S., No. 97), part i. (London, 1891); cf. A. C. Paues, *A Fourteenth-Century English Biblical Version* (Upsala Diss.) (Cambridge, 1902), p. lvi.
2. H. R. Bramley, *The Psalter and Certain Canticles ... by Richard Rolle of Hampole* (Oxford, 1884); cf. H. Middendorff, *Studien über Richard Rolle von Hampole unter besonderer Berücksichtigung seiner Psalmen-Commentare* (Magdeburg, 1888).
3. A. C. Paues, *A Fourteenth-Century English Biblical Version* (Cambridge, 1904), pp. xxiv. ff.
4. See Paues, *op. cit.* p. 210.
5. For a different view as to the authorship of the Wycliffite versions, see F. A. Gasquet, *The Old English Bible and Other Essays* (London, 1897), pp. 102 ff.
6. Sir F. Madden and Rev. J. Forshall, *The Holy Bible ... made from the Latin Vulgate by John Wycliffe and His Followers* (4 vols., Oxford, 1850), pp. xix., xxiv.
7. Cf. A. C. Paues, *The English Bible in the Fourteenth Century.*
8. See Foxe, *Acts and Monuments,* iv. 135 ff. (ed. Townsend, 1846).
9. Wilkins *Concilia,* iii. 317.
10. T. G. Law, The New Testament in Scots, being Purvey's Revision of Wycliffe's version turned into Scots by Murdoch Nisbet, c. 1520 (Scot. T. S., Edinburgh, 1901-1905).

Brief Comparison of Gothic and Anglo-Saxon

"Anglo-Saxon Laws, and at a later date in the Gospels. The English philologist will now be able to trace many words and phrases from the present time, 1865, to the translation of Tyndale in 1526, of Wycliffe in 1389, of Saxon about 995, and of the gothic about 360, a space of more than 1500 years. The gothic is a language of Low German origin, as well as the Anglo-Saxon and English, we are, therefore, not surprised to find many phrases apparently identical in Gothic, in anglo-Saxon, and in modern English."

GOTHIC	MODERN ENGLISH (not the KJB)	ANGLO-SAXON	VERSE
In bokem Psalmo.	In the book of Psalms.	On them Scalme	Lk. 20:42
Ik im tbata daur	I am the door	Ic com geat	Jn 10:9
Langai wheilai	For a long while	Langre tide.	Lk. 18:4
Naub lcitila wheila	Now a little while	Gyt sume liwile	Jn. 7:33
Whis brother	Whose brother	Hwoes brothor	Lk. 20:28
Kaurno whaitels	A corn of wheat	Hwaeteno corn	Jn. 12:24
Hardu-hairtei	Hardness of heart	heortan heardness	Mk. 10:5
Hardu ist thata waurd	Hard is that word	Heard is theos apraec	Jn. 6:60
Sibun brothryus	Seven brothers	Seofon gebrothru	Lk. 20:29
Wheitos swe snaiws	White as snow	Swa white swa snaw	Mk. 9:3
Yuka auhsne	Yokes of oxen	An getyme oxena	Lk. 14:19
Wha ist namo thein?	What is thy name?	Hwaet is thin nama?	Lk. 8:30
Galeiks ist maun	He is like a man	He ys gelic men	Lk. 6:48

THE GOTHIC translation of Ulphilas is the first, in date and importance, which claims attention in a brief notice of these four versions, and of their celebrated translators.[302]

---

[302] Joseph Bosworth and George Waring, *The Gothic and Anglo-Saxon Gospels in Parallel Columns with the Versions of Wycliffe and Tyndale* (John Russel Smith, London, 2nd Edition, 1874) p. ii and iii, preface.

Map of Lollardy in the 16th Century[303]
(Blue, no doubt, Red probable, p. 366-7)

303 Originally published in: G. M. Trevelyan, England in the Age of Wycliffe (London: Longmans, Green, 1909). From: http://www.lollardsociety.org/map.html

BIBLIOGRAPHY

Addis, William E.; and Thomas Arnold. *A Catholic Dictionary* Containing Some Account of the Doctrine, Disciplines, Rites, Ceremonies, Councils, and Religious Orders of the Catholic Church, Part II. London. Kessinger Publishing, 9th Edition. originally published, 1916.

Anderson, Christopher. *The Annals of the English Bible* www.williamtyndale.com/0johnwycliffe.htm. accessed 02/2008.

Armitage, Thomas. *A H*

Arnold, M.A., Thomas. *Select English Works of John Wyclif, Vol. I, Sermons on The Gospels For Sundays and Festivals.* Oxford. Clarendon Press. Edited from the originals by Thomas Arnold, M.A. of University College, Oxford. 1869.

Balasundaram, Subir. "John Wycliffe, the Father of the English Bible." http://lifegivingword.googlepages.com/john. accessed 04/2008.

Bagster, Samuel. *The English Hexapla.* Edmonton, Canada. Still Waters Revival Books. Paternoster Kow, London. Samuel Bagster and Sons, 1841.

Bosworth, D.D., Rev. Joseph, Professor of Anglo-Saxon, Oxford. *The* Gothic and Anglo-Saxon Gospels in Parallel Columns with the Versions of Wycliffe and Tyndale Arranged with Preface and Notes. London. Joseph Russell Smith. 2nd edition, 1874.

Bosworth, Joseph, and George Waring. *The Gothic and Anglo-*Saxon Gospels in Parallel Columns with the Versions of Wycliffe and Tyndale. London. John Russell Smith. 2nd Edition. 1874.

Brown, Ph.D., David L. *The Incomparable Book—The Holy Bible, The History of the English Bible.* Oak Creek, WI. Pastor David L. Brown, Ph. D. First Baptist Church, Oak Creek.

_________ *Our English Bible Heritage.* Oak Creek, WI. Pastor David L. Brown, Ph. D. First Baptist Church, Oak Creek.

Bruce, F. F. *The Canon of Scripture.* Downers Grove, IL. Intervarsity Press. 1988.

Cloud, David. "Jerome and the Latin Vulgate" Port Huron, MI. Way of Life Literature, FBIS. 2001.

_________ "Rome Destroyed Bibles." Port Huron, MI. Way of Life Literature, FBIS. 2001.

________ "John Wycliffe: The Father of the English Bible." Way of

Life Literature, FBIS. 2001.
________ "John Wycliffe and the Lollards" Port Huron, MI. Way of Life Literature. from the book Rome and the Bible: Tracing the History of the Roman Catholic Church and its Persecutions of the Bible and of Bible Believers. 2000.
Christian History Institute. "Into the Fires Goes Jerome of Prague." *Christianity Today International.* History Institute. 2007. accessed 06/09/2008 at http://chi.gospelcom.net/DAILYF/2001/05/daily-05-30-2001.shtml
Conant, Mrs. Hannah O'Brian Chaplin, *The English Bible.* New York. Sheldon, Blakeman & Co. J. J. Reed printers. 1856.
Connolly, K. *The Indestructible Book.* Grand Rapids, NY. Baker Books.
Cramp, J. M. *Baptist History.* Port Huron, MI. Way of Life Electronic Edition, 2003. First published in 1869.
Daniell, David. *The Bible in English, Its History and Influence.* New Haven & London. Yale University Press. ISBN 0-300-09930-42003. 2003.
Eliot, Samuel. *History of Liberty, Part II, The Early Christians.* Boston, MA. Little Brown and Company. 1853.
Ford, Samuel Howard. *The Origin of the Baptists: Traced Back by Milestones on the Track of Time.* Port Huron, MI. Way of Life Literature, FBIS. 2003.
Jobes, Karen H. and Moises Silva. *Invitation to The Septuagint.* Baker Academic. Grand Rapids, MI. 2000.
Ivemy, Joseph. *A History of the English Baptists,* Vol. 1. Port Huron, MI. Way of Life Electronic Edition, 2003.. First printed in London, 1811.
Khoo, Dr. Jeffrey. "Truth or Lies?" *The Burning Bush.* Singapore. Far Eastern Bible College. Vol. 12, Number 2, 2006.
Goadby, J.J. *Bye-Paths in Paptist History.* Port Huron, MI. Way of Life Electronic Edition, 2003. First published by Elliot Stock, London, 1871.
Jones *History of the Waldenses.*
Jurkowski, Maureen. "New Light on John Purvey." Oxford. *The English Historical Review,* Vol. 110, No. 439, Nov. 1995.
Grady, William P. *Final Authority, A Christian's Guide to the King James Bible.* Knoxville, TN. Grady Publications, Inc. ISBN 0-9628809-1-4. 2001.
Hallihan, C. P. "The Latin Vulgate." London. *Quarterly Review,* issue 579.
Hudson, Anne. "John Purvey: A Reconsideration of the Evidence for his Life and Writings" Los Angeles, CA. UCLA, Center for

Medieval and Renaissance Studies. *Viator*, Vol. xii.
Irvin, Dale T., and Scott T. Sunquist, *History of the World Christian Movement, Vol. 1, Earliest Christianity to 1453*. Maryknoll, NY. Orbis Books. Continuum International Group. ISBN:0567088669.
2001.
Lechler, G.V. "Hus, John." *A Religious Encyclopaedia or Dictionary of Biblical, Historical, Doctrinal, and Practical Theology*. Toronto, New York & London. Funk & Wagnalls Company. 3rd edition, Vol. 2. 1894.
Levy, Ian Christopher. *John Wyclif On the Truth of Holy Scripture*. Kalamazoo, Michigan. Medieval Institute Publications, Western Michigan University. 2001.
Mcarthur, Tom. *Concise Oxford Companion to the English Language*. Oxford. Oxford University Press. 1998.
McClure, Alexander. *Translators Revived*. "The Glorious History of the English Bible." Port Huron, WI. Way of Life Literature, FBIS. c. 1850.
McComb, M.A., D.D., Rev. Samuel. *The Making of the English Bible*. New York. Moffat, Yard, and Co. 1909.
Miller, Andrew. *Church History*. Port Huron, MI. Way of Life Literature Electronic Edition. 2003.
Moorman, Dr. Jack . *Forever Settled*. Collingswood, NJ. Dean Burgon Society Press. 1999.
Nix, William E. "Theological Presuppositions and Sixteenth Century English Bible Translation, Part 1" Dallas, TX. *Bibliotheca Sacra*, Dallas Theological Seminary. Vol. 124, Jan. 67.
Noble, Terrance P. "Version Information." *Wycliffe New Testament."* Introduction, Endnotes, Conclusion." www.biblegateway.com/versions/index.php?action=getVersionInfo&vid=53; accessed 6/16/2008.
Paues, Anna C. "Bible, English." Encyclopaedia Britannica, 11th Edition. 1911.
Preface to the 1611 King James Bible from http://m2.aol.com/AVBibleTAB/av/KJVpre.htm.
Riplinger, G. A. *In Awe of Thy Word*. Ararat, VA, A.V. Publications Corp., 2003.
Sergeant, Lewis. *John Wycliff, The Last of the Schoolmen and the First of the Reformers*. London. Knickerbocker Press. G. P. Putman's Sons. 24 Bedford Street. 1893.
Schaff, Phillip. *History of the Christian Church, Vol.1 - 8*. Reo, WI. Master's Christian Library, Ages Software. 1997.
Trevelyan, George Macaulay. *England in the Age of Wycliffe*. New York, London and Bombay. Longmans, Green, and Company.

1900.
Vance, Laurence M. *King James His Bible and Its Translators.* Pensacola, FL. Vance Publications. 2006.
Vaughan, The Rev. Robert. *Tracts and Treatises of John de* Wycliffe, D.D., Selections and Translations from his manuscripts and Latin Works. Hatton Garden, London. Blackburn and Pardon. The Wycliffe Society. 1845.
Waite, Pastor D. A. Waite, Th.D., Ph.D. *Defending the King James Bible.* Collingswood, NJ. Bible For Today
Ward, A. W. and A. R. Waller. *The Cambridge History of English Literature.* Cambridge, England. G. P. Putman and Sons. Cambridge University Press. 1910.
Westcott, Brooke Foss. "The English Bible" London. *Quarterly Review.* John Murray, printed by William Clowes & Sons. Jan & April, 1870.
Wetzel, Dr. R. C. *A Chronology of Biblical Christianity.* Rio, WI. Master Christian Library. Books For The Ages, Ages Software. 1995.
Williams, M.D., Ph.D., H.D. *The Attack on the Canon of Scripture.* Cleveland, GA. The Old Paths Publications, Inc. 2008.
_________"The Character of God's Words in Not Found in the 'G' But is Found in the Ancient Landmarks" Collingswood, NJ. Dean Burgon Society. *Dean Burgon Society Message Book,* #15, 2005.
_________*The Lie That Changed the Modern World.* Collingswood, NJ. Bible For Today Press. 2004.
Wylie, James A. *History of Protestanism, Vol. 1.* London, New York. Cassell and Company, Lmt. J. A. Wylie. 1808-1890.
Young, Jeff. "John Huss, The Prereformer" *Biblical Insights.* Dec. 2005. accessed 06/09/2008. www.lavistachurchofchrist.org/LVarticles/JohnHus

INTERNET SITES

http://news.bbc.co.uk/1/hi/world/4243727.stm
http://exposingchineseancestorworship.blogspot.com/2008/04/western-museums-with-chinese-artifacts.html
http://www.tpub.com/content/religion/14229/css/14229_109.htm
http://pow.reonline.org.uk/christianity.htm
http://www.americancatholicpress.org/Bishop_%20Perry_Black_Catholic_Worship.html
http://www.marypages.com/
http://www.britannia.com/history/biographies/joseph.html.

http://en.wikipedia.org/wiki/Fall_of_Constantinople
http://johnscorner.blogspot.com/2006/11/bible-translation-3-john-wycliffe.html.
http://www.greatsite.com/timeline-english-bible-history/john-wycliffe.html
http://www.answers.com/topic/lollardy
http://www.rasitesbooks.com/Wycliffe.html
http://lifegivingword.googlepages.com/john
http://www.mostholyfamilymonastery.com/Great_Western_Schism.html
http://www.newadvent.org/cathen/15367a.htm
http://lifegivingword.googlepages.com/john
http://www.lollardsociety.org/map.html.
http://www.answers.com/topic/john-purvey.
http://dictionary.reference.com/search?q=Carthusian
http://www.archives.gov/exhibits/featured_documents/magna_carta/
http://www.wardsbookofdays.com/31december.htm
http://www.crosbyheritage.co.uk/blog/entry/colins-little-known-facts-john-wycliffe-and-lutterworth/
http://www.greatsite.com/timeline-english-bible-history/john-wycliffe.html
http://www.bbc.co.uk/history/british/middle_ages/richardii_reign_07.shtml
http://www.bible-researcher.com/1911-wyclif.html
http://www.adullamfilms.org/

REFERENCE WORKS

Columbia Encyclopedia
Encyclopædia Britannica Online
Fox's Book of the Martyrs
The Martyrs Mirror
Concise Oxford Companion to the English Language

INDEX

ABOUT THE AUTHOR

Dr. Williams was born in Ft. Pierce, Florida. He was saved at the age of fourteen at his local Baptist church under Pastor J. R. White where he was active in the church youth group. His local church ordained him to preach the gospel. After graduating with honors from high school, he attended Stetson University where he met his wife, Patricia, and they were married in 1961. Starting in the ministerial program at Stetson and switching to pre-med in his junior year, he graduated with honors with a B.A. After Stetson, he taught high school at Eau Gallie, Florida for two years, and then continued his training at the University of Miami Medical School where he graduated with honors. Following his medical training, Dr. Williams and Patricia settled in New Port Richey, Florida where he practiced Family Medicine as a board certified family practitioner. He was active in his community as a hospital board member for twenty years, a chief-of-staff, president of the medical society, an advisory board member and president of Moody Bible Institute's Florida program, a board member of the Health Planning Commission, and a teacher at his local Baptist church. He helped develop and administrate a multi-specialist medical clinic with forty thousand patients and seventeen doctors. His Biblical training was obtained at Stetson University, Moody Bible Institute, and Louisiana Baptist University. After retirement, Dr. Williams has continued serving the Lord Jesus Christ as an associate pastor, a teacher, and as vice-president and representative for the Dean Burgon Society. He received a Ph.D. in Biblical studies at Louisiana Baptist University. He has traveled to many foreign lands where he has represented the Dean Burgon Society, teaching pastors and participating in evangelistic events. He is author of the several books, *The Lie That Changed The Modern World; Word-For-Word Translating of the Received Texts, Verbal Plenary Translating; Hearing the Voice of God; The Septuagint is a Paraphrase; The Pure Words of God;* and *The Attack on the Canon of Scripture,* in addition to many articles and booklets. Dr. Williams and his wife, Patricia have two sons and five grandchildren.

BOOKS BY DR. WILLIAMS

WORD-FOR-WORD TRANSLATING OF THE RECEIVED TEXT, VERBAL PLENARY TRANSLATING:

This 270 page perfect bound book may be purchased through www.BibleForToday.org or Amazon.com. There is a vital need for a book to inform sincere Bible-believing Christians about the proper techniques of translating the WORDS of God into the receptor languages of the world. No book like this one has ever been written. It is a unique and much-needed book. The very first requirement for any translation of the Bible is to have the proper WORDS of Hebrew, Aramaic, and Greek from which to translate. It is the contention of this book that the original verbally and plenarily inspired Hebrew, Aramaic, and Greek WORDS have been verbally and plenarily preserved in accordance with God's promises. These preserved WORDS are those received-text-WORDS which underlie the King James Bible. This volume emphasizes the requirement of a proper technique to be used in all translations of God's WORDS. It must be done in a verbally and plenarily translation technique. That is, the Hebrew, Aramaic, and Greek WORDS must be conveyed into the receptor languages, not merely the ideas, concepts, thoughts, or message. This technique is absent in all of the other manuals on Bible translation. Dr. Williams is not the usual sort of writer. He combines the meticulous skill of a Doctor of Medicine with the artistry and acumen of a Doctor of Philosophy to produce this grand volume. May translators and sincere Christians of all persuasions and professions use this important book worldwide! Amazon.com (type in book title) or The Bible For Today Press, BFT #**3302** ISBN 1-56848-056-3, Order by PHONE: 1-800-JOHN 10:9, Order by FAX: 856-854-2464, Order by MAIL: Bible For Today, 900 Park Avenue, Collingswood, NJ 08108"

THE ATTACK ON THE CANON OF SCRIPTURE, A POLEMIC AGAINST MODERN SCHOLARSHIP

This 272 page perfect bound book was released in January, 2008. ISBN 978-0-9801689-0-7. This 172 page book demonstrates the newest attack on the Words and books of the Bible by modern day scholarship. The changing methods for assaulting the Scriptures are important for those who are concerned about the relentless attempt to destroy them. In a remarkable polemic against modern scholarship, Dr. Williams outlines the most recent means many are using to undermine confidence in the Words of God received through the priesthood of believers. It will be available at Amazon.com. (type in book title) or at BibleForToday.org, BFT # **3345**.

THE LIE THAT CHANGED THE MODERN WORLD

This book is in hardback format, 440 pages in all. ISBN 1-56848-042-3. It is a factual defense not only of the King James Bible, but also of the Hebrew and Greek Words that underlie the King James Bible. The author is a medical doctor, now retired, who has researched this important topic thoroughly. May the Lord Jesus Christ use and honor this study in the days, weeks, months, and years ahead until our Lord Jesus Christ returns. It should be in every layman's library, every Pastor's library, every church library, every college library, every university library, and in every theological seminary library. It is available through Amazon.com (type in book title) or Bible For Today Press, www.biblefortoday.org, BFT # **3125**.

THE PURE WORDS OF GOD

This is a perfect bound 136 page book. ISBN 978-0-9801689-1-4. Dr. Williams' book, *The Pure Words of God,* clarifies the use of the word "pure" when it is used to define the Words of God. Should "pure" be applied to translations, to Traditional/Received Texts, or to critical texts? Once the correct application is explained, Dr. Williams clarifies God's commands to receive and keep His pure Words. It is available through Amazon.com (type in book title) or Bible For Today Press at www.biblefortoday.org, BFT #3344.

Look for other books to be released by Dr. Williams in the near future. One work, ***The Apostolic Origin of the Traditional Text*** is nearing completion and should be released in 2008. Another book, ***The Septuagint is a Paraphrase***, will be released in 2008.

www.ingramcontent.com/pod-product-compliance
Lightning Source LLC
LaVergne TN
LVHW020536100826
845148LV00010B/1482

* 9 7 8 0 9 8 1 7 3 3 9 8 2 *